P9-DDW-120

Reflections of an Affirmative Action Baby

Reflections of an Affirmative Action Baby

STEPHEN L. CARTER

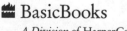
BasicBooks
A Division of HarperCollins*Publishers*

Library of Congress Cataloging-in-Publication Data

Carter, Stephen L., 1954–
  Reflections of an affirmative action baby/ Stephen L.
Carter.
     p.   cm.
  Includes bibliographical references (p.) and index.
  ISBN 0–465–06871–5
  1. Affirmative action programs—Law and legislation—
United States. 2. Race discrimination—Law and legisla-
tion—United States. 3. Afro-American lawyers—Biogra-
phy. 4. Carter, Stephen L., 1954–. I. Title.
KF4755.5.C37 1991
342.73′0873—dc20   91–70054
[347.302873]   CIP

To Enola,
for gifts *sine numero*
and *sine quibus non*

Contents

Acknowledgments

My friend Adebayo Ogunlesi first opened my mind a decade ago to many of the questions discussed in this book. We were both serving as law clerks for Justice Thurgood Marshall of the Supreme Court of the United States. After considerable argument, Bayo convinced me of the folly of the *Harvard Law Review*'s affirmative action membership program; ever since, he has been a playful and supportive (if occasionally mischievous) interlocutor. To Justice Marshall himself, as well as to Spottswood W. Robinson, III, of the United States Court of Appeals for the District of Columbia Circuit, another eminent jurist for whom it was also my privilege to serve as law clerk, I owe a debt that I can never repay. Each was a wonderful and inspiring teacher through his personal example of a simultaneous commitment to racial justice and intellectual endeavor.

As I have worked my way through this project during the past few years, many individuals have read, discussed, and criticized various parts of the book, and although mentioning all of them would be impossible, several deserve special words of thanks. In particular, my friends Lea Brilmayer, Harlon Dalton, George Jones, and Randall Kennedy have been patient and generous with unfailing encouragement and thoughtful suggestions. No doubt the book would have been better had I accepted more of them.

Other friends, colleagues, students, acquaintances, and correspondents who have taken time to read parts of the book or just to discuss the ideas underlying it include Bruce Ackerman, Barbara Bradley, Adrienne Davis, Peggy Davis, Drew Days, Richard Delgado, Ronald Feenstra, Henry Louis Gates, Jr., Alex Johnson, Harold Koh, Julius Lester, Jane Livingston, Michael McConnell, Martha Minow, Karen Odom, Michael Perry, Loretta Pleasant-Jones, David Plotke, Natalie Roche, Roberta Romano, Peter Schuck, Alan Schwartz, Suzanna Sherry, Thomas Sowell, Michael Stout, Wayne Turner, and Roger Wilkins.

The Dean of the Yale Law School, Guido Calabresi, has been generous and supportive, and in part through his generosity, I have been fortunate to have the services over the past five years of eight excellent research assistants, Anthony Ball, Yasmin Cader, Beth Deane, Karen Porter, Sushma Soni, Christopher Wray, John Yoo, and, especially, Denise Morgan. Each was a very fine and very busy Yale law student who was nevertheless willing to take time away from other work to help me with mine; and each has had a much larger role in shaping the final product than is suggested by the bare words "research assistant."

My editors at Basic Books, Martin Kessler and Linda Carbone, as well as my literary agent, Lynn Nesbit, have been tireless and careful readers of the several drafts of the book, and their assistance has been indispensable.

My mother, Emily Carter, died while the book was being written; I had told her about it, and she had looked forward to seeing it, which was only natural since some of my ideas were inspired by some of hers. She also would have disputed a great deal of it, which is all the more reason to wish that I had finished it earlier. My father, Lisle Carter, who read the manuscript with enormous care, encouraged me from the start. With his usual wisdom, he also warned me early on in the project that I was stepping into a world quite different from the sheltered academic life that I have heretofore led. Some who disagreed with me, he said, were not likely to be gentle. (Although Dad, who disagrees with much of the book, has never been anything else—on this matter, at least.)

My children, Leah Cristina Aird Carter and Andrew David Aird Carter, also gave generously, by putting up with Daddy's frequent distraction and occasional absences. Yes, Leah, Daddy has finally finished putting the pages together, and yes, Andrew, there may well still be mistakes in it.

Above all, I am indebted to my wife, Enola G. Aird, for tirelessly reading every word of the manuscript, most of them three or four times; for offering keen editorial advice and sharp, thoughtful criticism; for saving me sometimes from my own worst instincts and offering her own, which were almost always better; but more than any of that, for her solid, unwavering support—emotional, spiritual, and intellectual—through this experience and so many others. Now it is my turn to spend time with the children and Enola's to write a book of her own, and I hope and pray that I can provide for her a fraction of the love, support, and inspiration that she has always given to me.

S. L. C.
New Haven, Connecticut
March 1991

A Note on Terminology

In this book, I try to use the words *black* and *white* as adjectives rather than nouns because the book is about people, not about colors. Also, for reasons explained in the final chapter, I try to avoid using the word *minority,* choosing instead the term *person of color.* I also try to avoid the word *nonwhite* because of its implied assignment of what is normal and what is different. As the reader will quickly discover, I do not entirely succeed in attaining any of these goals, which helps illustrate the point I make several times in the book about the inadequacy of our language for discussing questions of race. For reasons set forth briefly in chapter 6, I do not use the term *African-American,* although I have no quarrel with those who prefer it.

On Being a Black Intellectual

T o be black and an intellectual in America is to live in a box. So I live in a box, not of my own making, and on the box is a label, not of my own choosing. Most of those who have not met me, and many of those who have, see the box and read the label and imagine that they have seen me.

The box is formed by the assumptions others make when they learn that I am black, and a label is available for every occasion. Some years ago, for example, when I was yet fairly new to the academic world, a white professor at another law school—a fine scholar, to be sure, but a gentleman I had never met—sent me a draft of an article he was writing in which he criticized some earlier work of mine about constitutional law. My essay, he wrote in the draft, showed a lack of sensitivity to the experience of black people in America. When he learned the color of my skin, rather than defend his claim of insensitivity he simply dropped it from the paper. In his eyes, my blackness evidently provided an immunity from the charge; perhaps he thought I possessed a special perspective on racial matters that he did not, or maybe he decided that it was unfair or racist for him, a white professor, to make such an ac-

cusation against a black one. Either way, he plainly decided
that as a white person, he had no right to criticize my views
on race. I am black, so there are things I simply know better
than white people do. "POSSESSES SPECIAL PERSPECTIVE," the
label reads; "DO NOT CHALLENGE ON MATTERS RELATING TO
RACE." Naturally, my colleague had to withdraw his criticism
of my insensitivity. To do otherwise would require looking
beyond the box.

Other labels, too, bedevil the black intellectual, and many
of them, as though required by a truth-in-advertising law, are
in the form of cautions. Cheek by jowl with assumptions
about the special perspective are assumptions about politics:
the presumptive label reads, "CAUTION: BLACK LEFT-WING AC-
TIVIST, HANDLE WITH CARE OR BE ACCUSED OF RACISM," but if
one criticizes some aspect (any aspect) of the dominant civil
rights paradigm, the label then becomes, "CAUTION: BLACK
NEOCONSERVATIVE, PROBABLY A NUT CASE"; one's field of scholarship: "CAREFUL: DISCUSS CIVIL RIGHTS LAW OR LAW AND
RACE ONLY"; and, not least, qualifications for one's position:
"WARNING! AFFIRMATIVE ACTION BABY! DO NOT ASSUME THAT
THIS INDIVIDUAL IS QUALIFIED!" True, it is possible in theory
to correct the misimpressions these labels create, but it is very
hard work, always carrying with it the risk—no, the likelihood—that when one label is successfully peeled away, the labelers will just replace it with another.

This societal insistence on rendering complexity simple,
on squeezing people into preformed boxes, is perhaps the principal reason that it is not easy to tell the story I wish to tell in
this book. As the twentieth century spins toward its close, it
has become something of a commonplace that it is hard to hold
an honest conversation about affirmative action, but in this
book I intend to try. It may be harder still to hold an honest
conversation about the reasons why it is hard to hold an honest conversation about affirmative action, but in this book I
intend to try to do that, too.

This book is fired by the experience of being a black professional who has lived his entire adult life in a world defined
in part by "benign" racial preferences. As our national debate

over the wisdom of affirmative action intensifies, the beneficiary's side of the saga cries out to be told, for there is a growing black professional class that tends to be spoken for rather than to. Professionals have been fortunate, able for the most part to avoid the debate over the mythic status of preferences, sitting on the sidelines as others argue in vitriolic tones. As William Julius Wilson pointed out something over a decade ago, one reason that affirmative action has been able to endure in the professions and in government without causing the sometimes severe interracial friction that has occurred in other labor markets has been the continued expansion of both sectors.[1] As we enter the 1990s, however, the smooth and steady growth in the corporate sector and, perhaps more radically, in government has ceased and might even be going into a period of reversal. Now we learn (and see by example) that the Republican Party plans to make racial preferences a major campaign issue in the 1990s, and nobody is sure how or even whether the Democratic Party plans to defend them. Add in the point that the farther one gets from college campuses, the fewer the white people who have ever been enthusiastic about racial preferences that benefit people of color. Put it all together and there is little reason to think that the professional sector will be immune from the clearly portended affirmative action shakeout.

My narrative, then, consists of two related stories. The first, which comprises part I, is the story of what it has been like for me as a black professional to come of age in the era of affirmative action, a time in which every professional who is not white is subjected to that extra degree of scrutiny that attaches to those who are suspected of having benefited, at some point in the development of their careers, from a racial preference. As I chronicle the ambivalence and frustration of the role of beneficiary (or suspected beneficiary), I sift the case for and against affirmative action in the professions, and propose a compromise that returns our systems of racial preference to their simpler, more defensible roots.

The second story, set forth in part II, chronicles the deepening divisions in the black community over the issue of affirmative action and the increasing isolation of those I call the black dissenters—professionals and intellectuals who have developed positions that are often sharply opposed to those for which the contemporary civil rights movement now fights. This second tale is the more painful to tell, because it exposes the pain and anguish that have led many black supporters of racial preference to lash out bitterly against the dissenting black intellectuals. But these battles must end, for the problems of our community are too complex for us to pretend that all of their solutions are already known. Besides, in an age when increasing numbers of black professionals are resolving their ambivalence by declaring a desire to put the issue of racial preferences behind them, a war of this kind can have only losers. The losers, however, will not be those who are doing the fighting; they will be instead the millions of black people whose lives will be left unaffected by the result. Silencing debate solves no problems; it only limits the range of possible solutions. That is why, as I explain in part III, the time has come for the black community to seek a reconciled solidarity, based not on a consensus on solutions but on a shared desire to solve our problems.

Mine, of course, is in a sense only one person's story; it is not the story of the race. I do not set up myself or my life as models for anyone else, white or black. I do not write in order to convince anybody that every black person starts life with the various advantages I had. I do suspect, however, that what I have to say will resonate with the lives of many other black professionals, for when I talk about the contradictions of affirmative action, about the desire to attain career success without it, and about the difficulty in discussing these issues, I see eyes light up and heads nod. After all those of us who have come of age professionally in the era of affirmative action have shared the distinctive and unique experience of being part of a professional world that for the first time is seeing in substantial numbers people like us—people with faces that are not white.

I call us the affirmative action babies. I know that this term is sometimes used pejoratively, but it is my intention to invert that meaning, to embrace the term, not reject it. Had I not enjoyed the benefits of a racial preference in professional school admission, I would not have accomplished what I have in my career. I was afforded the opportunity for advanced professional training at one of the finest law schools in the country, Yale, and I like to think that I have made the most of this privilege. So, yes, I *am* an affirmative action baby, and I do not apologize for that fact.

By the term *affirmative action baby,* I mean to imply only a temporal identification: that is the name, and an accurate one, of the civil rights age in which we live. I do not intend any comment on qualification, on merit, on smarts, on how we got where we are, or on any of the other code words that often pass for reasoned argument about racial preferences. We are who we are, and we are where we are. But no matter who we are or where we are, our lives and careers will always be marked, fairly or not, by the era in which we came of age.

My generation was in or about to start high school when a nation torn by violent racial strife and shattered by the murder of Martin Luther King, Jr., decided to try preferential admission and hiring policies as a form, it was hoped, of corrective justice. We entered college around the dawn of the era of affirmative action in admission. My law school classmates and I agonized as preferential policies went through their first major crisis, a partial rejection by the Supreme Court of the United States in the *Bakke* case.[2] And now, as I look around the classrooms at the Yale Law School, where I have taught for almost a decade, I realize that the bright and diverse students of color I see before me have a shot, and a good one, at being the last members of the affirmative action generation—or, what is better still, the first members of the post–affirmative action generation, the professionals who will say to a doubting world, "Here are my accomplishments; take me or don't take me on my merits."

In recent years, however, affirmative action has slipped its moorings and started to drift. The drift has been slow, so slow that it has scarcely been noticed, but it has carried the programs a long and dangerous distance from the relatively placid waters of the provision of opportunities for developing talent. Nowadays, affirmative action is being transformed into a tool for representing the "points of view" of excluded groups. The argument one now hears is that people of color have a distinctive voice, a vision of the world, that is not being represented in the places where vital decisions are made: the boardroom, the bureaucracy, the campus. In the new rhetoric of affirmative action, it seems, the reason to seek out and hire or admit people of color is that one can have faith that their opinions, their perspective, will be different from the opinions and perspectives of people who are white—who evidently have a distinctive set of views of their own. The unfortunate logical corollary is that if the perspective a particular person of color can offer is *not* distinctive, if it is more like the "white" perspective than the "black" one, then that person is not speaking in an authentically black voice—an accusation that has become all too common.

But part of the responsibility of the intellectual is to try not to worry about whether one's views are, in someone else's judgment, the proper ones. The defining characteristic of the intellectual is not (as some seem to think) a particular level of educational or cultural attainment, and certainly not a particular political stance. What makes one an intellectual is the drive to learn, to question, to understand, to criticize, not as a means to an end but as an end in itself. An intellectual believes in criticism in the purest sense of the word, and understands that to be a critic is not necessarily to be an opponent; an intellectual, rather, is an observer willing and able to use rational faculties to distinguish wisdom from folly. An intellectual is necessarily a skeptic. To proclaim oneself an intellectual—admittedly an awkward act in our simplistic times—is to demand the right to doubt.

But I am not just another intellectual. I am, both by societal fiat and by personal choice, a *black* intellectual, and in that capacity I see my role as one of trying, if possible, to foster reconciliation, to promote the educational conversation from which all of us who care about the future of black people will benefit. There is no reason for us to be at each other's throats when there is so much on both sides of the argument from which all can learn. Our task, I think, should be to find the common ground, to be at once realistic about the world and sensitive to each other.

Let us, then, be frank: there is good reason to think that we are looking toward the end of most racial preferences— which, lest we forget, have long been justified as "transitional." For those of us who have been positioned to take advantage of what it offers, the affirmative action era has been a decidedly mixed blessing. The prospect of its end should be a challenge and a chance; it does not portend disaster. We must never turn affirmative action into a crutch, and therefore we must reject the common claim that an end to preferences "would be a disastrous situation, amounting to a virtual nullification of the 1954 desegregation ruling."[3] Our economic condition improved steadily in the decades before the institution of affirmative action, and I have far too much faith in our competitive capacity to anticipate some apocalypse when, inevitably, the programs are cut back. In the meanwhile, we should be concentrating on constructive dialogue about how to solve the problems of the real and continuing victims of the nation's legacy of racist oppression: the millions of struggling black Americans for whom affirmative action and entry to the professions are stunningly irrelevant.

Mine is not, I hope, a position that will be thought inauthentically black. It is not, I think, evidence of that most fatal of diseases (for a black intellectual), neoconservatism;* my views on many other matters are sufficiently to the left that I do not imagine the conservative movement would want me. (Neither, I think, would the left—but that is fine with me, for it is best for intellectuals to be politically unpredictable.)

The argument I present in this book is generated by reason but fired by love. My concern is with the situation of black people in America, a situation about which we need an open

---

*In chapter 7, I catalogue what I take to be the reasons the term *black conservative* has come to be pejorative, at least among intellectuals.

and reasoned dialogue. Surely the abject and sometimes desperate circumstances that confront so many of us who have not been fortunate enough to gain access to college and professional school are reason enough for us to stop sniping at one another. If not, we can be sure of two things: first, as professionals and intellectuals, we who are black and middle class will likely endure; second, as they struggle through the violent prisons that many inner cities have become, millions of other black people may not. So perhaps, for a golden moment, we can pause in our quarreling and actually talk *to* one another, instead of continuing an endless, self-defeating argument over who is the authentic keeper of the flame.

On Being an Affirmative Action Baby

It is a hard thing to live haunted by the ghost of an untrue dream . . . to know that with the Right that triumphed, triumphed something of Wrong.
—*W. E. B. DuBois,*
The Souls of Black Folk

CHAPTER 1

Racial Preferences?
So What?

I got into law school because I am black.

As many black professionals think they must, I have long suppressed this truth, insisting instead that I got where I am the same way everybody else did. Today I am a professor at the Yale Law School. I like to think that I am a good one, but I am hardly the most objective judge. What I am fairly sure of, and can now say without trepidation, is that were my skin not the color that it is, I would not have had the chance to try.

For many, perhaps most, black professionals of my generation, the matter of who got where and how is left in a studied and, I think, purposeful ambiguity. Some of us, as they say, would have made it into an elite college or professional school anyway. (But, in my generation, many fewer than we like to pretend, even though one might question the much-publicized claim by Derek Bok, the president of Harvard University, that in the absence of preferences, only 1 percent of Harvard's entering class would be black.)[1] Most of us, perhaps nearly all of us, have learned to bury the matter far back in our minds. We are who we are and where we are, we have records of accomplishment or failure, and there is no rational reason that anybody—employer, client, whoever—should care any longer whether racial preference played any role in our admission to a top professional school.

When people in positions to help or hurt our careers *do* seem to care, we tend to react with fury. Those of us who have graduated professional school over the past fifteen to twenty years, and are not white, travel career paths that are frequently bumpy with suspicions that we did not earn the right to be where we are. We bristle when others raise what might be called the qualification question—"Did you get into school or get hired because of a special program?"—and that prickly sensitivity is the best evidence, if any is needed, of one of the principal costs of racial preferences. Scratch a black professional with the qualification question, and you're likely to get a caustic response, such as this one from a senior executive at a major airline: "Some whites think I've made it because I'm black. Some blacks think I've made it only because I'm an Uncle Tom. The fact is, I've made it because I'm good."[2]

Given the way that so many Americans seem to treat receipt of the benefits of affirmative action as a badge of shame, answers of this sort are both predictable and sensible. In the professional world, moreover, they are very often true: relatively few corporations are in a position to hand out charity. The peculiar aspect of the routine denial, however, is that so many of those who will bristle at the suggestion that they themselves have gained from racial preferences will try simultaneously to insist that racial preferences be preserved and to force the world to pretend that no one benefits from them. That awkward balancing of fact and fiction explains the frequent but generally groundless cry that it is racist to suggest that some individual's professional accomplishments would be fewer but for affirmative action; and therein hangs a tale.

For students at the leading law schools, autumn brings the recruiting season, the idyllic weeks when law firms from around the country compete to lavish upon them lunches and dinners and other attentions, all with the professed goal of obtaining the students' services—perhaps for the summer, perhaps for a longer term. The autumn of 1989 was different, however, because the nation's largest firm, Baker & McKenzie, was banned from interviewing students at the University of Chicago Law School, and on probation—that is, enjoined to be on its best behavior—at some others.

The immediate source of Baker & McKenzie's problems was a racially charged interview that a partner in the firm had conducted the previous fall with a black third-year student at the school. The interviewer evidently suggested that other lawyers might call her "nigger" or "black bitch" and wanted to know how she felt about that. Perhaps out of surprise that she played golf, he observed that "there aren't too many golf courses in the ghetto." He also suggested that the school was admitting "foreigners" and excluding "qualified" Americans.[3]

The law school reacted swiftly, and the firm was banned from interviewing on campus. Other schools contemplated taking action against the firm, and some of them did.[4] Because I am black myself, and teach in a law school, I suppose the easiest thing for me to have done would have been to clamor in solidarity for punishment. Yet I found myself strangely reluctant to applaud the school's action. Instead, I was disturbed rather than excited by this vision of law schools circling the wagons, as it were, to defend their beleaguered minority students against racially insensitive remarks. It is emphatically not my intention to defend the interviewer, most of whose reported questions and comments were inexplicable and inexcusable. I am troubled, however, by my suspicion that there would still have been outrage—not as much, but some— had the interviewer asked only what I called at the beginning of the chapter the qualification question.

I suspect this because in my own student days, something over a decade ago, an interviewer from a prominent law firm addressed this very question to a Yale student who was not white, and the student voices—including my own—howled in protest. "Racism!" we insisted. "Ban them!" But with the passing years, I have come to wonder whether our anger might have been misplaced.

To be sure, the Yale interviewer's question was boorish. And because the interviewer had a grade record and résumé right in front of him, it was probably irrelevant as well. (It is useful here to dispose of one common but rather silly anti-affirmative action bromide: the old question, "Do you really want to be treated by a doctor who got into medical school because of skin color?" The answer is, or ought to be, that the patient doesn't particularly care how the doctor got *into* school; what matters is how the doctor got *out*. The right question, the sensible question, is not "What medical school performance did your grades and test scores predict?" but "What was your medical school performance?") But irrelevance and boorishness cannot explain our rage at the qualification question, because lots of interviewers ask questions that meet the tests of boorishness and irrelevance.

The controversy is not limited to outsiders who come onto campus to recruit. In the spring of 1991, for example, students at Georgetown Law School demanded punishment for a classmate who argued in the school newspaper that affirmative action is unfair because students of color are often admitted to law school on the basis of grades and test scores that would cause white applicants to be rejected. Several universities have considered proposals that would deem it "racial harassment" for a (white?) student to question the qualifications of nonwhite classmates.* But we can't change either the truths or the myths about racial preferences by punishing those who speak them.

This clamor for protection from the qualification question is powerful evidence of the terrible psychological pressure that racial preferences often put on their beneficiaries. Indeed, it sometimes seems as though the programs are not supposed to have any beneficiaries—or, at least, that no one is permitted to suggest that they have any.

And that's ridiculous. If one supports racial preferences in professional school admissions, for example, one must be prepared to treat them like any other preference in admission and believe that they make a difference, that some students would not be admitted if the preferences did not exist. This is

---

*I discuss campus regulation of racial harassment in chapter 8.

not a racist observation. It is not normative in any sense. It is
simply a fact. A good deal of emotional underbrush might be
cleared away were the fact simply conceded, and made the beginning, not the end, of any discussion of preferences. For
once it is conceded that the programs have beneficiaries, it follows that some of us who are professionals and are not white
must be among them. Supporters of preferences must stop
pretending otherwise. Rather, some large segment of us must
be willing to meet the qualification question head-on, to say,
"Yes, I got into law school because of racial preferences. So
what?"—and, having said it, must be ready with a list of what
we have made of the opportunities the preferences provided.

Now, this is a costly concession, because it carries with it
all the baggage of the bitter rhetorical battle over the relationship between preferences and merit. But bristling at the question suggests a deep-seated fear that the dichotomy might be
real. Indeed, if admitting that racial preferences make a difference leaves a funny aftertaste in the mouths of proponents,
they might be more comfortable fighting against preferences
rather than for them.

So let us bring some honesty as well as rigor to the debate, and begin at the beginning. I have already made clear
my starting point: I got into a top law school because I am
black. Not only am I unashamed of this fact, but I can prove
its truth.

As a senior at Stanford back in the mid-1970s, I applied
to about half a dozen law schools. Yale, where I would ultimately enroll, came through fairly early with an acceptance.
So did all but one of the others. The last school, Harvard,
dawdled and dawdled. Finally, toward the end of the admission season, I received a letter of rejection. Then, within days,
two different Harvard officials and a professor contacted me
by telephone to apologize. They were quite frank in their explanation for the "error." I was told by one official that the
school had initially rejected me because "we assumed from
your record that you were white." (The words have always
stuck in my mind, a tantalizing reminder of what is expected
of me.) Suddenly coy, he went on to say that the school had

obtained "additional information that should have been counted in your favor"—that is, Harvard had discovered the color of my skin. And if I had already made a deposit to confirm my decision to go elsewhere, well, that, I was told, would "not be allowed" to stand in my way should I enroll at Harvard.

Naturally, I was insulted by this miracle. Stephen Carter, the white male, was not good enough for the Harvard Law School; Stephen Carter, the black male, not only was good enough but rated agonized telephone calls urging him to attend. And Stephen Carter, color unknown, must have been white: How else could he have achieved what he did in college? Except that my college achievements were obviously not sufficiently spectacular to merit acceptance had I been white. In other words, my academic record was too good for a black Stanford University undergraduate, but not good enough for a white Harvard law student. Because I turned out to be black, however, Harvard was quite happy to scrape me from what it apparently considered somewhere nearer the bottom of the barrel.

My objective is not to single out Harvard for special criticism; on the contrary, although my ego insists otherwise, I make no claim that a white student with my academic record would have been admitted to any of the leading law schools. The insult I felt came from the pain of being reminded so forcefully that in the judgment of those with the power to dispose, I was good enough for a top law school only because I happened to be black.

Naturally, I should not have been insulted at all; that is what racial preferences are for—racial preference. But I was insulted and went off to Yale instead, even though I had then and have now absolutely no reason to imagine that Yale's judgment was based on different criteria than Harvard's. Hardly anyone granted admission at Yale is denied admission at Harvard, which admits a far larger class; but several hundreds of students who are admitted at Harvard are denied admission at Yale. Because Yale is far more selective, the chances are good that I was admitted at Yale for essentially the same reason I was admitted at Harvard—the color of my skin made up for what were evidently considered other deficiencies in my academic record. I may embrace this truth as a matter of simple justice or rail against it as one of life's great evils, but being a member of the affirmative action generation means that the one thing I cannot do is deny it. I will say it again: I got into law school because I am black. So what?

II

One answer to the "So what?" question is that someone more deserving than I—someone white—may have been turned away. I hardly know what to make of this argument, for I doubt that the mythical white student on the cusp, the one who almost made it to Yale but for my rude intervention, would have done better than I did in law school.* Nor am I some peculiar case: the Yale Law School of my youth trained any number of affirmative action babies who went on to fine academic performances and are now in the midst of stellar careers in the law.

Even in the abstract, what I call the "fairness story" has never struck me as one of the more convincing arguments against preferential policies. The costs of affirmative action differ from the costs of taxation only in degree, not in kind. People are routinely taxed for services they do not receive that are deemed by their government necessary to right social wrongs they did not commit. The taxpayer-financed "bailout"

---

*It has always struck me as quite bizarre that so many otherwise thoughtful people on both sides of the affirmative action controversy seem to think so much turns on the question of how the beneficiaries perform. I would not dismiss the inquiry as irrelevant, but I am reluctant to say that it is the whole ball game. It may be the case, as many critics have argued, that the affirmative action beneficiary who fails at Harvard College might have performed quite well at a less competitive school and gone on to an excellent and productive career that will almost surely be lost because of the shattering experience of academic failure; but one must weigh this cost (and personal choice) against the tale of the student who would not have attended Harvard without affirmative action and who succeeds brilliantly there. It may be that those who do less well in school because of preferences outnumber those who do better, but such statistics are only the edge of the canvas, a tiny part of a much larger and more complex picture, and that is why I think the energy devoted to the qualification question is largely wasted.

of the weak or collapsed savings-and-loan institutions is one example. Another is the provision of tax dollars for emergency disaster assistance after a hurricane devastates a coastal community. The people who bear the costs of these programs are not the people who caused the damage, but they still have to pay.[5]

Like many, perhaps most, of America's domestic policies, affirmative action programs are essentially redistributive in nature. They transfer resources from their allocation in the market to other recipients, favored for social policy reasons. Much of the attack on affirmative action is fueled by the same instinct—the same American dream—that stands as a bulwark against any substantial redistribution of wealth. In America, most people like to think, it is possible for anyone to make it, and those who do not have been victims principally of their own sloth or lack of talent or perhaps plain bad luck— but not of anybody else's sinister plottings. Seymour Martin Lipset, among others, has argued plausibly that a stable democracy is possible only when an economically secure middle class exists to battle against radical economic reforms that the wealthier classes would otherwise resist by using means outside the system.[6] In America, that middle class plainly exists, and racial preferences are among the radical reforms it is willing to resist.

Sometimes the fervent opposition of the great majority of white Americans to affirmative action is put down to racism, or at least racial resentment, and I do not want to argue that neither motivation is *ever* present. But affirmative action programs are different from other social transfers, and the way they differ is in the basis on which the favored and disfavored groups are identified. The basis is race, and sometimes sex—and that makes all the difference.

I say that race is different not because I favor the ideal of a color-blind society; indeed, for reasons I discuss in chapter 9, I fear that the rhetoric of color blindness conflates values that are best kept separate. Race is different for obvious historical reasons: the world in general, and this nation in particular, should know well the risks of encouraging powerful institutions to categorize by such immutable characteristics as race. Besides, even were race as a category less controversial, there is still the further fairness argument, that the sins for which the programs purportedly offer compensation are not sins of the current generation.

Many proponents of preferential policies, however, insist that the current generation of white males deserves to bear the costs of affirmative action. "White males," we are told, "have had exclusive access to certain information, education, experience, and contacts through which they have gained unfair advantage."[7] In the words of a leading scholar, "[W]e have to say to whites, 'Listen, you have benefited in countless ways from racism, from its notions of beauty [and] its exclusion of minorities in jobs and schools.'"[8] The argument has a second step, too: "For most of this country's history," wrote one commentator, "the nation's top universities practiced the most effective form of affirmative action ever; the quota was for 100 percent white males."[9] The analogy is fair—indeed, it is so fair that it wins the endorsement of opponents as well as supporters of affirmative action[10]—but what does it imply? For proponents of preferences, the answer is clear: if white males have been for centuries the beneficiaries of a vast and all-encompassing program of affirmative action, today's more limited programs can be defended as simply trying to undo the most pernicious effects of that one. That is how, in the contemporary rhetoric of affirmative action, white males turn out to deserve the disfavored treatment that the programs accord.*

But there is risk in this rhetoric. To make race the determining factor not simply of the favored group but of the disfavored one encourages an analytical structure that seeks and assigns reasons in the present world for disfavoring one group. The simplest structure—and the one that has come, with mysterious force, to dominate the terms of intellectual

---

*Even accepting this dubious rhetorical construct, it is easy to see that racial preferences call for sacrifices not from white males as a group but from the subgroups of white males most likely to be excluded by a preference benefiting someone else—that is, the most disadvantaged white males, those who, by hypothesis, have gained the least from racism.

and campus debate—is what Thomas Sowell has called "social irredentism," an insistence that all members of the disfavored dominant group bear the mantle of oppressor.[11] Affirmative action, then, becomes almost a punishment for the sin of being born the wrong color and the wrong sex.

All of this carries a neat historical irony. The personalization of affirmative action, the specification of white males as the villains, has diluted the message of the black left of the 1960s and early 1970s, which often (but by no means always) joined forces with the white left to insist that the problems were systemic, not individual. In those halcyon days of campus radicalism, the race struggle was widely described as hand-in-glove with the class struggle. Racial justice was said to be impossible under capitalism, and the principal debate among radical students was over what form of socialism was best for black people—a separate society or an integrated one, central planning or local communities?

As for affirmative action, well, sophisticated nationalists understood that it was part of the problem. By funneling the best and brightest young black men and women into the white-dominated system of higher education, the critics argued, the programs would simply skim the cream from our community, co-opting into the (white) mainstream those who should have been our leaders. An attack on efforts to substitute enhanced educational opportunities for racial justice was a principal focus of Robert Allen's provocative 1969 book *Black Awakening in Capitalist America.* "The black student," Allen warned, "is crucial to corporate America's neocolonial plans."[12] The best and brightest among black youth, he argued, instead of criticizing capitalism from the outside, would be trained to serve it from the inside. Nationalist reviewers agreed. For example, Anne Kelley wrote in *The Black Scholar* that "the emphasis on higher education for black students" was part of a "neo-colonialist scheme" that was "designed to stabilize the masses."[13]

But the language of protest is quite different now, and the success of affirmative action is one of the reasons; to paraphrase John le Carré, it is hard to criticize the system when it has brought you inside at its own expense. Affirmative action programs in education are designed to move people of color into productive roles in capitalist society, and the best sign that they are working is the way the argument has shifted. White males have replaced "the society" or "the system" or "the establishment" in the rhetoric of racial justice, perhaps because the rhetoric of justice is no longer under the control of genuine radicals. The modern proponents of preferences rarely plan to spend their lives in community organizing as they await the revolutionary moment, and there is no particular reason that they should. They are liberal reformers, not radical revolutionaries; with the collapse of communism as a force in the world, nobody seems to think any longer that the solution is to burn everything down and start over. On campuses nowadays, especially in the professional schools, the students of color seem about as likely as their white classmates to be capitalists to their very fingertips; they have no desire to kill the golden goose that the (white male) establishment has created. Or, to switch metaphors, today's affirmative action advocates want mainly to share in the pie, not to see it divided up in some scientific socialist redistribution.

III

Which helps explain, I think, why the "So what?" that I advocate is not easy to utter. Students of color are in the professional schools for the same reason white students are there: to get a good education and a good job. Because so many people seem to assume that the beneficiaries of affirmative action programs are necessarily bound for failure, or at least for inferiority, there is an understandable tendency for people of color to resist being thought of as beneficiaries. After all, who wants to be bound for failure? (Especially when so many beneficiaries of racial preferences really *don't* succeed as they would like.)[14] Better not to think about it; better to make sure nobody else thinks about it either. Rather than saying, "So what?" better to say, "How dare you?"

I understand perfectly this temptation to try to make the world shut up, to pursue the fantasy that doubts that are not expressed do not exist. When I listen to the labored but heart-felt arguments on why potential employers (and, for that matter, other students) should not be permitted to question the admission qualifications of students of color, I am reminded uneasily of another incident from my own student days, a shining moment when we, too, thought that if we could only stifle debate on the question, we could make it go away.

The incident I have in mind occurred during the fall of 1978, my third year in law school, a few months after the Supreme Court's decision in *Regents of the University of California v. Bakke,*[15] which placed what seemed to many of us unnecessarily severe restrictions on the operation of racially conscious admission programs. The air was thick with swirling critiques of racial preferences, most of them couched in the language of merit versus qualification. Everywhere we turned, someone seemed to be pointing at us and saying, "You don't belong here." We looked around and saw an academic world that seemed to be doing its best to get rid of us.

So we struck back. We called the critics racist. We tried to paint the question of our qualifications as a racist one. And one evening, when the Yale Political Union, a student organization, had scheduled a debate on the matter (the title, as I recall, was "The Future of Affirmative Action"), we demonstrated. All of us.

Our unanimity was astonishing. Then as now, the black students at the law school were divided, politically, socially, and in dozens of other ways. But on this issue, we were suddenly united. We picketed the Political Union meeting, roaring our slogan *("We are not debatable! We are not debatable!")* in tones of righteous outrage. We made so much noise that at last they threw wide the doors and invited us in. In exchange for our promise to end the demonstration so that the debate could be conducted, we were offered, and we accepted, the chance to have one of our number address the assembly. That task, for some reason, fell to me.

I remember my rising excitement as I stood before the

audience of immaculately attired undergraduates, many of them still in their teens. There was something sweet and naive and appealing about the Political Union members as they sat nervously but politely in their tidy rows, secure (or, perhaps, momentarily insecure) in their faith that a commitment to openness and debate would lead to moral truth. But I set my face against the smile that was twitching there, and tried to work up in its stead a glower sufficient to convey the image of the retributive fury of the radical black left. (Having missed those days in college, I thought perhaps to rekindle them briefly.) And while some of the kids seemed annoyed at the intrusion, others looked frightened, even intimidated, which I suppose was our goal. I spoke briefly, pointing out that it was easy for white people to call for color-blind admissions when they understood perfectly well that none of the costs would fall on them. I carefully avoided the word *racism,* but I let the implication hang in the air anyway, lest I be misunderstood.

And then we marched out again, triumphantly, clapping and chanting rhythmically as though in solemn reminder that should the Political Union folks get up to any more nonsense, we might return and drown them out again. (A few of the undergraduates and one of the speakers joined us in our clapping.) We were, for a shining moment, in our glory; the reporters were there, tapes rolling, cameras clicking; in our minds, we had turned back the calendar by a decade and the campuses were in flames (or at least awash with megaphones and boycotts and banners and an administration ready to compromise); the school would meet us with a promise of justice or we would tear it down!

Then all at once it was over. We dispersed, returning to our dormitory rooms and apartments, our law review and moot court activities, our long nights in the library to prepare for class and our freshly cleaned suits for job interviews, our political differences and our social cliques. We returned to the humdrum interests of law school life, and suddenly we were just like everybody else again. Absolutely nothing had changed. *Bakke* was still the law of the land. There was no magic, the campus was not in flames, and there had never been a shining moment. There was only the uneasy tension of our dual existence. The peculiar uncertainty provoked by affirmative action was still with us, and our outrage at being reminded of its reality was undiminished. And as for the eager young minds of the Political Union, I suppose they held their debate and I suppose somebody won.

I V

The demonstration at the Political Union seems very long ago now, not only in time but in place: Could that really have been Yale? Could that really have been *us?* (I look around at the chanting faces in my memory and pick out their subsequent histories: this one a partner in an elite law firm, that one an investment banker, this one a leading public interest lawyer, that one another partner, this one in the State Department, that one a professor at a leading law school, this one a prosecuting attorney, that one in the legal department of a Fortune 100 corporation, and so on.) We are not the people we were then, but the fact that the debate was held over our boisterous objections seems not to have diverted our careers. We are a successful generation of lawyers, walking advertisements, it might seem, for the bright side of affirmative action. Our doubts, seen from this end of the tunnel, seem vague and insubstantial.

At the time, however, the doubts, and the anger, were painfully real. I do not want to suggest that the doubts have persisted into our careers or those of other black professionals—I am as irritated as anybody else by the frequent suggestion that there lurks inside each black professional a confused and uncertain ego, desperately seeking reassurance—but it is certainly true that as long as racial preferences exist, the one thing that cannot be proved is which people of color in my generation would have achieved what they have in their absence.

At this point in the argument many of us are told, as though in reassurance, "Oh, don't worry, you're not here because of affirmative action—you're here on merit." But it is not easy to take this as quite the compliment it is presumably meant to be. In the first place, it continues the opposition of merit to preference that has brought about the pain and anger to begin with. More important, and perhaps more devastating, it places the judgment on how good we are just where we do not want it to be: in the minds and mouths of white colleagues, whose arrogant "assurances" serve as eloquent reminders of how fragile a trophy is our hard-won professional status.

Very well, perhaps we were wrong in our youthful enthusiasm to try to stifle debate, but that is not the point of the story. The point, rather, is that our outrage was misdirected. Even at the time of my glowering diatribe, I realized that not all of what I said was fair. Looking back, I have come to understand even better how much of my message—our message—was driven by our pain over *Bakke* and the nation's changing mood. "Don't you understand?" we were crying. "We have fought hard to get here, and we will not be pushed back!"

Our anguish was not less real for being misdirected. Whether one wants to blame racial preferences or white racism or the pressures of professional school or some combination of them all, our pain was too great for us to consider for an instant the possibility that victory in the battle to "get here" did not logically entail affirmative action. We were not prepared to discuss or even to imagine life without preferences, a world in which we would be challenged to meet and beat whatever standards for admission and advancement were placed before us. We wanted no discussion at all, only capitulation. All we saw was that the Supreme Court had given us the back of its hand in *Bakke* (we even wore little buttons: FIGHT RACISM, OVERTURN BAKKE) and the forces of reaction were closing in.

Now that I am a law professor, one of my more delicate tasks is convincing my students, whatever their color, to consider the possibility that perhaps the forces of reaction are *not* closing in. Perhaps what seems to them (and to many other people) a backlash against affirmative action is instead (or in addition) a signal that the programs, at least in their current expansive form, have run their course. Or perhaps, if the programs are to be preserved, they should move closer to their roots: the provision of opportunities for people of color who might not otherwise have the advanced training that will allow them to prove what they can do.

My students tend to disagree, sometimes vehemently. The bad guys are out there, they tell me, and they are winning. And one of the reasons they are winning, as I understand it, is that they get to set the rules. A couple of years ago, for example, a student complained to me that people of color are forced to disguise their true voices and write like white males in order to survive the writing competition for membership on the *Yale Law Journal.* One critic has argued that university faculties employ a "hierarchical majoritarian" standard for judging academic work—a standard that is not sensitive to the special perspective people of color can bring to scholarship.[16] And all over the corporate world, I am led to believe, the standards of what counts as merit are designed, perhaps intentionally, to keep us out.

Nowadays, racial preferences are said to be our tool for forcing those bad guys—the white males who run the place, the purveyors, so I am told, of so much misery and the inheritors of so much unearned privilege—to acknowledge that theirs is only one way of looking at the world. Anyone who can't see the force of this argument is evidently a part of the problem. White people who ask whether the quest for diversity contemplates a lowering of standards of excellence are still charged with racism, just as in the old days. (The forces of reaction *are* closing in.) People of color who venture similar thoughts are labeled turncoats and worse, just as they always have been. (Don't they *know* that academic standards are a white male invention aimed at maintaining a eurocentric hegemony?) And through it all, the devotion to numbers that has long characterized the affirmative action debate continues.

Certainly the proportions of black people in the various professions are nothing to shout about. In my own field of law teaching, for example, a study prepared for the Society of

American Law Teachers shows that only 3.7 percent of faculty members are black at law schools that are, as the report puts it in an unfortunate bit of jargon, "majority-run."[17] In other professions, too, although the numbers have generally improved in recent years, the percentages of black folk remain small. On medical school faculties, for example, 1.9 percent of the professors are black.[18] On university faculties generally, just 4 percent of the faculty members are black. For lawyers and judges, the figure is 2.3 percent. For physicians, 3.3 percent. Financial managers, 4.3 percent. (And, as long as we're at it, for authors, 0.4 percent, about 1 out of 250.)[19]

But while we might agree on the desirability of raising these numbers, the question of strategy continues to divide us. To try to argue (as I do elsewhere in this book) that purported racism in professional standards is not a plausible explanation for most of the data is to risk being dismissed for one's naïveté. And as to my oft-stated preference for returning to the roots of affirmative action: well, the roots, as it turns out, had the matter all wrong. My generation, with its obsessive concern with proving itself in the white man's world, pressed an argument that was beside the point. Had we but understood the ways in which our experiences differ from those of the dominant majority, it seems, we would have insisted on an affirmative action that rewrites the standards for excellence, rather than one that trains us to meet them.

CHAPTER 2

The Representatives of the People

I n race-obsessed America, racial stereotypes are back in fashion. Having run out of ways to talk about our obsession, we have gone back to the basics—only now the stereotypers are the friends, not just the enemies, of people of color. The rising generation of black professionals, the one that was supposed to smash the racist stereotypes of inferiority and more, instead finds itself mired in the rhetoric of the 1960s, confronted with a network of expectations that to be black is to hold a certain set of views.

Consider: When Gary Franks, a wealthy conservative Republican who happens to be black, was running his ultimately successful race for a congressional seat in Connecticut, the *New York Times,* in an editorial endorsing his white opponent, offered as one argument the suggestion that Franks would "be a misfit in the Congressional Black Caucus."[1] Now, even assuming the truth of this supposition, what is one to make of it? The message, I suppose, is that Franks's blackness creates a special obligation to hold a particular set of views. One can only assume that had Franks presented views that made him fit more snugly (in the *Times*'s view) into the Black Caucus, he would have been a more attractive candidate.

Meanwhile, absent an editorial lambasting a white candidate for holding positions inconsistent with those of the Black Caucus, one must assume that the *Times* said what it did in the way it did because Franks is black. The Caucus is a fine and necessary organization, but where is it written that black people who do not share the views of its members are ineligible for public office? Evidently, and unfortunately, it is written in the *New York Times.* As a letter to the editor subsequently complained, the editorial was "an appalling effort to straitjacket members of particular groups into adopting a uniform position on a political litmus test."[2]

Appalling, perhaps. Uncommon, no. Indeed, far from being an aberration, the *Times* editorial on Franks is a comment on our turbulent times. Nowadays, if you know the color of somebody's skin, you know what the person values (or should value), what causes the person supports (or should support), and how he or she thinks (or should think). Skin color, it seems, is a perfectly acceptable proxy for lots of other things—but principally for holding, or being willing to espouse, the right views.

Consider another event, one that occurred on a slow news day a few months before the Franks editorial, when a member of the Congress of the United States, perhaps seeking a way of making his commentary more vivid, attacked a black public official as "a disgrace to his race." The scheme worked: the Representative, Fortney "Pete" Stark, was suddenly news everywhere. The official singled out for this cruel and preposterous insult was Louis Sullivan, Secretary of Health and Human Services under George Bush. Stark, who is white, was trying to argue that Bush administration health policies were harming the health of black Americans. Undoubtedly stunned by this personal assault, Sullivan responded with considerable punch: "I don't live on Pete Stark's plantation." In what must have been for them a lovely irony, conservative Republicans had the rare pleasure of demanding from liberal Democrats an apology for a racial epithet.[3]

Stark apologized, of course; that's politics. But the impulse that would lead a prominent member of the Congress to make such a remark in the first place is an important symbol of our racially charged times. The central fact in the story is the color of Sullivan's skin. Even granting for the sake of argument Stark's premise that the Bush administration's health policies were harming black Americans, no one would suppose that a white government official who carried them out was a disgrace to his race (although the white official might be considered a disgrace in some other sense). Stark's criticism of Sullivan, like the *Times*'s criticism of Franks, reflects the idea that black people who gain positions of authority or influence are vested with a special responsibility to articulate the presumed views of other people who are black—in effect, to think and act and speak in a particular way, the *black* way—and that there is something peculiar about black people who insist on doing anything else.

In an earlier era, such sentiments might have been marked down as frankly racist. Now, however, they are almost a gospel for people who want to show their commitment to equality. The rhetoric is everywhere. No government would imagine creating a commission to study any important problem without first ensuring adequate "minority representation." A university would find it unthinkable to search for a new chancellor with a committee that is entirely white. Corporate boards of directors are openly on the lookout for members who will "represent the interests" of people who are not white. (In a wonderful inversion of Say's Law, that supply generates demand, specialized executive search firms have sprung up to find candidates who will speak in the proper voice.)[4] Two recent studies of television news programs by Fairness and Accuracy in Reporting (FAIR) have informed us that through their choice of guests, the popular ABC news/interview program "Nightline" and the "MacNeil/Lehrer Newshour," the flagship of public television, both "overrepresent" the views of the corporate and national security establishment—represented, it seems, by white males—and "underrepresent" the presumably contrary views of women and people of color.[5] (Presumably the diligent researchers who prepared the report were not aware of the survey data suggesting that on many, perhaps most, controversial policy issues, including those regarding foreign affairs, the views of people of color tend to be similar to, or to the right of, the views of white males.)[6] In April 1990, when Derrick Bell, a prominent law professor at Harvard, announced his intention to take an extended unpaid leave of absence in protest of the school's continuing failure to grant tenure to a black woman, he argued for the hiring of people of color who are "willing by preference to embrace rather than reject the unique political and cultural perspectives of those this society places in subordinate status."[7] The theory underlying all of this seems to be that people who are not white have a distinct point of view that *must be represented,* which makes Pete Stark's error, if no less outrageous, at least considerably more understandable.

Viewpoint, outlook, perspective—whatever word is used, the significance is the same. We have come to a point in the evolution of our ways of talking about race when it is not only respectable but actually encouraged for public and private institutions alike to make policy based on stereotypes about the different ways in which people who are white and people who are black supposedly think. The reason we have come down this path has much to do with the problems plaguing racial preferences. Affirmative action, its once-bright promise tarnished by a growing awareness of its flaws and a rising opposition, is evidently in need of a new and less vulnerable guise. Indeed, Stark's expectation that Sullivan should take a particular position because of his race might be considered the sad but logical end toward which affirmative action has lately been moving us.

In this latter-day vision of affirmative action, black people in positions of prominence have become *representatives of their people.* Black people who have attained a measure of success in the white world are assumed—and, indeed, expected—always and everywhere to represent the race, not in the traditional and still-important senses of serving as role models for those who will come later or opening doors by proving their worth, but in a strange new sense of bringing excluded voices into the corridors of power, thereby articulating the interests of a constituency.

This obligation is different from the venerable (if not always venerated) vision of solidarity, the notion that successful people who are black owe support or inspiration to those who have not shared their advantages. Instead, the opportunities the civil rights movement opened up have been diluted by the imposition of a stereotype that the black people on the inside will hold a particular, and predictable, set of political positions—will be, in effect, black people of the right kind. Not only does this notion stereotype the black professionals whom it burdens; it also stereotypes the people themselves, the less fortunate, who become a faceless monolith without any of the richness or diversity that characterizes people of color. They become simply possessors of a "viewpoint" that the black people who reach positions of influence are expected to articulate. And what goes often unspoken yet clearly implied in all of this is that people of color who do not hold or represent this special viewpoint (whatever it is) are not the right people to fill these representational slots. As Derrick Bell has put it, "the ends of diversity are not served by people who look black and think white."[8]

Given its starting point, the argument is virtually seamless: successful black people who hold the "wrong" views do not belong on the inside because they are bringing nothing new to the table. They are expressing opinions that white males can express perfectly well. They are not bona fide representatives of the people.

How things have changed! In my own student days, the case for racial preferences in hiring or college admission might have been controversial, but at least it was clear. The dearth of black students in colleges and professional schools, like the dearth of black professionals generally, was understood to be a vestige of the nation's odious legacy of racist oppression. The schools, therefore, would reach out to bring into their student bodies highly motivated young people who might not have been admitted under the prevailing criteria but would nevertheless, if all went as planned, benefit from the opportunity for advanced training at a good school. And then they would graduate and go on to do . . . well, whatever it is that graduates do. They would be their own people, their obligation to their ethnicity discharged by the fact that they had taken full advantage of the opportunities offered.

Evidently, this is not quite the understanding any longer. Affirmative action programs are still around, and despite mounting political resistance (the Republican Party has already intimated plans to make racial preference a campaign issue in 1992), the pressure to expand them is considerable. But affirmative action of the 1990s is not the same as affirmative action of the 1970s. The ideals of affirmative action have become conflated with the proposition that there is a *black way to be*—and the beneficiaries of affirmative action are nowadays supposed to be people who will be black the right way.

This notion goes under the deceptive rubric of *diversity,* a wonderfully evocative word that conjures images of the Walt Disney Pavilion at the New York World's Fair in the mid-1960s, with its lines of smiling, fresh-faced audioanimatronic children, not noticeably different from one another except in skin color, singing about what a small world it is after all. (In my student days, it was more or less obligatory to see racism in images of this kind, and with some reason: we don't all look like Anglo-Saxons with painted faces, and we wouldn't want to, no matter how much Walter Disney, Sr., who never allowed a nonwhite face into his Mouseketeers, might have wished otherwise.)

This new conception of affirmative action might be called viewpoint diversity, because its goal is to diversify a professional world that is said to represent mostly the viewpoints of white males. Even if racial preferences have nothing to do with their attainments, members of the new generation of black professionals—whether sitting in a boardroom, crunching numbers in a computer room, lecturing in a classroom, or cutting political deals in a smoke-filled room—are widely expected, even encouraged, to speak on behalf of and in the voice of all the other people of color who are less fortunate than they.

But suppose the representatives speak in the wrong voice? What if they press views that are deemed not, in fact, to be the views of the people? The answer should be obvious: if they espouse the wrong views, they are not doing their jobs. They are not giving the people good representation. This notion, I think, helps explain the reason that some black activists—made incautious, perhaps, by the times in which we live—seem to reserve their most stinging rebukes not for white racists but for prominent black people who are not, in their view, representing the race as they should. This, surely, was the point of the harsh reprimand delivered by Representative John Conyers, who is black, to William Lucas, also black, who was at the time the Republican candidate for governor of Michigan and who, had he won, would have been the first elected black governor in the nation's history. Said Conyers, "I want to tell you that biologically he is black, but he is not in the spirit of Martin Luther King or the civil rights movement."[9] Just biologically black: Lucas, as Conyers saw it, was not a proper representative of his people.

This, perhaps, captures in a nutshell the problem Pete Stark had with Louis Sullivan and the editorial staff of the *Times* had with Gary Franks. The two black men did not fit the rhetoric. They did not express the proper views—the views of their proper constituents, not the voters at large, but the other black people, the people represented in the Black Caucus. Such eccentricity evidently provokes discomfort, for the proposition that people who are black can be neatly stuffed into boxes, with experiences and views that are predictably different from the views of people who are white, has practically become an article of faith among advocates of diversity. No one, I assume, would dispute the notion that there are substantial benefits to be gained from association with people unlike oneself. But as much as defenders of this new understanding of affirmative action might protest that it is not intended to suggest that people of color hold a *particular* set of views, it is difficult to make sense of the arguments any other way: after all, if the views of people who are not white turn out to be just the same as the views of people who are, the case for using race as a proxy for viewpoint diversity collapses.

The proposition that there is a right way and a wrong way to be black, and its logical corollary, that people who are black the wrong way are part of the problem rather than part of the solution, recalls the rhetoric of the 1960s and early 1970s, when the idea that one should be a black person of the right kind held a great deal of currency. Huey P. Newton, in his autobiography, lavished contempt upon Stokely Carmichael for trying to intervene on behalf of a black police officer threatened with dismissal from his post. The Black Panthers, said Newton, considered Carmichael's act "racist and suicidal." The reason? "If you support a Black man with a gun who belongs to the military arm of your oppressor, then you are assisting in your own destruction."[10]

That, perhaps, is the difficulty with black people who refuse to be representatives of the right kind, who, rather than bringing to the table a fresh and authentic perspective, instead confound the stereotypes of those who have brought them in by stating views that are . . . well, not what black people are supposed to say. The larger the number of black students and professionals who refuse to speak in the proper voice, the greater the difficulty for the theory holding that the reason to integrate elite institutions of education, commerce, and government is to bring that voice inside. And yet the notion that race is a good proxy for viewpoint remains a crucial premise of the modern diversity movement, a premise so unquestioned that, as we shall see, even the Supreme Court of the United States has pronounced itself unbothered by a federal agency's open assumption that it is true.

II

Once the search for people of color is envisioned as a process for the inclusion of particular views those people are presumed to hold, there is no logical stopping point. As it turns out, there may be no illogical stopping point, either. For example, if the dominance of the airwaves by white *studio guests* distorts public debate by excluding the purportedly different voices and views of people who are not white, how much worse must the situation be when the facilities where decisions are made on what views to broadcast are themselves *owned* by white people far out of proportion to their numbers in the population? Quite a bit worse, evidently; so much so that the Federal Communications Commission, a bit over a decade ago, adopted regulations designed to enhance "broadcast diversity" by granting preferences in certain circumstances to "minority" bidders for broadcast properties.

How exactly does minority ownership enhance diversity of programming?* The only possible answer lies in assuming that owners who are white and owners who are not will reach different conclusions about which programs to air. One might assume instead that minority owners, far from evidencing some distinct mode of thought, would face the same economic imperatives as white owners—pleasing the audience, attracting advertisers, and thus making money—but one would apparently be wrong.† For in 1990, no less an authority than the Supreme Court of the United States ruled that the government is perfectly free to make policy predicated on the assumption that racial diversity in ownership is a good proxy for programming diversity, an assumption that necessarily entails presuppositions about the ways black people and white people think.

The case was *Metro Broadcasting, Inc., v. Federal Communications Commission,* and the Court's reasoning is revealing. The minority ownership regulations, the Justices explained, were justified "primarily to promote programming diversity." And programming diversity, the Justices assured, "is an im-

---

*I use the word *minority* in this discussion, despite my dislike of it, because that is the jargon in which preferential transfer-of-ownership rules are described.
†And, as if to make sure that one is wrong, legislation has been introduced in the Congress to make it illegal for an advertiser to favor white-owned over minority-owned broadcast properties. Not a bad idea for a law, except that no rational advertiser will decline to use a medium programmed in a format that will sell its products, and in a consumer goods market, no irrational advertiser will stay in business. Presumably, it is not the intent of the drafters of the law to create a climate in which no matter the broadcast format minority-owned stations might choose, it will be presumptively illegal for advertisers to refuse to buy air time from them. One can only hope, therefore, that should the law be enacted, it will not be read to allow a case of discrimination to be made on the basis of statistics alone.

portant governmental objective."[11] Lest the point be missed, the Justices went on to defer to the FCC's judgment that "there is an empirical nexus between minority ownership and broadcasting diversity."[12] An empirical nexus: in other words, the "minority owners" whom the FCC policy is designed to produce will not bring to radio and television the same tired old views presented by the white males who have heretofore controlled the airwaves. *Au contraire:* the new owners will be representatives of the people!

Or will they? The four dissenting Justices, concerned about the majority's empirical conclusion, offered a stern caution: "Social scientists may debate how peoples' thoughts and behavior reflect their background, but the Constitution provides that the Government may not allocate benefits and burdens among individuals based on the assumption that race or ethnicity determines how they act or think."[13] I am confident that the majority got the result right, that the FCC rules are not prohibited by the Constitution.[14] But that is not the same as saying that the rules are a good idea. Indeed, there is a worrisome point here, and the dissenters found it: perhaps it is likely that black people, formed in the crucible of a racially divided society where they have too often been the losers, would in many instances develop a different politics than white people. Even so, one might remain concerned over the prospect of the government sorting out what the differences are likely to be—not only because there is no particular reason to have such faith in officialdom but, further, because placing government imprimatur on racial generalizations establishes an enormous pressure to conform. Imagine: It is not just the *Times* and Pete Stark and a few campus activists who think that black people should think a certain way if they want to be bona fide representatives—it is the government of the United States!

So it is not surprising that the five Justices in the majority squirmed a bit at the dissent's sharp riposte. After all, they were trying to help people of color, not to harm them, and certainly not to stereotype them. "The judgment that there is a link between expanded minority ownership and broadcast diversity," the majority wrote in an effort to reassure, "does not rest on impermissible stereotyping." Rather, it rests on the conclusion that "expanded minority ownership of broadcast outlets will, in the aggregate, result in greater broadcast diversity." There is nothing to get upset about, the Justices insisted: "The predictive judgment about the overall result of minority entry into broadcasting is not a rigid assumption about how minority owners will behave in every case."[15]

All right, not in every case: the image this language conjures is of a few eccentric "minority" owners who will make programming decisions not appreciably different from those made by owners who happen to be white. But in most cases, or at least in a substantial number, the Court, and the FCC that issued the regulations, *must* be assuming that most white owners and black owners will program differently. Otherwise, neither the FCC policy nor the decision makes any sense. Naturally, one might try to defend minority preferences in the transfer of broadcast properties on some other ground—for example, as a means for redistribution of wealth. But that is not what the FCC claims to be up to, and that is not what the Supreme Court has approved. Rather, the entire project of preference is justified by a claim that "broadcast diversity" can be enhanced by using skin color as a proxy for "certain" differing views; and a claim of that kind, no matter what fancy language is used to dress it up, does indeed rest on a racial stereotype. And yet in an age in which affirmative action has become a means for assuring representation of the people, the Court is right about one point: the stereotyping involved is certainly not "impermissible." On the contrary, it is common.

Still, one might ask, what difference does the stereotyping make? Surely it is at least *possible* that the FCC rules will lead to a greater diversity of viewpoint.[16] Besides, in a world as race-obsessed as ours, negative stereotypes abound; why not, then, make use of a few good ones? Indeed, on the surface, the rhetoric of representation must seem rather benign, at least in its attitude toward people of color. For do we not tend to have views of our own, ways of looking at the world that the white folks who run the place are unlikely to appreciate unless we are there to present it? Surely this new emphasis on drawing into the corridors of power the voices that have hitherto been excluded is simply another useful arrow in the quiver of racial justice—an arrow that must seem much needed in an age like ours, when playing to the nation's collective sense of guilt seems less hopeful a strategy for progress than it might once have been.

But unless one supposes that biology implies ideology, this movement to make race a proxy for views surely involves a category mistake. The American culture consists of a broad and interwoven set of subcultures, and the diversity ideal exalts particular subcultures, suggesting that there are reasons to value specially their political and aesthetic visions. The trouble is that race is not the same as culture, and there is no way of predicting whether a particular black person—a station owner, say—will adopt any particular cultural stance. The philosopher Anthony Appiah has put it this way:

> Talk of "race" is particularly distressing for those of us who take culture seriously. For, where race works—in places where "gross differences" of morphology are correlated with "subtle differences" of temperament, belief, and intention—it works as an attempt at a metonym for culture; and it does so only at the price of biologizing what *is* culture.[17]

All too often, the modern diversity movement seems to treat this important distinction as irrelevant and even irrational; the experience of oppression is assumed to be sufficiently widespread that by knowing the gross difference of race (meaning color) we can know immediately a good deal more about the subtle differences that determine what might properly be termed *culture*. And even the implied culture itself is then treated as less an aesthetic sensibility than a political one: the black people who are going about matters the right way, at least, will adopt the proper "temperament, belief, and intention."

Besides, to allow or, worse, to encourage the *state* to use racial differences as proxies for other differences is potentially quite dangerous to the cause of equality. Our sharp rhetorical arrows have a way of turning back on us, as any civil rights lawyer struggling to defend racial preferences against the ringing and eloquent (if a bit misleading) language of "color blindness" and "reverse discrimination" can testify. We may run similar risks by emphasizing the special perspective that people of color are said to bring to the table. By abandoning the vision of affirmative action in the professions as a tool for providing training so that students of color will have the chance to show what they can do, and treating it instead as a battle to bring into our most powerful institutions at all levels the points of view that have been excluded in the past, we risk opening a box that might have given even Pandora some pause. Indeed, even in this early stage of a defense of racial preferences based on a presumed diversity of viewpoints, some of the horrors already seem to be leaking out, for the use of racial stereotypes, once begun, is not easily cabined.

III

The idea that only the right sort of black person will do is fraught with magnificent ironies. Not the least of them is this: if people of color who *think like* people who are white are unable to represent their people correctly, then, *a fortiori,* people who *are* white clearly cannot do it. One stereotype leads to another, only this time the stereotype is of a person who is forbidden to act as a representative, rather than of a person who is required to act as one.

The proposition that a white person cannot possibly represent the true perspective of the people helps explain the ruckus in the early 1980s when the Harvard Law School hired Jack Greenberg, the longtime head of the NAACP Legal Defense Fund, to teach a course on law and race. Greenberg, to his apparent discredit, is white, and his invitation sparked a student boycott of his course. The protesters, while too savvy actually to insist that his white skin disqualified him from teaching the course, argued that the course should have been "taught by an instructor who can identify and empathize with the social, cultural, economic, and political experiences of the Third World communities"[18]—as a white person, evidently, cannot. Thus, they concluded, the course should be "taught in its entirety by a minority professor, most preferably a full-time professor."[19]

Although the impulse that inspires arguments of this kind is understandable—black people and white people are not exactly the same—the idea that only a person of color can truly empathize with "Third World communities" makes a villain, and perhaps an impossibility as well, of anyone who troubles to study a culture well enough to understand it and then purports to tell the culture's story. No wonder so much controversy erupted a few years back when Danny Santiago, author of *Famous All over Town,* an award-winning novel about an inner-city Chicano neighborhood, turned out to be a pseudonym for Daniel Lewis James, a screenwriter victimized by the 1950s blacklist, who happens to be white. I am not here concerned with the rights and wrongs of his imposture. What is fascinating, rather, is that few of the attacks on him went to the substance of the novel itself. Was its portrayal of barrio life accurate or not? Did the accuracy change with the ethnic identity of the author? (I am reminded of my white colleague's withdrawal of the charge that I was insensitive to the experience of black people.) These were not the principal questions. The problem, many critics said, was that the author had pretended to be something he was not: a Mexican-American. Had he really been one, it seems, his account (whatever its content) would have been acceptable. Instead, it was tainted by a false viewpoint. Even Alvin Pouissant, the distinguished psychiatrist, fell into this critical pattern, lamenting that James's subterfuge "gave the book an authenticity it did not have."[20] A white person, in other words, cannot possibly understand what it is like to be nonwhite; Daniel Lewis James, not even "biologically" anything else but white, was not even a plausible candidate for representative of the people.

Well, all right. Perhaps Daniel Lewis James should have owned up to his own ethnicity. There is a distinction, after all, between arguing that he should not have written the book and arguing that he should not have chosen Santiago as his *nom de plume,* and I take it that the critics were more concerned with the second objection.[21] Suppose, however, a very different case. Suppose that the author, born of white parents, had been adopted at birth by Mexican-American parents and raised by them in a barrio. Upon reaching maturity, he decided to write a novel. Would he then be entitled to write in the voice of an inner-city Chicano? Or would he be misrepresenting himself unless he wrote only in the voice of a white person raised as one?

This example is not as far-fetched as it might seem. The state of New Mexico has a law on its books restricting to enrolled members of groups registered with the Bureau of Indian Affairs the right to sell anything called "Indian art." This law has been described as consumer-protection legislation aimed at art fraud, and perhaps it is, as long as one is confident that what the consumer of "Indian art" wants is an object created by a person of a particular ethnic background rather than an object created in a particular way. In the late 1980s, however, *Business Week* (December 26, 1988) reported on the plight of an artist named John Redtail Freesoul, the official pipemaker of the Cheyenne-Arapahoe tribe in Oklahoma. Freesoul insisted that he was one-quarter Indian and argued that he should be allowed to sell his work as Indian art. The statute, however, leaves it to each tribe to determine its own membership, and those who are not accepted by any tribe cannot, under New Mexico law, call themselves Indian artists. (Freesoul is a member of the Redtail Hawk Society, but that is an intertribal organization.) Perhaps this is an inevitable outgrowth of tribal sovereignty. And yet I must suppose that this, too, is a triumph for the idea that white people cannot share or express the distinctive culture that racial oppression has spawned, because, at least as the state of New

Mexico sees it, no matter the quality of the work Freesoul might create, it can never be the work of a *real* Indian.

Jack Greenberg, in the eyes of the Harvard protesters, was evidently a bit like John Freesoul: he was offering wares that were not his to sell. He was not a bona fide representative of the people.

IV

The call for diversity of underrepresented voices comprises an effort to elide many of the arguments typically pressed against affirmative action: that it is unfair to those excluded from its benefits, that it stigmatizes its beneficiaries, and that in any case many of its beneficiaries are underqualified for the positions they are awarded. In an earlier era, when racial preferences were justified in terms of compensation for past discrimination or opening up opportunities, these arguments against the programs were always plausible. For example, the fact that someone has suffered an inadequate education because of America's legacy of racism (the very claim once pressed in favor of affirmative action for college and professional school admission) makes that individual less likely to be professionally successful than those who have had stronger educational backgrounds—thus the underqualification argument. If, on the other hand, one chooses to extend a hand in the name of opportunities to highly qualified people of color who are just short of succeeding without the special break, there are lots of people who are not white and not particularly disadvantaged, and lots of other disadvantaged people who are white and might also want a special break and might benefit from it—thus the unfairness argument.

But now look at the modern way. The unfairness argument is rejected because the advocates of diversity are simply trying to help powerful institutions in the society do a better job, by bringing inside a broader range of viewpoints than is offered by the "white male" perspective that has traditionally been dominant. The stigma argument is rejected because those who are hired to bring diversity into the executive suite or onto the campus should not be suspected of anything except embracing the perspective of the oppressed. The under-qualification argument is rejected because the fresh perspective this generation can offer is a qualification in itself; as an editor of the *Columbia Law Review* put it in justifying that journal's decision to adopt an affirmative action program, "diversity is part of quality."[22] The diversity approach to affirmative action, in short, seems to solve all the problems that have plagued programs of racial preference—unless, of course, one is troubled by the idea of racial stereotypes and wishes to challenge the notion that there is a correct and predictable way in which a person of color will differ in his or her analysis of an issue from a person who is white.

But the argument about embracing the perspective of the excluded solves too many problems too neatly; the fit is a little too snug. When a fresh approach seems so easily to escape so many of the problems of the old one, it is terribly tempting to conclude that it was designed that way. So I suspect that what might be happening here is a kind of reversal of what Richard Rodriguez once tried to do. In his fine but tragic book *Hunger of Memory,* Rodriguez describes his effort to avoid entanglement in our national thicket of racial preferences after graduate study by writing to all his potential employers and politely declining any benefits of affirmative action.[23] The advocates of diversity are also trying to avoid entanglement with affirmative action—not, as in the case of Rodriguez, because of a concern that the programs are unfair, but rather as a way of evading the more brutal difficulty, the fear that the programs hire people of color who will be charged with being less excellent than some white people who are turned away. If this is indeed a part of the motive force, then I fear that the diversity movement, like Richard Rodriguez, is trying to do the impossible. No one who is not white can opt out; in our color-conscious, preference-bound society, there is no escape from the affirmative action thicket.

CHAPTER 3

The Best Black

Affirmative action has been with me always. I do not mean to suggest that I have always been the beneficiary of special programs and preferences. I mean, rather, that no matter what my accomplishments, I have had trouble escaping an assumption that often seems to underlie the worst forms of affirmative action: that black people cannot compete intellectually with white people. Certainly I have not escaped it since my teen years, spent mostly in Ithaca, New York, where the presence of Cornell University lends an air of academic intensity to the public schools. At Ithaca High School in the days of my adolescence, we had far more than our share of National Merit Scholars, of students who scored exceptionally well on standardized tests, of students who earned advanced placement credits for college, and of every other commodity by which secondary schools compare their academic quality.

My father taught at Cornell, which made me a Cornell kid, a "fac-brat," and I hung out with a bunch of white Cornell kids in a private little world where we competed fiercely (but only with one another—no one else mattered!) for grades and test scores and solutions to brain teasers. We were the sort of kids other kids hated: the ones who would run around compiling lists of everyone else's test scores and would badger guidance counselors into admitting their errors in arithmetic (no computers then) in order to raise our class ranks a few notches. I held my own in this bunch, although I was forced by the norms of the fac-brat community to retake the Mathematics Level II achievement test to raise a humiliating score of 780 to an acceptable 800. (No one had yet told me that standardized tests were culturally biased against me.) Like the rest of the fac-brats, I yearned for the sobriquet "brilliant," and tried desperately to convince myself and everyone else who would listen that I had the grades and test scores to deserve it.

And yet there were unnerving indications that others did not see me as just another fac-brat, that they saw me instead as that black kid who hung out with the Cornell kids. There was, for example, the recruiter from Harvard College who asked to see those he considered the brightest kids in the school; I was included, so a guidance counselor said, because I was black. And when I decided that I wanted to attend Stanford University, I was told by a teacher that I would surely be admitted because I was black and I was smart. Not because I was smart and not even because I was smart and black, but because I was black and smart: the skin color always preceding any other observation.

But the worst of it came at National Merit Scholarship time. In those days (this was the early 1970s), the National Merit Scholarship Qualifying Test was a separate examination, not combined with the Preliminary Scholastic Aptitude Test as it later would be. When the qualifying scores came in, I was in heaven. Mine was the second highest in the school. I saw my future then—best fac-brat!—and awaited my National Merit Scholarship. Instead, well before the National Merit Scholarships were announced, I received a telephone call informing me that I had been awarded a National Achievement Scholarship, presented, in the awkward usage of the day, to "outstanding Negro students." Well, all right. If one wants more black students to go to college, one had better provide the necessary resources. So I wasn't insulted. College is expensive and money is money. But—I inquired politely as I saw my "best fac-brat" status slipping away—what about my possible National *Merit* Scholarship? The one not for the best black students, but for the *best* students?

The caller responded, a bit coldly, that she knew nothing about that. Well, I pressed on, if I accepted this, could I still be considered for that? Oh, no, of course not, she said. It was one or the other. And did I have to decide now? Well, yes. In a few days, anyway. But I was not to worry, she told me; I wouldn't win a National Merit Scholarship anyway. Oh, I said sadly. The decision is already made, then. Well, no, she responded. But the people who get National Achievement Scholarships are never good enough to get National Merit Scholarships.

I was stunned—the more so when, later, a number of white students who had lower test scores than mine and, I was sure, similar grades were awarded National Merit Scholarships. Could I have had one too? I will never know. What I do know is that I was faced with a bizarre rule under which, in order to receive a National Achievement Scholarship, I was required to forfeit any claim to a National Merit Scholarship. The lesson was clear: the smartest students of color were not considered as capable as the smartest white students, and therefore would not be allowed to compete with them, but only with one another.

I call it the "best black" syndrome, and all black people who have done well in school are familiar with it. We are measured by a different yardstick: *first black, only black, best black.* The best black syndrome is cut from the same cloth as the implicit and demeaning tokenism that often accompanies racial preferences: "Oh, we'll tolerate so-and-so at our hospital or in our firm or on our faculty, because she's the best black." Not because she's the best-qualified candidate, but because she's the best-qualified *black* candidate. She can fill the black slot. And then the rest of the slots can be filled in the usual way: with the best-*qualified* candidates.

This dichotomy between "best" and "best black" is not

merely something manufactured by racists to denigrate the abilities of professionals who are not white. On the contrary, the durable and demeaning stereotype of black people as unable to compete with white ones is reinforced by advocates of certain forms of affirmative action. It is reinforced, for example, every time employers are urged to set aside test scores (even, in some cases, on tests that are good predictors of job performance) and to hire from separate lists, one of the best white scorers, the other of the best black ones. It is reinforced every time state pension plans are pressed to invest some of their funds with "minority-controlled" money management firms, even if it turns out that the competing "white" firms have superior track records.[1] It is reinforced every time students demand that universities commit to hiring some pre-set number of minority faculty members. What all of these people are really saying is, "There are black folks out there. Go and find the best of them." And the best black syndrome is further reinforced, almost unthinkingly, by politicians or bureaucrats or faculty members who see these demands as nothing more than claims for simple justice.

Successful black students and professionals have repeatedly disproved the proposition that the best black minds are not as good as the best white ones, but the stereotype lingers, even among the most ardent friends of civil rights. In my own area of endeavor, academia, I hear this all the time from people who should know better. It is not at all unusual for white professors, with no thought that they are indulging a demeaning stereotype, to argue for hiring the best available professors of color, whether or not the individuals on whom that double-edged mantle is bestowed meet the usual appointment standards. I put aside for the moment the question of the fairness of the standards, for the white people I am describing have few doubts about *that;* I have in mind white people who argue with straight face for the hiring of black people *they themselves* do not believe are good enough to be hired without extra points for race. For example, one prominent law professor, a strong and sincere proponent of racial diversity, sent me a list of scholars in his field who might be considered for

appointment to the Yale faculty. The first part of the list set
out the names of the best people in the field; the second part,
the names of people who were so-so; and the last part, the
names of the leading "minorities and women" in the field,
none of whom apparently qualified (in his judgment) for even
the "so-so" category, let alone the best. I know that my colleague acted with the best of intentions, but the implicit invitation offered by this extraordinary document was to choose
between diversity and quality. I suspect that to this day he is
unaware of any insult and actually believes he was advancing
the cause of racial justice.

"No responsible advocate of affirmative action," argues
Ira Glasser, "opposes merit or argues . . . that standards
should be reduced in order to meet affirmative action goals."[2]
Perhaps not; but the language of standards and merit is slippery at best. I am reminded of a conversation I had some
years ago with a veteran civil rights litigator who, concerned
at charges that affirmative action sometimes results in hiring
unqualified candidates, drew a sharp distinction between *unqualified* and *less qualified.* An employer, he mused, does not
have to hire the *best* person for the job, as long as everyone
hired is *good enough* to do the job. Consequently, he reasoned,
it is perfectly fine to require employers to hire black applicants who are less qualified than some white applicants, as
long as the black candidates are capable of doing the job. A
tidy argument in its way, but, of course, another example of
an almost unconscious acceptance of a situation in which an
employer is made to distinguish between the best black candidates and the best ones.

Even our sensible but sometimes overzealous insistence
that the rest of the nation respect the achievements of black
culture might reinforce the depressing dichotomy: if we insist,
as often we must, that others appreciate "our" music and
"our" literature, we should not be surprised if those others
come to think of the best of our music and the best of our
literature as distinct from the best music and the best literature. Indeed, this is the implication of Stanley Crouch's vigorous argument (on which I here express no view) that white

critics accept a level of mediocrity from black artists, film-makers, and writers that they would never tolerate from creative people who are white.[3]

The best black syndrome creates in those of us who have benefited from racial preferences a peculiar contradiction. We are told over and over that we are among the best black people in our professions. And in part we are flattered, or should be, because, after all, those who call us the best black lawyers or doctors or investment bankers consider it a compliment. But to professionals who have worked hard to succeed, flattery of this kind carries an unsubtle insult, for we yearn to be called what our achievements often deserve: simply the best—no qualifiers needed! In *this* society, however, we sooner or later must accept that being viewed as the best blacks is part of what has led us to where we are; and we must further accept that to some of our colleagues, black as well as white, we will never be anything else.

II

Despite these rather unsettling pitfalls, many of us resist the best black syndrome less than we should, and one of the reasons is surely that it can bestow considerable benefits. Racial preferences are perhaps the most obvious benefit, but there are others. In high school, for example, I quickly stood out, if only because I was the lone black student in any number of honors and advanced placement courses. Perhaps my intellect was not unusually keen; although I did as well as anyone, I have always thought that with proper training, scoring well on standardized tests is no great trick. Nevertheless, other students and, eventually, teachers as well concluded that I was particularly sharp. These perceptions naturally fed my ego, because all I really wanted from high school was to be considered one of the best and brightest.

What I could not see then, but see clearly now, two decades later, is that while the perceptions others had of my abilities were influenced in part by grades and test scores, they were further influenced by the fact that students and teachers (black and white alike) were unaccustomed to the idea that a black kid could sit among the white kids as an equal, doing as well, learning as much, speaking as ably, arguing with as much force. In their experience, I was so different that I had to be exceptional. But exceptional in a specific and limited sense: the best black.

College was not much different. My college grades were somewhat better than average, but at Stanford in the era of grade inflation, good grades were the norm. Nevertheless, I quickly discovered that black students with good grades stood out from the crowd. Other students and many of my professors treated me as a member of some odd and fascinating species. I sat among them as an equal in seminars, my papers were as good as anyone else's, so I had to be exceptionally bright. In their experience, it seemed, no merely ordinarily smart black person could possibly sit among them as an equal.

In law school, the trend continued. I was fortunate enough to come early to the attention of my professors, but all I was doing was playing by the rules: talking in class with reasonable intelligence, exhibiting genuine interest in questions at the podium later, and treating papers and examinations as matters of serious scholarship rather than obstacles to be overcome. Lots of students did the same—but, in the stereotyped visions of some of my professors, not lots of black students. Here was the best black syndrome at work once more: I was not just another bright student with an enthusiastic but untrained intellect; I was a bright *black* student, a fact that apparently made a special impression.

The stultifying mythology of racism holds that black people are intellectually inferior. Consistent survey data over the years indicate that this stereotype persists.[4] Such incidents as those I have described, however, make me somewhat skeptical of the familiar complain that because of this mythology, black people of intellectual talent have a harder time than others in proving their worth. My own experience suggests quite the contrary, that like a flower blooming in winter, intellect is more readily noticed where it is not expected to be found. Or, as a black investment banker has put the point, "Our mistakes are amplified, but so are our successes."[5] And it is the amplification of success that makes the achieving black student or professional into the best black.

When people assign to a smart black person the status of best black, they do so with the purest of motives: the curing of bewilderment. There must be an explanation, the reasoning runs, and the explanation must be that this black person, in order to do as well as white people, is exceptionally bright. What I describe is not racism in the sense of a design to oppress, but it is in its racialist assumption of inferiority every bit as insulting and nearly as tragic. The awe and celebration with which our achievements are often greeted (by black and white people alike) suggest a widespread expectation that our achievements will be few. The surprise is greater, perhaps, when our achievements are intellectual, but other achievements, too, seem to astonish. The astonishment, moreover, takes a long time to fade: even, or perhaps especially, in the era of affirmative action, it seems, the need to prove one's professional worth over and over again has not receded.

III

Affirmative action, to be sure, did not create this particular box into which black people are routinely stuffed. Throughout the long, tragic history of the interaction between white people and people of color in America (it is too often forgotten that there were people of color here before there were white people), the society has treated white as normal and color as an aberration that must be explained or justified or apologized for. Black people have always been the target of openly racist assumptions, perhaps the worst among these being that we are a stupid, primitive people. Every intellectual attainment by black people in America has been greeted with widespread suspicion. When the American Missionary Association and other abolitionist groups established black colleges in the South after the Civil War and determined to offer to the freed slaves and their progeny classical educations (Eurocentric educations, I suppose they would be called on today's campuses), emulating those available at the best Northern schools, editorialists had a field day. By the turn of the century, a standing joke had it that when two black students met on the campus of one of these colleges, the first greeted the second with, "Is yo' done yo' Greek yet?" The joke has faded from national memory, but its import, I fear, remains part of the nation's swirling racial consciousness.

Small wonder, then, that every black professional, in our racially conscious times, is assumed to have earned his or her position not by being among the best available but by being among the best available blacks. Any delusions to the contrary I might have harbored about my own achievements were shattered a few months after I was voted tenure at the Yale Law School. Late one night, a reporter for the campus newspaper called my home to say that the paper was doing a story about my promotion. Why was that? I wanted to know. Lots of law professors earn tenure, I said. Oh, I know, said the reporter, unabashed. Still, wasn't it true that I was the first black one? But that was the luck of the draw, I protested. It could as easily have been someone else. And besides, I wanted to shout, but dared not; besides, that isn't why I was promoted! (I hope.)

My protests mattered not a jot, and the newspaper ran its story. A banner headline on the front page screamed that the law faculty had, for the first time, voted to promote a black professor to tenure. The tone of the article—years of lily-whiteness in the academy was its theme—suggested that my promotion was simple justice. But justice of a special sort: not the justice of earned reward for a job well done, but the justice due me as a professor who happens to be black. Whether I was a strong scholar or a weak one, a creative thinker or a derivative one, a diligent researcher or a lazy one, a good teacher or a bad one, mattered less to the newspaper than the fact that I was a black one. Evidently I had finally arrived, had I but the gumption to acknowledge it, as one of the best blacks.

I muted my protest, however. I did not complain, to the newspaper or to others, that I felt oppressed by this vision of tenure as an extension of affirmative action. Like many other black professionals, I simply wanted to be left alone to do my work. My hope, then as now, was that if I earned a place in the academic world, it would be for the seriousness of my research and the thoughtful contributions I hoped to make to legal knowledge—not for the color of my skin. Most of the scholarship I have committed has related to the separation of powers in the federal government, the regulation of intellectual property,* and the relationship of law and religion—to the lay person, perhaps not the most thrilling of topics, but, for me, intellectually engaging and lots of fun. I have always relished the look of surprise in the eyes of people who, having read my work in these areas, meet me for the first time. My favorite response (this really did happen) came at an academic conference at the University of Michigan Law School, where a dapper, buttoned-down young white man glanced at my name tag, evidently ignored the name but noted the school, and said, "If you're at Yale, you must know this Carter fellow who wrote that article about thus-and-so." Well, yes, I admitted. I did know that Carter fellow slightly. An awkward pause ensued. And then the young man, realizing his error, apologized with a smile warm enough to freeze butter.

"Oh," he said, "*you're* Carter." (I have since wondered from time to time whether, had I been white and the error a less telling one, his voice would have been inflected differently: "You're *Carter.*" Think about it.) Naturally, we then discussed the article, which happened to be about the separation of powers, and by way of showing the sincerity of his apology, he gushed about its quality in terms so adulatory that a casual observer might have been excused for thinking me the second coming of Oliver Wendell Holmes or, more likely, for thinking my interlocutor an idiot. (That gushing is part of the peculiar relationship between black intellectuals and the

---

*Intellectual property is the field of law governing rights in intangible creations of the mind and includes such subjects as patents, copyrights, and trademarks.

white ones who seem loath to criticize us for fear of being
branded racists—which is itself a mark of racism of a sort.) I
suppose I should have been flattered, although, if the truth is
told, I quickly gained the impression that he was excited more
by the political uses to which my argument might be put than
by the analysis in the article itself.

But there it was! The Best Black Syndrome! It had, as
they say, stood up and bitten me! Since this young man liked
the article, its author could not, in his initial evaluation, have
been a person of color. He had not even conceived of that possibility, or he would have glanced twice at my name tag. No, if
the work was of high quality, the author had to be white—
there was no room for doubt! The best blacks don't do this
stuff!

And if you're black, you can't escape it! It's everywhere,
this awkward set of expectations. No matter what you might
accomplish (or imagine yourself to have accomplished), the
label follows you. A friend of mine who works in the financial
services field—I'll call him X—tells the story of his arrival at
a client's headquarters. The client had been told that a supervisor was on the way to straighten out a particularly knotty
problem. When my friend arrived, alone, and gave his name,
the client said, "But where is the supervisor? Where is Mr.
X?" With my friend standing right in front of him, name
already announced! My friend, being black, could not possibly
be the problem solver who was awaited. He was only . . . THE
BEST BLACK! The winner of the coveted prize!

And that's the way it works. You don't even need to
worry about a National Merit Scholarship—you've got a program of your own! This is the risk some critics see in setting
up Afro-American Studies departments: Isn't there a good
chance that the school will dismiss the professors in the department as simply the best blacks, saying, in effect, don't
worry about the academic standards the rest of us have to
meet, you've got your own department? The answer is yes, of
course, the school might do that—but that isn't an argument
against Afro-American studies as a discipline, any more than
it's an argument against hiring black faculty at all. It's just

an admission that this is the way many of the white people who provide affirmative action programs and other goodies tend to think about them: there's Category A for the smart folks, and Category B for the best blacks. It's also a reminder to all people of color that our parents' advice was true: we really do have to work twice as hard to be considered half as good.

This is an important point for those who are trapped by the best black syndrome. We cannot afford, ever, to let our standards slip. There are too many doubters waiting in the wings to pop out at the worst possible moment and cry, "See? Told you!" The only way to keep them off the stage is to make our own performances so good that there is no reasonable possibility of calling them into question. It isn't fair that so much should be demanded of us, but what has life to do with fairness? It was the artist Paul Klee, I believe, who said that one must adapt oneself to the contents of the paintbox. This is particularly true for upwardly mobile professionals who happen to be people of color, for people of color have had very little say about what those contents are.

So we have to adapt ourselves, a point I finally came to accept when I was in law school. In those days, the black students spent lots of time sitting around and discussing our obligations, if any, to the race. (I suppose black students still sit around and hold the same conversation.) In the course of one such conversation over a casual lunch, I blurted out to a classmate my driving ambition. It infuriated me, I said, that no matter what we might accomplish, none of us could aspire to anything more than the role of best black. What we should do for the race, I said, was achieve. Shatter stereotypes. Make white doubters think twice about our supposed intellectual inferiority.

A few years later, I foolishly imagined that I had attained my goal. It was the fall of 1981, and I was a young lawyer seeking a teaching position at a law school. I had, I was certain, played my cards right. In my law school years, I had managed to get to know a professor or two, and some of them liked me. I had compiled the right paper record before setting out to hunt for a job: my résumé included practice with a well-regarded law firm, good law school grades, service on the *Yale Law Journal,* and a spate of other awards and honors, including a clerkship with a Justice of the Supreme Court of the United States. One might have thought, and I suppose I thought it myself, that someone with my credentials would have no trouble landing a teaching job. But what people told me was that any school would be happy to have a black professor with my credentials. (Did a white professor need more, or did white professors just make their schools unhappy?) In the end, I was fortunate enough to collect a flattering set of job offers, but the taste was soured for me, at least a little, by the knowledge that whatever my qualifications, they probably looked more impressive on the résumé of someone black.

There is an important point here, one that is missed by the critics who point out (correctly, I think) that affirmative action programs tend to call into question the legitimate achievements of highly qualified black professionals. Yes, they do; but that is not the end of the story. A few years ago, in a panel discussion on racial preferences, the economist Glenn Loury noted that the Harvard Law School had on its faculty two black professors who are also former law clerks for Justices of the Supreme Court of the United States. (As I write, I believe that the number is three.) It isn't fair, he argued, that they should be dismissed as affirmative action appointments when they are obviously strongly qualified for the positions they hold. He is right that it isn't fair to dismiss them and he is right that they are obviously qualified, but it is also true that there are nowadays literally dozens of similarly qualified candidates for teaching positions every year. It is no diminution of the achievements of the professors Loury had in mind to point out that there is no real way to tell whether they would have risen to the top if not for the fact that faculties are on the lookout for highly qualified people of color. The same is surely true for many black people rising to the top of political, economic, and educational institutions.

There is a distinction here, however, that even the harshest critics of affirmative action should be willing to concede. Hiring to fill a slot that must be filled—the black slot, say—is not the same as using race to sort among a number of equally qualified candidates. Put otherwise, yes, it is true that the result of racial preferences is sometimes the hiring of black people not as well qualified as white people who are turned away, and preferences of that kind do much that is harmful and little that is good. But preferences can also be a means of selecting highly qualified black people from a pool of people who are all excellent. True, employers will almost always claim to be doing the second even when they are really doing the first; but that does not mean the second is impossible to do. And if an employer undertakes the second method, a sorting among the excellent, then although there might be legitimate grounds for concern, a criticism on the ground of lack of qualification of the person hired cannot be among them.

Ah, but are our analytical antennae sufficiently sensitive to detect the difference? I am not sure they are, and the sometimes tortured arguments advanced by the strongest advocates of affirmative action (I include the argument for viewpoint diversity discussed in chapter 2) occasionally leave me with a bleak and hopeless sense that all people of color who are hired for the tasks for which their intellects and professional training have prepared them will be dismissed, always, as nothing more than the best blacks. And I draw from all of this two convictions: first, that affirmative action will not alter this perception; and, second, that white Americans will not change it simply because it is unjust. Consequently change, if change there is to be, is in *our* hands—and the only change for which we can reasonably hope will come about because we commit ourselves to battle for excellence, to show ourselves able to meet any standard, to pass any test that looms before us, in short, to form ourselves into a vanguard of black professionals who are simply too good to ignore.

And that, I suppose, is why I relish the reactions of those who have liked my work without knowing I am black: in my mind, I am proving them wrong, as I promised I would at that lunch so many years ago. No doubt my pleasure at the

widened eyes is childish, but it is sometimes a relief to be sure
for once that it is really the work they like, not the-unex-
pected-quality-of-the-work-given-the-naturally-inferior-
intellects-of-those-with-darker-skins. It is a commonplace of
social science, a matter of common sense as well, that an observer's evaluation of a piece of work is frequently influenced
by awareness of the race of the author. Happily, I have found
that people who like my work before they learn that I am
black do not seem to like it less once they discover my color.*

   And when those who read my work *do* know that I am
black? Well, any prejudices that the readers might bring to
bear are, at least, nothing new. John Hope Franklin, in his
sparkling essay on "The Dilemma of the American Negro
Scholar," details the struggles of black academics during the
past century to have their work taken seriously by white
scholars.[6] Although progress has obviously been made, the
struggle Franklin describes is not yet ended, which means I
have to face the likelihood that many white scholars who read
my work will judge it by a different standard than the one
they use to judge the work of white people. Perhaps the standard will be higher, perhaps the standard will be lower, perhaps the standard will simply involve different criteria—but
whatever the standard, all I can do is try to carry out the
instruction that black parents have given their children for
generations, and make the work not simply as good as the
work of white scholars of similar background, but better.
Sometimes I succeed, sometimes I fail; but to be a professional is always to strive. And while I am perfectly willing to
concede the unfairness of a world that judges black people
and white people by different standards, I do not lose large
amounts of sleep over it. A journalist friend recently told my
wife and me that he is tired of hearing black people complain
about having to work twice as hard as white people to reach
the same level of success. He says that if that's what we have

---

*Often, however, they do suddenly assume that I must possess a special expertise in
the most sophisticated quandaries and delicately nuanced esoterica of civil rights law,
areas that take years of careful study to master, no matter the contrary impression
given by the sometimes simpleminded reporting on civil rights law in the mass media.

to do, that's what we have to do, and it would not be a bad thing at all for us as a race to develop that habit as our defining characteristic: "Oh, you know those black people, they always work twice as hard as everybody else." If you can't escape it, then make the most of it: in my friend's racial utopia, it would no longer be taken as an insult to be called by a white colleague the best black.

IV

My desire to succeed in the professional world without the aid of preferential treatment is hardly a rejection of the unhappy truth that the most important factor retarding the progress of people of color historically has been society's racism. It is, rather, an insistence on the opportunity to do what the National Merit Scholarship people said I would not be allowed to, what I promised at that fateful lunch I would: to show the world that we who are black are not so marked by our history of racist oppression that we are incapable of intellectual achievement on the same terms as anybody else.

In a society less marked by racist history, the intellectual achievements of people of color might be accepted as a matter of course. In *this* society, however, they are either ignored or applauded, but never accepted as a matter of course. As I have said, however, the general astonishment when our achievements are intellectual carries with it certain benefits. Perhaps chief among these is the possibility of entrée to what I call the "star system." The characteristics of the star system are familiar to anyone who has attended college or professional school or has struggled upward on the corporate ladder, and it has analogues in sports, the military, and other arenas. Early in their careers, a handful of individuals are marked by their teachers or supervisors as having the potential for special success, even greatness. Thereafter, the potential stars are closely watched. Not every person marked early as a possible star becomes one, but the vast majority of those who are never marked will never star. Even very talented individuals who lack entrée to the star system may never gain attention in the places that matter: the hushed and private conference rooms (I can testify to their existence, having sat in more than a few) where money is spent and hiring and promotion decisions are made.

Getting into the star system is not easy, and the fact that few people of color scramble to the top of it should scarcely be surprising. The reason is not any failing in our native abilities—although it is true that only in the past decade have we been present as students in numbers sufficient to make entry more plausible—but the social dynamics of the star system itself. Entrée is not simply a matter of smarts, although that helps, or of working hard, although that helps, too. The star system rewards familiarity, comfort, and perseverence. It usually begins on campus, and so do its problems. One must get to know one's professors. Most college and professional school students are far too intimidated by their professors to feel comfortable getting to know them well, and for many students of color, already subject to a variety of discomforts, this barrier may seem especially high. When one feels uneasy about one's status in the classroom to begin with, the task of setting out to get to know the professor personally may seem close to insuperable. The fact that some students of color indeed reap the benefits of the star system does not alter the likelihood that many more would never dream of trying.

Exclusion from the star system is costly. Anyone left out will meet with difficulties in being taken seriously as a candidate for entry-level hiring at any of our most selective firms and institutions, which is why the failure of people of color to get into the star system makes a difference. Still, there is an opportunity here: because so little is expected of students of color, intellectual attainment is sometimes seen as a mark of genuine brilliance. (None of the merely ordinarily smart need apply!) So the best black syndrome can have a salutary side effect: it can help those trapped inside it get through the door of the star system. Certainly it worked that way for me. (Who *is* this character? my professors seemed to want to know.) The star system, in turn, got me in the door of the academy at the entry level. (From the doorway, I would like to think, I made the rest of the journey on my own; my achievements ought to speak for themselves. But in a world in which I have heard my colleagues use the very words *best black* in discussions of faculty hiring, I have no way to tell.) So, yes, I am a beneficiary of both the star system and the best black syndrome. Yet I hope it is clear that I am not a fan of either. The star system is exclusionary and incoherent; the best black syndrome is demeaning and oppressive. Both ought to be abandoned.

Consider the so-called glass ceiling, the asserted reluctance of corporations to promote people of color to top management positions. If indeed the glass ceiling exists, it is very likely a function of the star system. If people of color tend to have trouble getting in good, as the saying goes, with their professors, they are likely to have as much or more trouble getting in good with their employers. And if, once hired, people who are not white face difficulties in finding mentors, powerful institutional figures to smooth their paths, then they will naturally advance more slowly. Oh, there will always be some black participants in the star system, not as tokens but as people who have, as I said, taken to heart the adage that they must be twice as good. (One need but think of Colin Powell or William Coleman.) Still, plenty of people of color who are merely as good as or slightly better than white people who are inside the star system will find themselves outside. The social turns do not work for them, and their advancement on the corporate ladder will be slow or nonexistent.

To be sure, the star system cannot get all of the blame for the dearth of people who are not white in (and, especially, at the top of) the professions. That there is present-day racism, overt and covert, might almost go without saying, except that so many people keep insisting there isn't any. But one should not assume too readily that contemporary discrimination explains all of the observed difference. Groups are complex and no two groups are the same. With cultural and other differences, it would be surprising if all group outcomes were identical. When the nation's odious history of racial oppression is grafted onto any other differences that might exist, the numbers are less surprising still. What would be surprising would be if we as a people had so successfully shrugged off the shackles of that history as to have reached, at this relatively early stage in the nation's evolution, economic and educational parity.

But the star system is not exactly blameless, either. Any system that rewards friendship and comfort rather than merit will burden most heavily those least likely to find the right friends.[7] It is ironic, even awkward, to make this point in an era when the attack on meritocracy is so sharply focused, but the claims pressed by today's critics in that attack—bigotry, unconscious bias, corrupt and malleable standards, social and cultural exclusion—are among the reasons that led other ethnic groups in the past to insist on the establishment of measurable systems for rewarding merit. The star system is a corrupt and biased means for circumventing the meritocratic ideal, but its corruption should not be attributed to the ideal itself.

V

None of this means that affirmative action is the right answer to the difficulties the star system has spawned. Among the group of intellectuals known loosely (and, I believe, often inaccurately) as black conservatives, there is a widely shared view that the removal of artificial barriers to entry into a labor market is the proper goal to be pursued by those who want to increase minority representation. The economist Walter Williams often cites the example of cities like New York that limit the number of individuals permitted to drive taxicabs. No wonder, he says, there are so few black cabdrivers: it's too difficult to get into the market. Consequently, says Williams, New York should abolish its limits and, subject only to some basic regulatory needs, open the field to anyone. This, he says, would automatically result in an increase in black drivers—assuming, that is, that there are black people who want to drive cabs.

Other strategies, too, are easy to defend. For example, it is difficult to quarrel with the idea that an employer concerned about diversity—whatever its needs and hiring standards—should be as certain as possible that any candidate search it conducts is designed to yield the names of people of color who fit the search profile. After centuries of exclusion by design, it would be a terrible tragedy were black and other minority professionals excluded through inadvertence. Mari Matsuda has argued that a serious intellectual ought to make an effort to read books by members of groups not a part of his or her familiar experience, and I think she is quite right.[8] It is in the process of that determined reading—that searching—that the people who have been overlooked will, if truly excellent, eventually come to light.

The example can be generalized. Searching is the only way to find outstanding people of color, which is why all professional employers should practice it. Although the cost of a search is not trivial, the potential return in diversity, without any concomitant lowering of standards, is enormous—provided always that the employer is careful to use the search only to turn up candidates, not as a means of bringing racial preferences into the hiring process through the back door. For it is easy, but demeaning, to conflate the goal of searching with the goal of hiring, and to imagine therefore that the reason for the search is to ensure that the optimal number of black people are hired. It isn't. The reason for the search is to find the blacks among the best, not the best among the blacks.

If this distinction is borne firmly in mind, then an obligation to search will of course provide no guarantee that the statistics will improve. But I am not sure that a guarantee is what we should be seeking. People of color do not need special treatment in order to advance in the professional world; we do not need to be considered the best blacks, competing only with one another for the black slots. On the contrary, our goal ought to be to prove that we can compete with anybody, to demonstrate that the so-called pool problem, the alleged dearth of qualified entry-level candidates who are not white, is at least partly a myth. So if we can gain for ourselves a fair and equal chance to show what we can do—what the affirmative action literature likes to call a level playing field—then it is something of an insult to our intellectual capacities to insist on more.

And of course, although we do not like to discuss it, the insistence on more carries with it certain risks. After all, an employer can hire a candidate because the employer thinks that person is the best one available or for some other reason: pleasing a powerful customer, rewarding an old friend, keeping peace in the family, keeping the work force all white, getting the best black. When the employer hires on one of these other grounds, it should come as no surprise if the employee does not perform as well as the best available candidate would have. There will be times when the performance will be every bit as good, but those will not be the norm unless the employer is a poor judge of talent; and if the employer consistently judges talent poorly, a second, shrewder judge of talent will eventually put the first employer out of business.[9] That is not, I think, a web in which we as a people should want to be entangled.

Racial preferences, in sum, are not the most constructive method for overcoming the barriers that keep people of color out of high-prestige positions. They are often implemented in ways that are insulting, and besides, they can carry considerable costs. Although there are fewer unfair and arbitrary barriers to the hiring and retention of black professionals than there once were, many barriers remain, and the star system, although some few of us benefit from it, is prominent among them. But if the barriers are the problem, then it is the barriers themselves that should be attacked. Should the star system be brushed aside, our opportunities would be considerably enhanced because many of the special advantages from which we are excluded would vanish.

Getting rid of the star system will not be easy. I have discovered through painful experience that many of its most earnest white defenders—as well as many of those who pay lip service to overturning it but meanwhile continue to exploit it—are also among the most ardent advocates of hiring black people who, if white, they would consider second-rate. They are saying, in effect, We have one corrupt system for helping out our friends, and we'll be happy to let you have one for getting the numbers right. Faced with such obduracy, small wonder that racial preferences seem an attractive alternative.

But people of color must resist the urge to join the race to the bottom. The stakes are too high. I am sensitive to Cornell University Professor Isaac Kramnick's comment that even if a school hires some black professors who are not first-rate, "it will take till eternity for the number of second-rate blacks in the university to match the number of second-rate whites."[10] Point taken: one can hardly claim that elite educational institutions have been perfect meritocracies. However, the claim that there are incompetent whites and therefore incompetent blacks should be given a chance is unlikely to resonate with many people's visions of justice. Because of the racial stereotyping that is rampant in our society, moreover, any inadequacies among second-rate white professionals are unlikely to be attributed by those with the power to do something about it to whites as a whole; with black professionals, matters are quite unfairly the other way around, which is why the hiring of second-rate black professionals in any field would be detrimental to the effort to break down barriers.

The corruption of the meritocratic ideal with bias and favoritism offers professionals who are not white an opportunity we should not ignore: the chance to teach the corrupters their own values by making our goal excellence rather than adequacy. Consider this perceptive advice to the black scholar from John Hope Franklin, one of the nation's preeminent historians: "He should know that by maintaining the highest standards of scholarship he not only becomes worthy but also sets an example that many of his contemporaries who claim to be the arbiters in the field do not themselves follow."[11] The need to beat down the star system should spur us not to demand more affirmative action but to exceed the achievements of those who manipulate the system to their advantage.

Besides, the star system does not taint every institution to an equal degree. Some hiring and promotion processes actually make sense. If we rush to graft systems of racial preference onto hiring processes rationally designed to produce the best doctors or lawyers or investment bankers or professors, we might all hope that the professionals hired because of the preferences turn out to be as good as those hired because they are expected to be the best, but no one should be surprised if this hope turns to ashes. Painful though this possibility may seem, it is consistent with a point that many supporters of affirmative action tend to miss, or at least to obscure: racial preferences that make no difference are unimportant.

Racial preferences are founded on the proposition that the achievements of their beneficiaries would be fewer if the preferences did not exist. Supporters of preferences cite a whole catalogue of explanations for the inability of people of color to get along without them: institutional racism, inferior education, overt prejudice, the lingering effects of slavery and oppression, cultural bias in the criteria for admission and employment. All of these arguments are most sincerely pressed, and some of them are true. But like the best black syndrome, they all entail the assumption that people of color cannot at present compete on the same playing field with people who are white. I don't believe this for an instant; and after all these years, I still wish the National Merit Scholarship people had given me the chance to prove it.

CHAPTER 4

Racial Justice on the Cheap

S o far, I have told only one side of the story; I have explained why affirmative action is at best a mixed blessing for those of us who are its beneficiaries. I have not talked much about those who are excluded from its benefits. And I don't mean the white people who are left out; I mean the black people who are left out. What has happened in black America in the era of affirmative action is this: middle-class black people are better off and lower-class black people are worse off. Income stratification (the difference between the median income of the top fifth and the bottom fifth of earners) in the black community has increased sharply, even as it has softened in the white community.[1] At the same time, recent studies have shown considerable occupational convergence between black and white workers at the high end: that is, the number of black people in higher-paying professional positions is growing faster than the number of white people.[2] And at the elite educational institutions where, as Robert Klitgaard reminds us, affirmative action is both most hotly contested and most vigorously pursued,[3] the programs are increasingly dominated by the children of the middle class. One need not argue that affirmative action is the *cause* of increasing income inequality in black America to understand that it is not a solution.

Against this background, it is something of a puzzle that critics of affirmative action continue to be told they do not appreciate the disadvantage of the black people who are most deprived. The degree of one's support for affirmative action in the professions bears no relation to the degree of one's concern about the situation of the black people who are worst off, for the programs do them little good. In this sense, affirmative action, to borrow from W. E. B. DuBois, has been haunted by the ghost of an untrue dream. All the efforts at seeking to justify racial preferences as justice or compensation mask the simple truth that among those training for business and professional careers, the benefits of affirmative action fall to those least in need of them.[4] None of this is necessarily the *fault* of affirmative action, because the forces that work to determine who gains and who loses socioeconomic advantage are complex. A society like ours, which tends to be a bit parsimonious when it comes to fairness that requires taxes, will obviously choose the cheapest among its various options for providing what will be described as racial justice. If the nation adopts the civil rights agenda involving racial preferences, the costs of which fall invisibly, and rejects the civil rights agenda requiring the expenditure of money to help the worst off among us, the true inheritors of the decades of oppression, that is not the fault of a civil rights leadership that has promulgated both. It is the fault of a society that prefers its racial justice cheap.

In the meanwhile, the glowing language of compensation persists, as does my puzzlement. I cannot understand the vehemence with which the programs are defended if they do not live up to their promise. I cannot understand the logic (although I do understand what one might call the political rationale) of insisting that the situation of all black people is the same. And it is that continuing puzzlement, I think, that led me to what was probably my first expressed doubt about affirmative action or, at least, about its propriety for middle-class kids like me.

II

"You *are* disadvantaged," I am told, with gentle insistence. "Racism has marked you. It has held you back, as it has held all of us back." It is the spring of 1977, and I am in my first year of study at the Yale Law School. The speaker is another black student, two years ahead of me, and his words are meant to reassure.

"I don't know if that's true," I say, shaking my head. My mother and father are both college graduates, I am thinking. My father at the time of this conversation is an educator, formerly a practicing lawyer, as was his mother before him. My mother at the time is an aide to Georgia State Senator Julian Bond. I can trace middle-class ancestry a good way back, on both sides of the family. But I refrain from laying all of this out, because I do not want to play into the racist stereotype (as I then thought of it) of the child of the black professional who is better off than many disadvantaged white kids.

"It *is* true," my friend argues, as though in consolation. "Every black person is marked by racism."

Still I shake my head, knowing that he is right that I have been marked by racism, wanting to believe that the marking is as profound and defining as my friend insists, but still not certain. I want with all my heart to believe, for it is an era of willed convictions, even, perhaps especially, on university campuses, where we are supposed to be learning to think for ourselves. My annoying tendency to take free intellectual inquiry seriously is what has provoked this conversation. The afternoon is wearing on. We are in my dormitory room, a dusty gray cubbyhole snuggled up among the rafters. The window leaks. In winter, the room is so cold that I can keep apple juice chilled on the inside sill. My room overlooks a vast walled cemetery, final resting place of, among others, Noah Webster, Eli Whitney, and all the presidents of Yale. Students jog in the cemetery and are occasionally mugged, although it is not politically correct to dwell on the point. Yale is, after all, the oppressor.

"You *are* disadvantaged," my friend keeps repeating. I sit uneasily on the bed, waiting for the expected reassurance to take hold. The speaker styles himself a radical intellectual, much admired by me and some others for the suffering we imagine him to have experienced. "Racism is systemic," he says firmly, as though announcing a credo. "It touches us all."

We are having this meeting at my behest. I am suffering from an analytic confusion, the fruit of a year spent listening to other students talk about affirmative action and making a number of often fatuous suggestions of my own. My confusion comes because, I am certain, I would not have been admitted to law school—not to Yale, anyway—had I been white. And because I am unable to visualize myself as a victim of societal oppression, systemic or otherwise, I worry that an affirmative action program that would admit me to law school has unfairly deprived someone else of a place.

"Nonsense," my friend assures me, growing impatient with my intellectual self-indulgence. "Racism is *systemic,*" he reminds me; and as I nod slowly, pretending to understand, I am secretly turning this talismanic incantation over and over in my mind. I want to ask him, "But what does that *mean?*" Is being forced to sit for the Law School Admission Test (at that time, the racism of the test was very much an article of faith among students of color, as I suppose it is still) the same as being murdered by the Klan? All over the country, but rarely seen at places like Yale, there are black people who are truly disadvantaged. (Years later, William Julius Wilson would choose this phrase as the title of a fine book about the futility of pretending what my friend and I were pretending that day in my dorm room: that all black people are similarly situated.) There are black people stricken with the most abject circumstances, genuine victims of oppressive societal neglect, people who struggle through lives that a middle-class kid like me can scarcely imagine. If special admission programs are meant as compensation for that disadvantage (which was, back in the 1970s, the way they were defended, the contemporary concept of "diversity" not yet having been unearthed),

surely some of these others, the truly neglected, are more deserving than I. That is why I wonder what it means to say
racism is systemic, for to claim that racism has touched me in
the same way it has touched some of those who mug in the
cemetery seems to drain the word *racism* of all its power. I do
not ask, however; the minefield of racial politics is far too
difficult to negotiate, at least if, like me, one wants to be
thought of as politically correct.

Racism touches me, I am told. It has held me back. I am
disadvantaged. I nod and agree.

"It's systemic," my friend repeats, and in those dog
days, the late summer of the modern (post-Memphis) civil
rights movement, I understand perfectly well what he means.
The institutions of capitalist society, we have been taught at
the feet of the theorists of black power, are structured by racist commitments and are satraps of racist authority. The system is the enemy; it is capable only of self-interest, never of
justice. Which is why the same friend, on another occasion,
reprimanded me for suggesting that affirmative action programs showed the society's good faith in trying to undo its
racist legacy. "When somebody gives you some tiny part of
what you deserve," he grumbled, "you don't go around saying
Thank you."

So I repeat the magic words, the catechism of our shared
faith. Yes, racism has touched me. Yes, I am disadvantaged.
Yes, I belong. As for my friend, he is plainly relieved that I
have abandoned, at least for now, my brief moment of apos-
tasy: another soul has been saved for the movement, which
then, as now, needs all the souls it can get.

III

Except that I lied. I did not repent. Not of the tough part of
my views: my unwillingness to accept the idea that I have
suffered serious disadvantage because of systemic racism. As
to the claim that racism has touched me . . . well, that one is
easy to embrace. Racism has done more than touch me. It has

helped to shape me, just as the modern diversity movement would insist. As my friend laid out for me the line that, in his view, I should have been taking, incidents tumbled through my mind, the racial complications of a middle-class background: the way that the members of my racially integrated Boy Scout patrol when I was in the sixth grade drew straws to see who had to leave and form a new patrol, as ours was too big, and the six or seven white kids—who never showed their straws to anybody—all got to stay, while the three of us who were black and one who was Asian-American puzzled over our short straws. (Actually, one of the black Scouts was absent, but he got a short straw, too—I don't remember how.) More uncomfortable memories: the elderly white man who dug his elbow into my ribs as I sat next to him on a city bus in the nation's capital, nearly a decade after the successful conclusion of the Montgomery bus boycott, and pointed toward the back to show me where I should be sitting. I must have been about fourteen years old.

And more: the white kid in my junior high school in Washington, where, when I started the seventh grade, whites outnumbered blacks by something like 150 to 1, who called my hair a Brillo pad and giggled as I blushed quite invisibly. His friend, who nudged him and said, in a voice intended to carry, that he shouldn't say that, I might pull a knife. (Perhaps it would have been better if I had; the nickname "Brillo" stuck with me for three dreary years, and after the school was more thoroughly integrated through court-ordered busing, even the other black kids began to use it—I hope unthinkingly.) And I remember a white friend of mine from the same school who punned for my benefit on the name of a favorite drugstore, calling it "Nigger's." And the white guidance counselor at my high school in Ithaca, New York, who, unable to square the evidence of his eyes—my skin color—with the record I brought with me at transfer, put me a year ahead in math, where I belonged, but in a section two levels below the highest, where I did not. I remember the young white men in the car that pulled up next to me one night in Palo Alto while I was in college and tossed an egg and a racial epithet. The egg, at least, struck home. And the young white men in another car who did the same thing on a beautiful summer night in an Atlanta suburb, except that they threw a soft-drink bottle and their aim wasn't as good (although with Coca-Cola spattering everywhere, it didn't have to be). And I remember now, perhaps most sharply of all (although it had not yet occurred at the time of my dorm room conversation), the Yale professor who told me during my second year of law school that I was the best black student he had ever taught, implying, whether he knew it or not, that I was eligible for no higher honor than that.

I could go on and on. Every black person could. Surely, however, these experiences are relatively minor in the universe of racist transgressions. I have never been denied a promotion, a job, an education, shelter, or food. I have never been beaten within an inch of my life. I have never been arrested for something I didn't do, or treated with contempt by a system that refuses to believe. I have never gazed out at a bleak and uncaring world, certain that there is no place for me in it. I have never felt so overwhelmed by hopelessness or hostility or despair that I have turned to drugs or crime or some combination of the two. In short, my experience of the worst forms of privation is entirely vicarious. So, yes, the incidents I mention have marked me, but it would be folly to pretend that I have been damaged in the way the society so often damages through indifference those whom it could, by spending a little more money, protect.

Very well: I am marked, so the theory my friend was espousing up in the dreary Yale dormitory is partly correct. The rest of his argument, however, seems not to work, because it is not so easy to see how the marks left by these incidents and others like them have hindered my progress through the various tests white society sets up. On the contrary: incidents of racism have always fueled in me a burning desire to smash their racist faces in—but only metaphorically. I am sensitive to the punchline of the old joke, attributed to Malcolm X but actually of somewhat earlier vintage, that a black man with a Ph.D. is still called a nigger. But my answer has never been to say, "There are racists who want to stop me, so why bother?" Roger Wilkins has written that the answer is just to do your work and ignore them,[5] and sometimes I try to do just that. More often, however, my answer has been to try to show an often doubting, arrogant, and insensitive white world that whatever their best can do I can do, except that I can do it better. My answer has been overachievement.

The premise isn't true, of course. I can't do everything better than everybody else can. (And many things I can't do at all—advanced physics, for example, as I discovered as an undergraduate, to my chagrin.) But what I am describing is a statement less of fact than of attitude. Perhaps I can't hit the members of my Boy Scout troop over the head with my résumé, and nothing I might accomplish would alter the conviction of that old white man on the bus that I was not good enough to take the seat beside his. Nevertheless, those encounters have fueled in me a burning need for achievement in a white world that once wanted no part of me. Yes, I am marked, and the scars, I am sure, are permanent. But they are not the scars of disadvantage.

It is fashionable for black critics of affirmative action to point to the difficulties they have overcome in their lifetimes without anyone's offer of a leg up. I can't do that because I haven't suffered as others have. Oh, I could spin stories that make my life sound more difficult than it was. Like how I lived on Convent Avenue in Harlem as a child. Or how I walked to the bus stop under the watchful eyes and bayonets of the National Guard troops who patrolled my Washington neighborhood during the riots following the murder of Martin Luther King, Jr., in 1968. And both tales would be no more than the unvarnished truth.

Except that when I lived in Harlem, my father was a lawyer and the Harlem of the 1950s, while not, perhaps, New York City's most fashionable address, was a relatively stable community with lots of middle-class families. And as for the National Guard, well, the troops were there, armed and tense, but matters were more complex than the tale alone might suggest. The many black kids who were bused from the inner city to my mostly white junior high school in Northwest Washington, D.C., talked earnestly of the horrors being wreaked in their neighborhoods. I had no such tales to share. My family lived in Cleveland Park, a clean, quiet neighborhood of picturesque old homes and lovely, tree-lined streets far from the inferno at the city's center. Today, although moderately integrated, Cleveland Park is one of the few neighborhoods in the city that remain predominantly white. At the time of the riots, it was almost entirely white. Our neighbors included Walter Mondale and Eugene McCarthy, and the National Guard troops deployed around the neighborhood were there principally to protect white lives and white property against wholly imaginary threats. The roadblocks around Cleveland Park were established to keep most black people *out;* in the central part of the city, where most of the black folks lived, the purpose was quite the other way around.

This, I suppose, is why some of my friends, puzzled by my writing on affirmative action, mark it down to the peculiarity of my background—born to the silver spoon, never having known what it is to want, and so on. But that criticism, or explanation, actually helps to make my point. The programs were said to compensate for the present effects of past discrimination, and, even in 1977 when that difficult conversation took place, I was worried that there didn't seem to be any present effects in my life. No, I was more than worried: I was very nearly ashamed, which is why I had called on my friend for reassurance. I recalled the poignant line—is it from Richard Nixon's account of his childhood in *Six Crises?*—that we had hardships but did not consider them particularly hard. My family was far from wealthy, but we were certainly well above the poverty line—as, it happens, most two-parent black families were then and are now, no matter what image of black people the mass media, with their obsessive focus on urban street crime, have reinforced over the past two decades.*

---

*For two-parent black households, the poverty rate in 1969 was about 20 percent and has since dropped to around 15 percent.[6]

Why, then, the insistence—and not only by my friend who was so impatient to reassure me, but by civil rights advocates as well—that all black people are, in effect, in the same boat, and that the boat itself is on its way to the bottom? The structure of affirmative action programs in admission, and the predictable reaction to them by a rational university, offers a simple explanation: *The most disadvantaged black people are not in a position to benefit from preferential admission.* No one seriously imagines otherwise. No rational institution of higher learning would act otherwise. A college does not want to waste its resources. Surely, in assembling a class, the school will select those most likely to succeed. And if the college indulges a special admission program for the benefit of disadvantaged students, it will select for admission through that program those disadvantaged students most likely to succeed.*

The problem is that the truly disadvantaged are not likely to succeed in college: their disadvantage—perhaps the fruit of systemic racism, to use my friend's term—has taken that opportunity from them. How is the elite college or professional school, under pressure to diversify its student body, to resolve the dilemma? Simple: make race a proxy for disadvantage and then, ignoring other aspects of their background, admit as students those among the nonwhite applicants who seem most likely to succeed. That way, there is less risk. Everyone is happy.

I V

Everyone is happy, that is, as long as the case can be made that *every* student of color is disadvantaged by racism, which means that a program designed to help the disadvantaged is serving its function as long as it admits people of color. This

---

*Similarly (although the point is often overlooked), the demise of affirmative action in college admission would not help the most disadvantaged white people, because they, like the most disadvantaged black people, are also not in a position to take advantage of higher education. As Joel Dreyfuss and Charles Lawrence III have noted, when the Supreme Court imposed limits on preferential admission programs, "the real winners [were] the country's economically and educationally privileged."[7]

approach was the only way to make sense of racial preferences
in admission as they were justified in the mid-1970s, and at
the time of my disturbing conversation, there was even a theory available to support this view: the theory of institutional
racism. On my bookshelf, now as then, is *Black Power,* the
powerful ideological manifesto of the radical black left of the
1960s, in which the authors, Stokely Carmichael and Charles
V. Hamilton, distinguish *individual* racism, "which can be re-
corded by television cameras"—the bombing of a church by
white terrorists, for example—from *institutional* racism:

> The second type is less overt, far more subtle, less identifiable
> in terms of *specific* individuals committing the acts. But it is no
> less destructive of human life. The second type originates in
> the operation of established and respected forces in the society,
> and thus receives far less public condemnation than the first
> type.[8]

Individual racism, according to Carmichael and Hamilton, is
something the society is willing to condemn and even, in many
cases, to prevent. But the society "does nothing meaningful
about institutional racism." And there is more:

> This is not to say that every single white American consciously
> oppresses black people. He does not need to. Institutional rac-
> ism has been maintained deliberately by the power structure
> and through indifference, inertia and lack of courage on the
> part of white masses as well as petty officials. Whenever black
> demands for change become loud and strong . . . [t]he line be-
> tween purposeful suppression and indifference blurs.[9]

The theory of institutional racism has had a rocky intellectual history, but it has the plain virtue of unpacking the
pretense that racism exists only in specific and limited acts by
individuals. This point, I fear, is sometimes missed in the contemporary neoconservative effort to defend an antidiscrimination law based only on wrongs done to particular individuals.
Much of modern civil rights law is built on a bilateral paradigm, under which all that really matters is what specific enti-

ties do intentionally to other specific entities: a firm to an employee, a landlord to a tenant, a school district to its black students. Carmichael and Hamilton, however, understand the possibility that there is more to freedom and equality than undoing bilateral discriminatory deeds. The history of the United States has been marked by more than discrete overt acts of discrimination, featuring instead an evil far greater than the sum of its discriminatory parts. I have in mind what might be thought of as racist *oppression,* the systematic subjugation of black people as a group, an oppression that is passing into history but leaving a frightful legacy.

I am certainly not one who would argue that every present-day disadvantage suffered by people of color finds its cause in contemporary racism, but it is obvious that many of our problems have roots in historical racism. If the nation's only response to its racist legacy is to prevent individuals from doing what the society did for so long, much injustice will never be undone. Much more is needed, and the Great Society's much ballyhooed War on Poverty, whatever the weaknesses or failures of some particular policy initiatives, is an example of the kind of societal commitment that is required even now. The litany is familiar, and the neoconservative attack on it merely sharpens the points.

The neoconservative critics are surely correct in saying that what we need more than anything else is to build toward a world in which individual initiative and talent, rather than government programs, will be decisive in the distribution of resources. But although there are more opportunities for people of color now than ever before, there are barriers, too; and while the proposition put by such theorists as George Gilder and Charles Murray that an unfettered market will remove the barriers without the assistance of government programs (and largess) has obvious political appeal, it is ultimately unpersuasive.[10] Racial justice *isn't* cheap. We need, for example, vast improvements in medical care for poor children. It is inexcusable that our inner cities have infant mortality rates higher than those in much of the Third World. And if, as critics suggest, the problem is not the unavailability of services but the behavior of parents,[11] then it is inexcusable that our society cares so little about educating parents to take better care of their children. We need educational improvements, especially at the preschool level. It is true, as the critics hasten to point out, that there is little evidence that money spent on new educational programs leads ineluctably to greater educational achievement. But there is plenty of statistically reliable evidence that better preschool programs produce better achievement later, especially in mathematics,[12] and plenty more that education proceeds best in school environments that are stable and safe[13]—two conditions that it costs money to bring about. And while it is also true that the most important determinant of educational achievement is family socioeconomic circumstance,[14] this only points to improvement in the social infrastructure of inner-city communities as a bare necessity for progress—even if, obviously, a tremendously expensive one. (To paraphrase the columnist George Will, who was in turn parodying President Bush, if we have the will we'll open the wallet.)

All of this is consistent with the theory of institutional racism: there is much at stake that bilateral solutions will not cure. But none of these are civil rights programs, and all of them are targeted at the worst off among us, the people to whom affirmative action programs will never provide much help, even if they are the people in whose names the programs are often justified. I recognize that this brief litany of needed programs, when recapitulated here in the can't-do 1990s rather than the can-do 1960s and 1970s, has a pie-in-the-sky quality that must seem terribly naive. I have no illusion that a world in which there are fewer resources allocated by racial preference will miraculously see a concentration of societal resources where they are most needed. But it is useful nevertheless to sketch what is really required, as a way of illustrating just how good a bargain on racial justice America is getting if programs of affirmative action are all that is required to give.

Still, for the reasons that I have set out in the foregoing chapters, I am hardly an unabashed fan of affirmative action. To the extent that the programs are to be preserved, they should be returned to their roots—not the *ideological* roots, the notion that they are helping the truly disadvantaged by compensating for the legacy left by centuries of oppression, but the *metaphorical* roots, the once-dynamic image of the programs as means for promoting progress by ensuring opportunities that might not otherwise exist for people of color to show what they can do.

V

I begin at the beginning. Given the logic of all that I have said, I often feel that I should oppose all racial preferences in admission to college and professional school. But I don't. When the law school admission season rolls around during the winter, I find myself drawn to the folders of applicants who are not white, as though to something rare and precious. Those folders I give an extra bit of scrutiny, looking, perhaps, for reasons to recommend a *Yes.* I am not trying to get the numbers right and I do not believe that the standards applied by colleges or professional schools are racist; rather, I find myself wanting others to have the same leg up that I had. The question is whether I can square this instinct with what I have said about the damage that preferences do. One of the principal mistaken emphases (or perhaps a public relations problem) of the modern diversity movement that I described in chapter 2 is that it often seems in its rhetoric to press toward circumventing or eradicating standards, rather than training us and pushing us until we are able to meet them. There is an important distinction between this modern approach and the more traditional understanding of affirmative action as a program that would help a critical mass of us gain the necessary training to meet the standards of our chosen fields rather than seeking to get around them. Not the least of the difficulties is that the more time we spend arguing that various standards for achievement are culturally inappropriate, the more other people are likely to think we are afraid of trying to meet them.

My own view is that, given training, given a chance, we as a people need fear no standards. That is why I want to return the special admission programs to their more innocent roots, as tools for providing that training and that chance for students who might not otherwise have it. A college or university is not fulfilling its educational missions if it fails to take a hard look at the applicant pool to be sure that it is not missing highly motivated students—some of them people of color, some of them not—who might not be "sure things" but who show good evidence of being positioned to take advantage of what the school can offer. This means taking risks, but that is what higher educational institutions ought to be doing—not to fill a quota or to look good on paper or to keep student activists quiet, and certainly not to bring into the student body a group of students who will thereafter be called upon to represent the distinctive voices of oppressed people (imagine the brouhaha were a professor to take this idea seriously in calling on students in class discussion), but because the purveying of knowledge, the reason universities exist, is a serious enterprise, and one professors should undertake joyfully, even when it isn't easy and even when there is a risk of failure.

Of course, the students who are admitted because a school has decided to take a chance on them will not look as good on paper as those who are admitted because they are sure things; and the odds are that those with the better paper records will be the better performers, too, which is why grades and test scores are considered in the first place. The school, then, is admitting more than one group of students. Many students are admitted because of their paper qualifications, and these are the ones on which the school is likely to pin its highest hopes for academic attainment. The rest are admitted because they have benefited from one preference or another: legacy (as children of alumni are sometimes called), athlete, geography, even in some places music. And some receive a preference because of race.

All the beneficiaries of preferences, not just those who have earned a place through racial preferences, would have been excluded had only a paper record been used. But although every college has its stereotypes of the dumb jock and the stupid legacy, there is a qualitative difference between these characterizations and the conscious or unconscious racial nature of similar comments about the beneficiaries of racially conscious affirmative action. For just as a different standard for admission or hiring reinforces a double standard for the measurement of success, it also reinforces a double standard for the consequence of failure. When a person admitted because of membership in a special category does not succeed, that lack of success is often attributed to others in the same category. The stereotype of the dumb jock exists because of the widespread perception (a correct one) that athletes are frequently admitted on paper records for which other students would be rejected. When people of color are admitted in the same fashion, the damage is worse, because the double standard reinforces an already existing stereotype, and because the stereotype, like the program, sorts explicitly according to race. Consequently, if our success rate at elite colleges turns out to be lower than that of white students (as, thus far, it is), we can scarcely avoid having the fact noticed and, in our racially conscious society, remembered as well.

This risk is a predictable consequence of double standards and cannot be avoided. It can, however, be reduced. The best way to reduce the risk would be to eliminate racial preferences, and over time, as the competitive capacity of people of color continues to improve. A more immediate solution is for those students who are admitted as a consequence of affirmative action, while on the college campus and while in professional school and while pursuing their careers—in short, *for the rest of their professional lives*—to bend to their work with an energy that will leave competitors and detractors alike gasping in admiration. The way to turn this potential liability into a powerful asset is to make our cadre of professionals simply too good to ignore.

To accomplish this goal, the first thing that an opportunity-based affirmative action must do is to abandon the pretense that it will in any significant way compensate for present educational disadvantage. Programs of preferential admissions will not wipe away the lingering effects of struggling through the inner-city public schools about which the nation long ago ceased to care. To bring onto college campuses students whose academic abilities have been severely damaged by the conditions in which they have been forced to learn would be a recipe for failure. At best, affirmative action can take those students of color who have already shown the greatest potential and place them in environments where their minds will be tested and trained, the campuses of elite colleges and professional schools.

Besides, the evidence has long suggested, and recent studies have confirmed, that educational disadvantage is but one of a cluster of problems reducing the likelihood that students of color will attend or complete college. In the past decade, despite rising test scores,[15] a higher rate of high school graduation, and affirmative action programs galore, college attendance by black students is down. In particular, the proportion of black youth aged eighteen to twenty-four who have been enrolled in college has plummeted. In 1976, 33.4 percent of that group were or had been enrolled in college, representing nearly half of black high school graduates; this compared very favorably with the 33.0 percent of white youth of the same age with enrollment experience, representing 40 percent of white high school graduates. Ten years later, although the high school graduation rate rose, the percentage of black youth with enrollment experience dropped to 28.6 percent, representing only 37.4 percent of high school graduates, while the equivalent percentages for white youth barely changed at all.[16]

Debate over the causes of this decline continues, and some of the candidates—for example, the rising involvement with the drug culture, the large number of young black men caught up in the criminal justice system, and the appeal of competing career choices, such as the military—are beyond the control of educational institutions. (Besides, the drug culture and criminal justice arguments are plainly insufficient to explain why the rate of high school graduation would be *up* so sharply.) There is common agreement, however, that a principal difficulty is the high cost, especially at the nation's most exclusive universities, which makes alternative career choices more attractive. This is why preferential financial assistance (for all its obvious problems) might actually be a more logical and efficient solution than preferential admission. As this manuscript was being completed, a debate erupted over the decision (subsequently modified) by the United States Department of Education to deny federal funds to schools offering preferential financial aid packages on the basis of race.* This decision, defended on the ground that federal aid should be administered in a color-blind manner, created a dilemma for colleges interested in keeping both minority recruitment and academic standards at high levels. If one argues that affirmative action is impermissible, then schools are left with only the market mechanism—money—as a tool for enticing onto their campuses excellent students who are not white. A genuine believer in market solutions should allow participants in the market to bid for scarce resources—and by all accounts, first-rate students of color are such a resource. One might want to argue that this bidding is not fair, but if colleges can rely on neither preferential admission nor bidding to attract students who are not white, they plainly can do no more than pay lip service to the ideal of "minority recruitment."

VI

With the proper goal in mind, then, a degree of racial consciousness *in college and perhaps professional school admission* can plausibly be justified—but just a degree, and just barely. The educational sphere is the place for action because the proper goal of all racial preferences is opportunity—a chance at advanced training for highly motivated people of color who, for whatever complex set of reasons, might not otherwise have

*The compromise resolution was that schools may not use federal funds for racially preferential scholarships but may fund such scholarships from other sources.

it. So justified, the benefit of a racial preference carries with it the concomitant responsibility not to waste the opportunity affirmative action confers. What matters most is what happens *after* the preference.

I call this vision of professional achievement and racial preference the affirmative action pyramid, and it works much as the name implies: The role of preference narrows as one moves upward. And although I do not want to say arbitrarily *This is the spot,* what is clear is that as one climbs toward professional success, at some point the preferences must fall away entirely. Possibly a slight preference is justified in college admission, not as a matter of getting the numbers right, and certainly not as a matter of finding the right set of hitherto excluded points of view, but as a matter of giving lots of people from different backgrounds the chance—only the chance—to have an education at an elite college or university. But when that opportunity has been exercised, when the student has shown what he or she can do, the rationale for a preference at the next level is slimmer. So an even slighter affirmative action preference for professional school admission, while possibly justified on similar grounds, is less important, and a little bit harder to defend, than a program at the college level.

And when one's training is done, when the time comes for entry to the job market, I think it is quite clear that among professionals,* the case for preference evaporates. The candidate has by this time had six or seven or eight years of training at the highest level; it is a bit silly, as well as demeaning, to continue to insist that one's college and professional school performance is not a very accurate barometer of one's professional possibilities. The time has come, finally, to stand or fall on what one has actually achieved. And, of course, as one passes the point of initial entry and moves up the ladder of one's chosen field, all of the arguments run the other way; the time for preference has gone, and it is time instead to stand

---

*I make no claim here about the propriety of affirmative action in labor markets demanding less in the way of educational credentials.

proudly on one's own record. The preferences cannot go on forever. Sooner or later, talent and preparation, rather than skin color, must tell.

The question of the ability of people of color to meet professional standards should be distinguished from the separate question of the fairness of the standards themselves. Naturally, one must be wary of attributing fairness or neutrality to any particular set of professional standards simply because the standards exist; it is all too easy to suppose that those whom the standards fence out are excluded because they deserve to be and those whom the standards allow in have earned their places. As the British historian J. R. Pole has demonstrated, it has long been a feature of the American character to justify whatever social and economic lines happen to exist as fair and perhaps natural, even as the line drawers, and the lines themselves, have shifted over time.[17] Recent years, moreover, have seen increasing documentation of the connection between attitudes toward race and much of the original impetus (and original design) for drawing lines to measure intellect.[18]

For the committed professional, however, an argument of this kind can quickly become moot. The professions, after all, are in a sense defined by their standards, and most professionals of whatever color are far too busy proving themselves to spend time quibbling over the fairness of standards for medical board certification or law firm partnership. True, the standards for academic tenure are currently under assault as embodying a bias against people of color, but away from the campuses, I doubt there are many black professionals for whom the satisfaction of "I forced them to change their standards to take account of my cultural background" can compete with the thrill of "They did their worst, and I beat them at their own game." The distinction has nothing to do with fairness or cultural identity or self-actualization; the point is to gain what might be called The Edge, what every professional driving toward the top of his or her chosen field wants to hold over all the others, the competition, who are grabbing for the same brass ring.

VII

Any notion that we should demand to be treated just like any-body else also runs afoul of one of the great and frightening complexities of our age: standardized testing. On nearly every standardized test that one can name, whether for aptitude, achievement, admission, or employment, the median scores of black candidates lag well behind the median scores of white candidates.* On most tests, the gap has been narrowing, but it continues to exist. Given the multitudinous societal rewards that are distributed in part on the basis of standardized test scores, black people as a group will continue to run behind until our scores are raised.

America places greater emphasis on standardized testing than any other country in the world. Often, test results are misused, serving as a crutch, a single quantitative means for sorting applicants rather than one important factor in a mix of qualifications. And they are all too frequently misunder-stood, treated as though they measure aptitudes that are in-nate rather than skills that are learned. Consequently, in a racially conscious society, it is scarcely surprising, but cer-tainly frightening, that many people seem to think that the tests reveal racial differences in genetic inheritance.

For many civil rights advocates, the contemporary solu-tion is to get rid of the tests and their quantitative evidence of the continuing disadvantage with which racism, with its bru-tal force, has burdened us. The term that has been coined to explain the difference in median test scores is "cultural bias"; in other words, the tests measure traits that some people, be-cause of their backgrounds, are less likely to possess. The im-portant question, however, is not whether the measured traits are culture-specific, but whether measuring them is useful to the tester.

*The use of the word *median,* while frequently overlooked, is important. The scores of black candidates tend to be clustered around a lower point than the scores of white candidates, but this gives no information about the *actual* score of any particular candidate. A given black candidate might fall in the 99th percentile, even if most black candidates score far lower; and a given white candidate might fall in the 1st percentile, even if most white candidates score far higher.

Consider: If a test is not good at predicting job or professional school performance and is also racially exclusionary, getting rid of it is a very good idea, but the reason to get rid of it is not that it is racially exclusionary but that it is a poor predictor. This helps everybody, not just candidates who are black, because, as Derrick Bell has pointed out, it "increase[s] the likelihood that those selected, regardless of race, will fulfill the needs of the position."[19] That is what it means for a test (or any other qualification) to be job-related, which, although sometimes expensive to demonstrate, is all that the courts have required employers defending discrimination cases to show.

The trouble is that many of the tests on which black scores lag behind white ones are not poor predictors of the performance of black people—or rather, if they are poor predictors, black people are not disadvantaged by those poor predictions. Many standardized tests tend to *overpredict* the performance of people who are black; that is, the actual job performance or school performance is likely to be slightly *worse* on average than what one would expect, given the scores.

This fact, well supported by considerable and varied social science data, has led to some peculiar forms of argument. An example may be drawn from the National Research Council's very extensive study of the General Aptitude Test Battery, perhaps the most frequently used employment test. The report concluded that using the same formula to predict the job performance of both white and black candidates who sat for the test "would not give predictions that were biased against black applicants." On the contrary, "[i]f the total-group equation does give systematically different predictions than would be provided by the equation based on black employees only, it is somewhat more likely to overpredict than to underpredict."[20]

Does the report then conclude that the use of a single norm for the GATB does not discriminate against black candidates and, in fact, might even be helpful? Well, no, not exactly. One must be careful of the results, the report explains, because "there may be bias against blacks in the primary criterion measure used in the studies—supervisor ratings." Why? Because "[u]sually the supervisors were white."[21] The idea seems to be that the GATB predicts only supervisors' ratings, which, for black employees, might not be an accurate measure of job performance.

To their credit, the report's authors give the same careful attention to studies of supervisor bias that they do to studies of test bias. The difficulty with their thesis is that the empirical work does not clearly bear it out, leading to this awkward conclusion: "Although common sense suggests that evaluations of the performance of blacks or women might well be depressed to some degree by prejudice, it is difficult to quantify this sort of intangible (and perhaps unconscious) effect."[22]

The other possibility—the one that goes mysteriously unmentioned in the otherwise very comprehensive report—is that on this particular point, common sense is wrong. That there is a degree of racism is hardly a surprise, but in an era when highly skilled labor is at a premium, perhaps the supervisor bias is small. Perhaps it does not exist. Or perhaps, as I suggested in an earlier chapter, the bias works the other way: perhaps white supervisors, deeply imbued with stereotypical notions of black laziness and stupidity, are so astonished when black employees turn in outstanding performances that the ratings are *higher* than they would be for similarly performing whites. There is, as far as I know, no empirical support for any of these explanations either; but if the guide is to be common sense, these are as sensible as anything else.

Besides, if one concludes that supervisor ratings are too biased to be used as a measure of job performance, one trembles at the edge of a precipice of paradox. When it is not possible to hire everybody, one must sort among the potential employees *somehow.* Ordinarily, the most sensible means is to try to guess something about the candidate's future—that is, to make a prediction. One might reasonably argue over whether a college or professional school should try to predict grades or future life performance.[23] But it is difficult to see how an employer has any choice but to try to predict job performance, for there is no other reason to hire an employee except to do the job. If an employer is suddenly to be told that for black employees, it is not legitimate to measure performance by either quantitative measures (standardized tests, said to be biased) or subjective measures (supervisor ratings, also said to be biased), there comes the question whether the performance of black employees can be evaluated based on *anything*. It does not seem to strike a blow for equality to argue to employers that after hiring black employees with lower test scores than white employees who are turned away, an employer may not rely on supervisor evaluations (or, evidently, anything else) in deciding how well they have done.

This is a problem on the campuses too, where in the more extreme rhetoric of the diversity movement, a strong undercurrent suggests that mainstream professors—the Eurocentric white males who run the place—are not qualified to evaluate the work of scholars of color who are bringing the voices of the oppressed into the debate. But such an argument is self-defeating. After all, if mainstream faculties are incapable of evaluating the work of these new faculty members, who ought to do the evaluations? Indeed, how can those of us who are black—relatively young and inexperienced scholars that most of us still are—tell whether our work is any good? I suppose we could limit our universe of discourse and ask only one another. But then perhaps white scholars should ask only one another about the quality of their work, too, and I'm not sure what basis we would have for objection. True, it might be protested that white scholars have been asking only one another for decades—but I have always thought that those of us who are not white are moving into academia to change that process, not justify it.

VIII

In the long run, gaining The Edge we seek means beating the tests, too, and I am confident that we will. Ideally, a phaseout of affirmative action in professional employment should be accompanied by what Nathan Glazer has described as "vigorous attention to the elements in the education of blacks that lead to those test scores of all types that are at present a substantial barrier to black achievement."[24] In the meanwhile, even as we preserve temporarily a degree of racial preference in admission, our goal must be the creation of a cadre of black professionals who, by being too good to ignore, refute all the racist stereotypes. If affirmative action opens some doors at the level of college or professional school entry, fine; let us then be unembarrassed about it. Thereafter, our job—and it *is* a job, one we should undertake cheerfully on behalf of our people, for it is far more important in the long run than speaking the right words in the right voice—is to make the most of the opportunities affirmative action creates. And our strategy must be to insist, once the door is open, on being treated no differently than anybody else. Only then will we be able to look boorish interviewers and colleagues (and the genuinely racist ones, too) squarely in the eye and say in response to the qualification question I discussed in chapter 1, "Sure, I got into law school because I'm black—so what?"

The alternative is to pretend that the untrue dream that has haunted affirmative action is the reality. Rather than returning programs of racial preference to their simpler roots, we can instead continue our pretense that all black people are damaged in their competitive capacities by racism, and that the damage is something that will be undone if only we can get the casualties into the right school. We can continue to argue for a world in which there are two standards of achievement, the white and the black. We can continue to fight for the proposition that blackness is a good proxy for culture, and culture, in its turn, a good proxy for political opinions, so that our battle to integrate America becomes a struggle to make the authentic voices of our people heard in the corridors of power. And if we continue that fight, we necessarily continue to argue that there is a right way and a wrong way to represent the people, and that a black person in a position of power who presents the wrong views is betraying the birthright that blackness confers.

But if we travel down this less happy path, this path of accusation and avoidance, then we are not, after all, the beneficiaries of affirmative action: we are its victims.

PART II

On Being a Black Dissenter

Someone must have felt something very
deeply to have cried out these long sounds
of despair refusing to die.
  —*Ayi Kwei Armah*,
    The Beautyful Ones Are Not Yet Born

CHAPTER 5

Silencing Dissent

Each December, my wife and I host a holiday dessert for the black students at the Yale Law School, where I teach. We offer pastries and eggnog, a blazing fire, and quiet music, and our hope is to provide for the students an opportunity to unwind, to escape, to renew themselves, to chat, to argue, to complain—in short, to relax. For my wife and myself, the party is a chance to get to know some of the people who will lead black America (and white America, too) into the twenty-first century. But more than that, we feel a deep emotional connection to them, through our blackness: we look at their youthful, enthusiastic faces and see ourselves. There is something affirming about the occasion—for them, we hope, but certainly for us. It is a reminder of the bright and supportive side of solidarity. Talking with the students is fun: they are bright and engaging and earnest, and we have every reason to think that the future of our people is in capable hands.

True, we don't always agree with their views, nor they with ours (nor my wife with me, for that matter), but one of the reasons to train young minds is to enable us to differ, and to discuss our differences. Indeed, although I know it sounds fatuous, I take faith in dialectical interchange to be a touchstone of intellectual endeavor: only by reasoning together will we advance human knowledge. As a law student many years ago, censured by others for jumping down the throats, as they put it, of those with whom I disagreed, I defended my instinct (although perhaps not my manners) by insisting that I had as much right to criticize the views of others as they had to express them. As a teacher, I maintain the same view; so I feel free, even obliged, to dispute with my students, and I hope they feel the same about me.

Of course, from time to time, one of these young people expresses an opinion that strikes me as not only wrong but a little silly (such as the student who recently insisted, with no supporting data and only the flimsiest of anecdotal evidence, that most black people arrested for felonies are innocent) or disturbing (such as the students who argue vehemently that white students or professors who make racially offensive remarks ought to be disciplined). Expressing silly or disturbing ideas does not make black students different from any other students, or, indeed, from most adults, myself included; and a university community is a particularly appropriate place to debate ideas that in other contexts might seem outrageous. Still, at such moments, I fear that a weakly conceived ideology may be clouding their analytical faculties, and that is when I begin to worry a little.

But, as I said, Yale is an academic community, and where should these views be ventilated and debated if not here? True, some of my colleagues, at Yale and elsewhere, are inclined to warn that the students and their ideas are actually dangerous, but I tell them not to worry. The students are young, their minds are growing, they are testing theses and will ultimately reject most of them—as we did. So my wife and I continue to host our party, continue to engage them in discussion, and continue not to worry too much.

It may be that we should worry a little more, not so much about these students as about the examples being set for them by their elders. The black community in the United States, its always-fragile unity shattered in the more than two decades since the assassination of Martin Luther King, Jr., is at a dangerous but important moment in its history. Enormous progress has been made in the struggle for equality, but the problems that remain, particularly those related to drugs and education, often seem insurmountable. All too few new ideas are being generated, and some of the old ones—such as the need for widespread systems of racial preference in college admission and employment—seem increasingly irrelevant, yet are defended with a desperation that often turns to virulence.

I worry about what messages we are sending to these kids who will one day be the leaders of our community and our country. In particular, I worry about the message conveyed by the righteous fury that many of the current leaders of the black community direct toward dissenters from the traditional civil rights agenda—especially when the dissenters are black and when the agenda involves preferences. Racially conscious affirmative action, I fear, has become for some powerful voices in black America a kind of shibboleth and, like other shibboleths, has come to be used as a convenient device for separating friends from enemies. (We are *not* debatable.) And on college campuses, the rallying cry of "diversity" has become a shibboleth, too; and any person of color who does not agree that the reason to hire more people of color is to liberate the voices that racism has stifled, to represent the special perspective that people of color bring, evidently sacrifices his or her birthright. As an intellectual struggling to escape from the box of other people's preconceptions, I find the development of a loyalty test particularly distressing.

The word *shibboleth* has come into contemporary dialogue as a reference to a thing that is beyond criticism. I am using the word, however, in its original sense, as recounted in chapter 12 of the Book of Judges, which tells the story of the defeat of the Ephraimites at the hands of the Gileadites. After being put to rout, the Ephraimites found their retreat cut off by the Gileadites, who had prudently garrisoned the escape routes. Anyone desiring to pass was asked whether he was an Ephraimite, and if he denied it:

> Then they said unto him, Say now Shibboleth: and he said Sib-
> boleth: for he could not frame to pronounce it right. Then they
> took him, and slew him at the passages of Jordan: and there
> fell at that time of the Ephraimites forty and two thousand.[1]

Thus, to be true to its origins, *shibboleth* should be used as a
metaphor for a test that determines who is a genuine member
of a group. The shibboleth must always be pronounced correctly, with careful attention to every nuance; those unable to
say it right are outsiders who warrant destruction.

Thus, when I say that affirmative action has become a
shibboleth for many of the most powerful voices in black
America, I mean that there is now a correct way to talk about
racial preferences—as simple justice, the minimum a racist
society ought to offer the victims of its oppression, a *sine qua
non* of our progress as a people—and an incorrect way—as
unfair, illicit, denigrating, counterproductive, or unnecessary.
Group membership is determined by the tale one chooses: a
black person (or, nowadays, an African-American) who tells
the wrong tale—who mispronounces the shibboleth—is a traitor and an outsider. And traitors are much worse than adver-
saries; for every nation hates most the betrayer from within.
In the black community, our response to the dissent that we
label treason is often painfully straightforward: the dissenters
face ostracism, expulsion, official death. We purge them.

II

Purges are never pretty. They are not meant to be. The more
ruthless and complete the campaign in which one's opponents
are eliminated, the more emphatic the warning sent to those
who might dissent in the future: Beware, the message reads.
See how we deal with those who deny the official word. Don't
get on the wrong side, or you could be next.

A purge is, in its essence, a denial of the right to think.
It punishes those who disagree with the established view or
with a newly minted view being made into the established one.

And when a purge is under way, the intellectuals, with no protection in sight, are usually among the first to go. One is reminded of what someone said of the Russian anarchist Mikhail Bakunin: on the first day of the revolution, he is a treasure; on the second day, he should be shot. Of course, everyone hates the intellectuals, for to be an intellectual is to be a free thinker and a freer critic, to accept no proposition as beyond analysis or dispute, and to serve as a roaming adversary of all that is perceived as foolish, ill conceived, or simplistic.

It is our habit to think of the purge as one of the repulsive habits of the old Soviet state (although things are now quite different there), or as a kind of minor political earthquake that intermittently rumbles across the Third World. But we have purges of our own, too, and while some of them are orderly—for example, the reconstitution of the entire leadership of the federal bureaucracy each time a new president takes office—many others are decidedly unattractive. Few Western-style purges are more disheartening, and more threatening to freedom, than the disdainful treatment of intellectuals who dare to challenge fashionable academic orthodoxy. And a particularly tragic example of this treatment is the isolation of intellectual dissenters who happen to be black.

Regrettably—but perhaps understandably—the black community is one in which dissent is often stifled. Evidently, a good deal turns on solidarity, on not revealing to the world that some black people who have thought deeply about the problems facing our community disagree with the traditional civil rights consensus on either their causes or their cures. And the single proposition on which dissent seems to be least tolerated is the desirability of extensive systems of racial preference. That is our shibboleth, and black dissenters who instead say *sibboleth* are treated as outsiders.

Black dissenters are an easy target, in the sense that they are easy to find. This is the result of a peculiar form of affirmative action, one practiced all too often by those in a position to make or at least to influence public policy—the award

of celebrity status to that interesting curiosity, the conservative thinker who happens to be black. This was brought home
nicely in the early 1980s when Walter Williams, a black economist, declared that "most people in U.S. soup kitchen lines
have a few coins in their jeans they'd rather keep for items
not handed out free—like wine, dope, or cigarettes."[2] Williams has long been vilified by many black leaders for his vehement disdain of traditional civil rights strategies, and criticism of his startling comment was only to be expected; but it
was left to Glenn Loury, another black economist who would
shortly be vilified himself for his attacks on racial preferences, to deliver the most stinging rebuke—not so much of
Williams himself but of the media establishment that had
made him a star. After expressing his "surprise and disbelief" that Williams made his assertion "without any data,"
Loury went on to say:

> I think the liberal press is partly responsible for the phenome-
> non which is Walter Williams. If Ralph D'Arge were to have
> said the same thing, no one would be able to read about it in
> *USA Today,* because D'Arge (obviously an arbitrary choice) is
> white, about as well respected in the economics profession as
> Williams, but not of an "interesting" racial group. It is ab-
> surd that Williams' views, as inane as they sometimes are,
> should be so widely considered, simply because the man is a
> black economist. Applying the notion of affirmative action to
> press coverage of conservative economists is surely an instance
> of taking a good idea a bit too far![3]

In search of the better man-bites-dog story, our media of mass
communication do exactly what Loury charges. They make ce-
lebrities of black people who disagree with other black people.
And not just the media: in an awkward and perhaps unknow-
ing alliance with those scholars (discussed in chapters 2 and
9) who insist that the voices of people of color ought to carry
special weight in debate about civil rights, policy makers and
intellectuals seem to accept the notion that skin color can add
legitimacy—especially when the policy makers are propounding ideas that they have reason to think will leave them open

to charges of racism. Indeed, while educated Americans can probably recognize the names of the leaders of most major civil rights organizations, I doubt that many could easily call to mind the principal academicians, black or white, whose theoretical work underlies much of the contemporary civil rights agenda. But the names of the black scholars who are in dissent—the Lourys, the Thomas Sowells, the Shelby Steeles—are very likely familiar to American intellectuals.

Nowadays the label applied to the dissenters by their critics is "black conservatives"—as though the spirit of intellectual independence that leads critics to dissenting positions can be defeated if it is reduced to an insult. For make no mistake: the vision of large numbers of black activists has sufficiently diverged from the vision of most of the American people that the word *conservative* is thought to describe something unwholesome. Perhaps this is understandable when one considers that over history, the mantle of conservatism has been proudly worn by opponents of every part of the civil rights agenda (see chapter 7). The trouble with treating the word *conservative* as an insult is that the American people continue to vote for "conservative" presidents by huge majorities; even Jimmy Carter, the last elected Democratic president, often positioned himself to the right of the party mainstream in his first campaign, especially during the primary season. (Who can forget his campaign promise to preserve the "ethnic purity" of our neighborhoods?) In electoral politics, it is *liberal,* not *conservative,* that has somehow become a dirty word, and in recent years, black politicians searching for a broad base have shunned the "L-word" with about the same care as have white ones.

Besides, the routine application of "conservative" to the dissenters I am discussing seems incorrect. Sometimes it is an error even in simple descriptive terms, as when William Julius Wilson, a black sociologist at the University of Chicago, was dismissed as a "neoconservative" following the publication in 1978 of his *The Declining Significance of Race.* In that book Wilson argued that "the problems of subordination for certain segments of the black population and the experiences of social advancement for others" are associated less with race than with economic class and suggested, quite reasonably, that a continuing emphasis on civil rights rather than on economic justice would do little to help the worst off among us.[4] As Wilson himself felt constrained to point out when reflecting on the criticism years later, "I am a social democrat, and probably to the left politically of an overwhelming majority of these critics."[5] As I have no doubt made clear, I am not a fan of labels; but if the word *conservative* is to be accurately used, perhaps it ought to apply to the mainstream civil rights organizations, which insist, in the face of considerable evidence to the contrary, that preferences are the indispensable key to the education and advancement of professionals of color. Surely this unwillingness to let go, to try something new, to search for something better, is the very essence of conservatism. When Randall Kennedy, a black law professor at Harvard, declared himself a "radical" because he wants to eliminate the color line for evaluation of scholarship, many people laughed; but he was semantically correct. The idea that scholars of color can be hired and promoted without regard to color is, in the academic world, a very radical concept. The idea that color must and should be taken into account is nowadays a very old-fashioned—that is to say, conservative—one.

Plainly, there is no reason that the views of the black leadership, or of black people generally, need be closely congruent to those held by others. Freedom to think, freedom to criticize, freedom to be different are at the heart of the American enterprise. In fact, a black leadership that stands to the left of the country as a whole can provide an important service, for it is vital that sensitive, thoughtful criticism come from every corner. After all, if no one points out our nation's flaws, they might go forever unnoticed and thus forever uncorrected. And if the cost of that free criticism is that some things will be labeled flaws that are not, the cost is surely one that any free society must be willing to pay.

The mistake is in thinking that because a position represents a consensus, questioning that position is a crime and dissenting from it is high treason. To be sure, black intellectuals who question the wisdom of racial preferences and other parts of the civil rights agenda are thrusting themselves into heated controversies and, in the rough-and-tumble world of political debate, must expect to take their lumps. No one has a right to have his or her views prevail, and nobody who speaks is beyond criticism. Unfortunately, in their anger at the dissenters, some influential figures in the black community have strayed near or across the line between pointed rebuttal and personal attack. Black people who have come to reject the position of civil rights organizations on preferences are excoriated, often through the use of terms to which white dissenters would never be subjected. Because some of the figures who have strayed past the line are individuals for whom I have held lifelong respect, I find criticizing their views particularly painful. But their personal attacks are matters of public record.

Take the case of Shelby Steele. A professor of English at San Jose State, Steele in 1990 published a provocative book, *The Content of Our Character,* in which he asserted, among other themes, that black people spend so much energy crying racism that we tend to miss the genuine opportunities for advancement available to us. Racism, according to Steele, is receding as a force in American society, and it is time the black community recognized that fact. By investing our efforts in affirmative action, he says, we are bolstering a stereotype that holds us unable to make any progress, as they say, on our own.

Perhaps Steele paints too rosy a picture of American society; as it happens, I think that he does.[6] But he is thinking in fresh and compassionate ways, and hardly deserves this broadside from the writer Amiri Baraka: "To me, he's a basket case. I don't consider him knowledgeable about society at all. He seems to me somebody totally shaped by reaction."[7] Of course, Baraka, who also called Steele's ideas "regressive," is not exactly noted for a tendency toward understatement. But what, then, can one make of this blast from John Lewis, a veteran of the civil rights movement who now sits in the Congress of the United States?

There are these people, Steele in particular, sitting in their ivory towers far removed from the problems of poor, downtrodden black Americans. He's one of those who feels very comfortable articulating the position that the victim is responsible for his own situation.[8]

Accusing the dissenters of blaming the victim is common in the public dialogue on race. Thomas Sowell, the black economist who has been inveighing against racial preferences for about as long as they have been around, and who has been subjected to the same charge, protests that it represents a category mistake: "By making the issue *who* is to blame, such arguments evade or pre-empt the more fundamental question—whether this is a matter of blame in the first place."[9] But Sowell himself is evidently thought to be so dangerous that (according to news reports) some civil rights leaders threatened to boycott a meeting with President Bush on revamping the nation's civil rights laws if Sowell were invited. So it ought to be unsurprising that Sowell, too, comes in for his share of chilly blasts, such as this unusually intemperate comment from Carl Rowan, a distinguished and thoughtful black journalist:

> Okay, Sowell has a right to be a conservative and to articulate far-right views. But I must exercise my right to say that Vidkun Quisling, in his collaboration with the Nazis, surely did not do as much damage to the Norwegians as Sowell is doing to the most helpless of black Americans. Sowell is giving aid and comfort to America's racists and to those who, in the name of conservatism and frugality, are taking food out of the mouths of black children, consigning hundreds of thousands of black teenagers to joblessness and hopelessness, and making government a party to at least the partial resegregation of America.[10]

There are many more comments where these came from. Take, for example, the assertion by Benjamin Hooks, head of the National Association for the Advancement of Colored People, that Glenn Loury's views are "treasonous."[11] Other critics suggest ulterior motives for the dissenters. Martin Kilson, who teaches at Harvard, has asserted, "Neoconservative analysts like Glenn Loury address these issues for their own Reaganite public policy purposes."[12] And, of course, there is also simple name calling, as when the late Clarence Pendleton, during his term as head of the Civil Rights Commission, spoke at Yale Law School, and some of the posters announcing his address were defaced with the epithets Oreo and Uncle Tom—evidently referring to his rather mainstream political stance in opposition to racial preferences.*

Or take once more the case of Randall Kennedy, who has made the perfectly plausible suggestion that mainstream academia should not accept on faith what has become an article of faith for the campus branch of the diversity movement: the claim by some nonwhite scholars that people of color write about racial oppression in a distinctive voice that lends them a special credibility and a uniquely valuable perspective. This contention, Kennedy argued in the *Harvard Law Review,* requires evidence, not enough of which has been presented.[13] As an intellectual, Kennedy no doubt expected to spark a dialogue. But the immediate response to his article has been a whispering campaign, an effort to discredit him, a suggestion that he has done something wrong. According to Kennedy's critics, his work will set back the cause of progress. Even if he has a right to his views, the critics seem to think, he ought to know better than to express them in a forum where they will fall into the hands of racists. He is black, after all, and that limits what he should feel free to say.

But the example that should probably be most troubling is the unpardonable abuse of Julius Lester. The purging of Lester is a recent and unhappy reminder of how fragile a flower is the right to doubt when the doubter is black and challenges the community's orthodoxy. Back in the 1960s, Lester was a mainstream black leftist, involved in such groups as the Organization of Latin American Solidarity and Ber-

*To my astonishment, this incident of vandalism provoked considerable debate within the law school, among students and faculty alike, over whether the defacing was objectionable and, stranger still, whether "Oreo" and "Uncle Tom" are racial epithets. Evidently, the politics of the name callee can determine the wrongfulness of the name caller.

trand Russell's International War Crimes Tribunal. Like many black leftists, then and now, Lester was also accused (whether fairly or not) of anti-Semitism. Today Julius Lester is Jewish; he is also a dissenter who evidently has criticized too many icons, among them Jesse Jackson. Lester's colleagues in the Afro-American Studies Department at the University of Massachusetts at Amherst, liking neither Lester nor his views, criticized, mocked, and finally banished him: following the publication of *Lovesong* (1988), his moving but controversial memoir of his journey toward Judaism, Julius Lester was drummed out of the Afro-American Studies Department, despite his tenure. The final break came when he wrote in *Lovesong* what he evidently had previously said in private about a campus lecture by James Baldwin, one of the great figures of twentieth-century literature, who had lectured in one of Lester's courses: "I know that he is not an anti-Semite, but his remarks in class were anti-Semitic, and he does not realize it."[14] For his colleagues, this was the last of many straws. They issued a statement sharply disputing his comments about Baldwin, and concluded: "While Prof. Lester has the right to publicly characterize James Baldwin in any way that he might desire, the actual results can only be depicted as capricious, irresponsible and damaging in a most pernicious way."[15] They demanded that Lester leave their ranks. He did so, moving to the Judaic and Near Eastern Studies Department.

Since Lester's departure, his colleagues have lambasted him publicly as "self-serving and devious" and as engaging in "adolescent exhibitionism," further accusing him of having "a vicious attitude towards blacks and black organizations" and charging that he "can't seem to avoid stereotypical attacks on the black community."[16] It is plain from his book, written before his exile but after the handwriting was on the wall, that Lester, at least, will never be convinced that the colleagues who tormented him were untouched in their motivations by any breath of anti-Semitism. I suspect that their motivations were a good deal more complex than he paints them, but there can be little doubt that they disliked him intensely, and that a part of the reason was the views he expressed. With some notable exceptions, such as the late Clarence Pendleton and, more recently, Shelby Steele, prominent figures in the black community have greeted Lester's treatment by his colleagues with a thundering silence.

All right, fine. So a lot of names are called. Isn't that what an open and unfettered marketplace of ideas is all about? Freedom takes no predictable course; one can no more give instruction on how to be free than on how to be black. "The burden of democracy," says Stanley Crouch, "is that you will get not only a Thurgood Marshall but an Alton Maddox, a Martin Luther King *and* an Al Sharpton—the brilliant, the hysteric, the hustling."[17] Didn't Richard Tawney say that true freedom means you are free to tell me to go to hell and I am free not to go? Not even the framers of the First Amendment imagined that there was hidden somewhere in its vague language a requirement of good manners. If debate is to be robust, it will sometimes be unruly. And if debate is to be unruly, then some feelings are likely to be bruised.

To be black and a dissenter on civil rights issues, then, requires a reasonably thick skin. It is scarcely surprising that an ethnic community that feels itself isolated from and threatened by a larger hostile group perceived as hostile, should weave an ideology of solidarity requiring its own members to mute their criticisms of the community's policies or its leaders; countless other groups have responded to perceived threats in exactly the same way. Besides, the open dissenters are mostly scholars, and it is in the nature of the scholar to upset other people. As the political theorist Judith N. Shklar has put it, "Scholars do not directly serve the intangible or material interests of most citizens, but they offend the sensibilities and aspirations of many."[18]

Still, this leaves the black dissenter in an uncomfortable position. Many black professionals, although expressing privately the same views that prominent dissenters express publicly, mute their public votes. These private dissenters are understandably reluctant to "offend the sensibilities and aspirations" of other black people, sometimes because they agree that public disagreement would be harmful, but just as often, I suspect, because of their unwillingness to face the personal attacks, the slurs on their loyalty, that an open break frequently sparks. It is unfortunate that so many critics seem to think that the price one must pay for dissent is one's birthright: if you take the wrong position, you are thinking white; and if you think white, then you're not really black. A tragedy, of course, and a painful one, but in the end the response must be the same: not only must an intellectual refuse to pay the stated price for the right to think; an intellectual must refuse to acknowledge anyone else's authority to decide that the price must be paid.

III

I do not mean to suggest that the vitriol runs only one way. Some of the dissenters have chosen their words poorly when describing those who disagree with them. Loury refers to the rhetoric of such controversial leaders as Jesse Jackson as "demagoguery,"[19] and Sowell has accused the leadership of the traditional civil rights organizations of being "oblivious to things that don't bring money to them or get whitey."[20] Shelby Steele dismisses the orthodox civil rights agenda as a "party line,"[21] a term that, as he undoubtedly knows, carries heavy historical baggage. It is no excuse to say that the other side started it, for just as it takes two to have a reasoned debate, it takes two to have a nasty argument. But the battle is in an important sense an unequal one, for the dissenters lack a black power base from which to intimidate their opponents. It is unlikely (although not, I suppose, inconceivable) that Loury or Sowell will soon accuse their critics of looking black and talking white.

But the differences may not be irreconcilable. In an effort to establish dialogue, several groups have sponsored debates between the "conservatives" and figures whose views are closer to the mainstream. Prominent dissenters were invited to the African-American summit in New Orleans in 1989, although few of them attended, several citing as the reason for their refusal the participation of Louis Farrakhan.* (Conference organizers defended the invitation to Farrakhan on the plausible, if wrenching, ground that they did not want to exclude any views from the debate.) And the National Urban League, a civil rights organization that Glenn Loury singles out for rare praise, repaid the compliment by inviting Loury to address its convention as well as to participate in its annual report on the state of black America.

Still, the ungentle truth remains: that black intellectuals who dissent from the orthodoxy are all too often silenced by *ad hominem* criticism from many of the leaders of the black community, as well as from other intellectuals, who ought to know better. The attacks are generally far harsher than those launched against white opponents of the traditional civil rights agenda. The attacks are obviously fueled by an anger stemming from a deep worry about the consequences of the dissent. It is not simply that those who attack them believe the dissenters to be wrong; in an era when much of the civil rights agenda is under siege, they consider the dissenters' views terribly damaging. The source of the anger is less the dissenters' positions than the color of their skin. The point seems to be that *black* dissenters are dangerous because there are in this world racists who would willingly use the dissenters' views against the black community.

The point is not entirely groundless. Putting to one side the issue of what racists do, it is certainly true that even well-meaning white intellectuals and policy makers, when offering proposals they fear will upset black people, often seem to believe that they will be insulated from any charge of racial bias if only there is a black person to whom they can point as a supporter of the controversial policy. One recalls, for exam-

---

*Even this dissent—staying away—was not without its costs in name calling. One delegate, referring to Jewish concerns over Farrakhan's description of Judaism as a "gutter religion," shot back, "I'm sick and tired of having white folks tell us when we can meet and who we can talk to."[22] The many prominent figures in the black community who cited the invitation of the controversial Muslim leader as their reason for not attending, and the many others who gave no reason, were accused of bowing to white pressure, a notion that presupposes that no black person could rationally reach the decision that anything about Farrakhan is objectionable.

ple, President Bush's veiled references to the race of Colin Powell, chairman of the Joint Chiefs of Staff, and Michael Williams, an Education Department official, both of whom are black, in defending his administration against charges of racial insensitivity in sending a disproportionately black armed force to the Persian Gulf and restricting the availability of federal funds for college scholarships targeted at people of color. (Whether he knows it or not, the president was implicitly endorsing the thesis that black people have a uniquely valuable perspective on matters pertaining to race.)

It is difficult to believe, however, that the ability of a policy maker to point to a handful of black supporters will alter the opinions of many people, white or black. Given the reality of power relations in the United States, it is bizarre to insist that criticism of the civil rights orthodoxy by black people is more dangerous than the same criticism by people who are white. One must envision a huge mob of white fence-sitters, willing to do things "our" way as long as we are unanimous but ready to swing in some other, more racist direction should they learn of a split within the ranks of our community. This strikes me as an implausible portrait of the white American electorate. And, even if true, the claim that racists lie in wait for the words of black dissenters is ultimately beside the point, for if there were no black dissenters, a true racist would simply use something else.

Because those of us who are black live in a nation that still struggles (not always as hard as it should) to overcome its past, a belief in the importance of supporting one another, a love for our people in all their diversity—in short, solidarity—might seem crucial to our survival and our progress. But the desire for solidarity is an inadequate excuse for the stifling of dissent. As Henry Louis Gates, Jr., has put the point, "It is wrong for anyone to feel motivated to police a so-called party line to which all African American intellectuals are supposed to kowtow."[23]

The censors have matters backward. Free thinking is not treason; on the contrary, it is the greatest service individuals can perform for their communities. A long chain of black intellectuals, from W. E. B. DuBois to Zora Neale Hurston to James Baldwin to today's prominent dissenters, has openly proclaimed its unwillingness to be bound by what other, more popular figures in the black community announce as the "right" solutions to the difficulties that racism has spawned, and our understanding has ultimately been richer for it. Our community needs dissent, it needs dialogue, it needs all the fresh ideas it can get. But the message of the vehement criticism of Loury and Sowell and Steele and the rest is that dissent cannot be tolerated because the risks are too great. It is as though our responsibility as people who are black is to decline the invitation offered by our education—that is, the invitation to think for ourselves.

IV

I am familiar with a very tiny corner of the landscape I describe, because of some dissenting ideas of my own. In September 1989, an essay of mine entitled "Racial Preferences? So What?" appeared on the opinion page of the *Wall Street Journal*.[24] There I argued that racial preferences have real beneficiaries, an innocuous enough point, I would have thought. And, I continued, nobody who is black and who supports affirmative action who has been its beneficiary should be insulted if identified as one. When I wrote this op-ed essay, in fact, I thought the point so clear that it should become a starting point for debate over the preferences themselves. I never imagined that simply stating the proposition would itself be a political act.

My intention was to alter slightly the terms of the debate. Instead, I found myself the subject of debate. I received dozens of letters from around the country. Some were friendly, several complimenting me on my "honesty" and "courage." (I like to think of myself as honest, but those who used the word *courage* were a bit skittish about letting me know what I was supposed to be afraid of.) Other letters, from correspondents I took to be white, thanked me for saying what had to be said, and these I put aside with a certain angry tightening of the lips and, I might add, a degree of guilt; for although I cannot sugarcoat what I am trying to say, it is not my purpose in writing on these subjects to make white people more comfortable. Other white writers were patronizing, informing me, as though I had doubts, that I needn't worry, I was clearly smart. (The *Journal* essay, I should explain, included the story of my admission to law school that I recount in chapter 1.) To my chagrin, however, of those letter writers who identified themselves as people of color, few were supportive. On the contrary: They had found the enemy, and it was me.

One correspondent informed me that by "publicly criticizing" Harvard, I had "aided white bigots and injured [my] white supporters." He concluded his letter: "Shame on you." Another writer referred to my piece as a "shallow self-deprecating essay that showed little or no understanding of what affirmative action really accomplishes." The same writer added that my "sarcastic remarks" were "indicative of the cynicism and insecurity that is typical of a new emerging class of neo-conservative, black middle-class intellectuals who find themselves increasingly alienated from a growing black 'underclass' and grappling with their fears of not being accepted, professionally and socially, by their white peers," and chided me for "worrying about whether or not the corporate world or [my] peers earnestly respect [my] accomplishments."

Some black students at Yale criticized me, too, although in the hierarchical relationship between teacher and student, their words were naturally more restrained. A few students quarreled with my use of the word *preferences* to describe racially conscious affirmative action programs, suspecting, evidently, that the word implied a value judgment. Some suggested that I had underestimated the force of white racism or, at the very least, overestimated the willingness of white people to be fair. Several argued that whatever my personal views, I ought to air them within the group—that is, among black people—but not where white people could read them, misunderstand them (perhaps intentionally), and misuse them. The idea, I suppose, was that we ought to be working toward, and

presenting, a united front on the question of preferences. One
student, in casual conversation, argued that for a member to
refuse to subordinate his or her views to the group's, at least
on minor matters, is in effect a denial of the group's legitimacy, perhaps of its very existence.

I do not consider any of these comments, from students
or from correspondents, actually hostile. Rather, like many of
the criticisms of black dissenters, they are cries of anguish
and disbelief. And underlying them all, I think, is an awkward but urgent plea, the seductive call of group identity:
Don't betray the group, says the siren song; you belong to the
group, stay with us, don't leave us, don't betray us! The anguish, moreover, is sincere, the plea entirely ingenuous. My
dissent, they are saying in effect, is threatening the group itself; and as a member of the group, I owe greater loyalty than
that.

This, of course, is the crucial point, and it possesses a
"one-for-all-and-all-for-one" communitarian quality that can
seem quite attractive. The world, in this model, is a chilly and
inhospitable place, and if the group does not hang together, its
members will assuredly hang separately. The impression of
solidarity matters nearly as much as solidarity itself. Every
defector weakens the group. That is why we felt it so important, back in the 1970s, to turn out *all* the law school's black
students to picket the Yale Political Union. (We nearly did
it.) That is why an acquaintance of mine, who happens to be a
member of the Communist Party, tried to convince me that
my family and I have an obligation to do as his family does, to
live "with the people" in a predominantly black inner city.
(Every defector from the inner city weakens the social structure of the neighborhood.) That is why my dissent, if I choose
to express it, should be shared only with the group, not with
(hostile) outsiders.

The logic is clear, although not unassailable, and once I
even believed it; more than that, I *felt* it, I *knew* that the
group was all-important. But it was easier to know that truth
when, as a law student, I fancied myself a *leader* of the group.
(My perception was not necessarily correct.) To discover, as

the years pass, that other would-be leaders might prefer to treat me as a follower has not been an experience of unadulterated pleasure. And yet even today, I agree that I owe the group loyalty. When I am attacked for moving to a predominantly white suburb, I *do* feel a pang of guilt—I will not deny it—but in the end I must do what I think best for my family. When I am told that some of the views I express cause pain to many black people, I feel deeply pained in return. If I believed that my views actually threatened the progress of black people, I would naturally hesitate to express them. But this is where I part company with my critics. For just as I deny the right of the group (or any of its members) to tell me what to think, I deny the right of the group (or any of its members) to decide for me whether expressing my views will do harm or good. Loyalty itself can be the motive force for respectful dissent.

Actually, I am not sure that the would-be silencers disagree with this point, although they may think they do. I wonder who, in their view, is entitled to define "the group's" position or to decide whether the group is harmed. (I have inquired into this point, but have not had a satisfactory answer.) I suspect that each of those who so vehemently criticize the dissenters would, quite correctly, claim this right for herself or himself. I very much doubt that they would want a plebiscite. Many of the complaints about my essay seem to suggest that criticizing racial preferences is itself a mark of disloyalty, which leads me to wonder how many of the counter-critics are aware of consistent polling data demonstrating that a plurality, and perhaps a majority, of black Americans oppose racial preferences.[25]

I do not, of course, cite that majority sentiment as my authority. The entire point of the argument is that the majority view is irrelevant to the intellectual, whose authority must be the authority of reason. The views I express must be the ones I have reasoned out, not the ones that will make me popular. It is painful to take positions that powerful voices in the black community (including my students, the powerful voices of the future) insist are doing damage; it is painful to hear friends of long standing warn that my views are likely to be misconstrued and misused. But the task of the intellectual, finally, is to answer not the cautions of friends but the call of the mind.

V

For those of us holding dissenting views, to content ourselves with silence would represent a tragic rejection of our history as a people. The battle for the right to read, the right to learn, the right to question and to think and to understand and to challenge, has been fought at far too great a cost for us now to pretend that the struggle was really about having a black orthodoxy rather than a white one imposed upon us. As Glenn Loury has put the point: "I've got to have the freedom to go where my intellect leads me, in view of the opportunities the civil rights struggle made possible."[26] We of all people—we who are black—ought to understand the costs of silencing independent voices.

But trying to silence dissent is nothing new for us. I often wonder whether the silencers are aware of how often the same technique has been used by leaders of the black community to silence the voices that today's silencers and name callers would no doubt consider progressive. For while there is a magnificent tradition of black intellectual dissent in the United States, there is no comparable tradition of black intellectual tolerance; our history as a people has been to cast out those whose views make us uncomfortable, often on the insubstantial basis that the dissenter does not speak for black people (as though that is the intellectual's goal) or that the dissenter is a tool of white people (as though no black person would, unaided, come to the dissenting position).

The argument that dissenters from orthodoxy do not speak for the black community is an old and vicious form of silencing. It was used to shattering effect in the age when Booker T. Washington was the only black intellectual whose views mattered. In the early years of the twentieth century, as

Washington laid out his program of industrial training for
the black masses and of postponing the fight for political and
social rights, a small number of black intellectuals slowly
lined up against him.[27] The opposition, in turn, drove Washington himself into an anti-intellectual fervor, and he railed
against his black critics, who were, he said, "ignorant in regard to the actual needs of the masses of colored people in the
South today," because "[t]hey know books but they do not
know men."[28]

I never appreciated the force of Washington's ability to
punish those who criticized him until I spent a summer, many
years ago, doing research in the archives of Atlanta University. My undergraduate major was history, and I was writing
a senior honors thesis about the financial and public relations
difficulties that confronted Atlanta University because of its
decision to shelter W. E. B. DuBois, perhaps the most prominent black intellectual of the early twentieth century and
eventually Washington's most articulate critic. It was in the
course of my research in the archives that I first came across
the name of George A. Towns.

Towns, a young black professor with a Harvard degree
and one of Atlanta University's most popular instructors, was
a shining example of all the American Missionary Association,
which founded the school, had claimed that the freedmen
would, with education, accomplish. For the university itself, his
presence was a source of pride—at least until July 30, 1903.

That was the night of what was known at the time as the
Boston Riot, which was not really a riot at all but a demonstration against Booker T. Washington himself as well as
against his organization and his ideas. Led by a group known
as the Boston radicals, the demonstrators interrupted a
speech by Washington by hooting and hissing (and, according
to some accounts, tossing pepper into the audience). Among
those arrested was William Monroe Trotter, the Harvard-edu-
cated scion of a well-to-do black family. Trotter, editor of the
Boston Guardian, was at the time perhaps Washington's most
vociferous opponent. He rejected an offer of probation and
went to jail.

It was at that point that Towns made his mistake: he wrote Trotter a letter of support. "[Y]ou have my sympathy," the young professor wrote, "and I believe you have the sympathy of most of the educated and thinking Negroes of the United States who are opposed to letting white people select and set up our leaders before whom we should all fall down and worship without a question or any suggestion of dissent." Towns advised Trotter not to despair, and added: "There are more with you than with him of Negroes who think and who count for something according to the reckoning of the best people."[29]

Trotter promptly published the letter in the *Guardian,* and almost at once, Horace Bumstead, the university's president, began to feel the pressure from Washington's supporters, who included many of the school's principal financial backers. Bumstead immediately sent Towns a complaint: "The publication in the Guardian of your letter to Mr. Trotter is making serious trouble for me and I fear will work considerable injury to the University and its cause." He reprimanded the young scholar for obscuring "the fact that he [Trotter] had done anything worthy of punishment." But Trotter was grateful, and wrote warmly to Towns, "Few letters I have received while here in this stone prison have made me feel as good as yours."

How Towns must have agonized! Did he prefer the goodwill of Trotter, the dissenter, or of Washington, who spoke for the larger group? I found in the archives five different drafts of a letter of apology. Towns finally settled on one he liked and sent it along to Bumstead. Unfortunately for Towns, an apology was not all the worried university president needed; he also wanted Towns to produce a statement to the effect that Trotter had published the original letter without his consent—which would have been difficult, since the letter included as a postscript the words "Publish if you wish." In the end, outside pressures (Bumstead denied that the pressure came from "Mr. Washington or Tuskegee") forced the school into action. The executive committee of the Board of Trustees unanimously adopted a statement recording its "great astonishment and profound regret that such a letter could have been written, much more al-

lowed to be published, by a professor in Atlanta University."
The committee denied that it was trying to stifle academic freedom, but argued that harming the university was an abuse of
that freedom. A copy of the statement was sent to Booker T.
Washington, although he was said not to be the source of the
pressures. In his final letter on the subject to Towns, Bumstead
suggested that the statement was not a censure but a necessary
response to adverse publicity. Not long after, Towns resigned
from the Atlanta University faculty.

So much for academic freedom. So much for tolerance
of dissent. Both proved too expensive, too harmful to the
group. In his autobiography, DuBois reflected on what it was
like to live and think and criticize in the era of Washington's
hegemony:

> Things came to such a pass that when any Negro complained or
> advocated a course of action, he was silenced with the remark
> that Mr. Washington did not agree with this. Naturally the
> bumptious, irritated, young black intelligentsia of the day de-
> clared: "I don't care a damn what Booker Washington thinks.
> This is what I think, and *I have a right to think.*"[30]

This protest was no mere intellectual conceit. Like Towns,
DuBois himself was ultimately forced from his teaching position at Atlanta University largely because his continuing and
increasingly fervent opposition to Washington's program was
hurting the school's fund-raising efforts. For DuBois, in fact,
the problem of ostracism was a continuing one. When he opposed some policies of the Universal Negro Improvement Association, the populist back-to-Africa movement led by Mar-
cus Garvey, Garvey dismissed him as "purely and simply a
white man's nigger."[31] The UNIA, in fact, voted in 1924 to
dismiss DuBois "from the Negro race" because he was "an
enemy of the black people of the world."*

There are other sad moments in our intellectual history

---

*DuBois himself, to be sure, was equally ungentle with his rhetoric. When Garvey's
repeated proclamations that the United States was "a white man's country" and his
insistence on "racial purity" and an end to "amalgamation" led to circulation of
rumors of a deal between the UNIA and the Ku Klux Klan, DuBois swiftly blasted
Garvey as "without doubt the most dangerous enemy of the Negro race in America
and the world."[32]

when black dissenters from orthodoxy were routinely silenced. Prominent examples are the Harlem Renaissance between the world wars, when artists and writers simply had to be left to be in, and the Un-American Activities investigations of the 1950s, when leftist black intellectuals were virtually expelled from the black mainstream. Many a great thinker in our history, from Arna Bontemps to Ida B. Wells to James Weldon Johnson to Paul Robeson, has chafed under the pressure to conform or be ostracized. It is appalling to contemplate that some among us apparently want to return to the days when black intellectuals were ostracized if they got the shibboleths wrong. By this point in our history, we as a people should have learned a lesson about the importance of permitting, encouraging, even cherishing, critical thinking. By encouraging open and robust debate about the problems confronting our community, we can march upward toward a better tomorrow. If instead we choose to stifle the voices of dissent, it is hard to see how we will get anyplace at all.

CHAPTER 6

On Contenting Oneself with Silence

About forty years ago, Langston Hughes wrote a poignant little story called "Professor," about an educator at a segregated black college who needs a tiny donation for his school and therefore stands stoically and takes all sorts of patronizing abuse from a wealthy white philanthropist and a white professor no smarter or more accomplished than he. The professor of the title, T. Walton Brown, reasons that only by staying silent will he be able to get the money and, with money, the chance to "carry his whole family to South America for a summer where they wouldn't need to feel like Negroes."[1] In the end Professor Brown gets what he wants, but Hughes cleverly leaves us with an unspoken question: Is Brown to be admired for his stoicism or condemned for his cowardice?

Judging from the rhetoric I described in chapter 5, some supporters of the traditional civil rights agenda must see black intellectuals who disagree with them as successors to Professor Brown—ambitious individuals who remain silent to gain the respect of powerful white people. The story works at least as well, however, the other way around, as a description of the relationship of the dissenter not to influential people

who are white but to influential people who are black. In order
to avoid becoming an outcast, in order to gain what the dissenter not infrequently desires—the respect, the admiration,
even the friendship of other black people—the dissenter might
well choose to remain silent, to bear stoically the insistence on
a path he or she considers profoundly misguided. All too
often, the alternative is to find oneself being accused of being
only biologically black.

Indeed, among the criticisms black dissenters must suffer, perhaps the harshest is the one that says their views are a
betrayal, a symbol of disloyalty, perhaps even a rejection of
the group, as though we are still Gileadites trying to identify
the Ephraimites. The dissenters' motives are impugned; they
are denied the possibility of intellectual honesty. Instead, they
are often accused of self-hatred, of despising the group itself—even, as a recent letter to the *New York Times* put it, of
building their careers by fronting for white people who are
afraid to own up to their attacks on black people.[2]

These are not casual insults. The thought that a black
person would attack other black people because, as a friend of
mine has suggested, there is a lucrative market for such attacks is grotesque. Unfortunately, it is far from implausible:
even in Nazi extermination camps there were *Kapos* who led
their own people to slaughter. But the idea that any black
person who publicly criticizes a particular approach to black
progress is a traitor is worse than grotesque; it is vicious. For
black people who cherish their racial identity, such words cut
deeply. And, inevitably, they leave scars—which is, I suppose,
what is intended.

Similarly, the suggestion that dissenters yield their
group identity by failing to pronounce the shibboleths as
many in the group believe they should be pronounced is horri-
fyingly cruel; for if the group identity is lost, a vital aspect of
personality likely goes with it. Group identity is indispensable
to human identity. We know ourselves through both our
knowledge of others and theirs of us. Throughout human history, ethnicity has been fundamental to group identity.
"Every individual," according to the political scientist Har-

old Isaacs, "wherever he may be located on this chaotic landscape, has to shape or re-shape his sense of the content and
meaning of his identification with his primary group, the
group in which he finds himself by virtue of where, when, and
to whom he is born." He adds: "In this set of his identifica-
tions, his 'race' or the color of his skin will continue to have
special meaning to him and to all to whom he relates."[3]

In America today, this is virtually a truism. Our sense of
who we are means that we proclaim our race with pride, but
even if we did not, our racially conscious nation would still
assign racial identity and assume "special meaning" for it.
For many of us, race is the first thing that is noticed about us
when we board a bus or enter a store or walk into a classroom.
Sometimes the effect of the first racially conscious impression
is disastrous, as when a white citizen decides that race is a
good proxy for criminal intent, and opts for a bit of self-
help—for example, by shooting the source of the fear. A principal point of the Black Power movement of the 1960s was to
convince the victims of racist oppression that the problem lay
with the white people, not the black, and that we did not have
to try to be like them in order to be valuable human beings.
Still, a little bit of this can easily become too much: a recent
survey of students in the public schools of the District of Columbia revealed that a substantial number of black teens consider studying, going to class, and trying to achieve as ways
of attempting to be white. These findings are well borne out by
other social science data,[4] and friends and relatives of mine
have reported the same syndrome, albeit anecdotally. (In fact,
when I reflect on such studies as these, my own high school
days, when the other black students referred to me, in a tone
half-respectful but half-mocking, as "the professor," take on
a considerably grimmer cast.) Apparently, the black kids who
believe in hard work and academic achievement have more and
more trouble convincing classmates that they value their heritage and do not reject the group.

Children are impressionable; criticisms from their
friends make a difference in their lives, and if verbal attacks
on achieving students turn out to be common, we face a prob-

lem that no remedial government program will be able to solve. I cannot help wondering where our children learn this behavior. Who teaches them that words can wound, and that words purporting to deny one's racial identity sometimes wound most of all? I am not suggesting that our children are mimicking the attacks on black dissenters; the pathology is surely more complicated than that. Besides, much of what they know about the way exclusion can cut at the soul is no doubt gleaned from their own sense of exclusion from a larger society perceived as racist. At the same time, if in their formative years they are already convinced that the way to stop other kids from going against the group is to deny them their birthright, how will they respond to dissenters when they are adults?

I do not know the answer. But I worry about the models I see. I worry when one of the nation's leading black scholars charges recklessly that black neoconservatives "spout white-racist rhetoric."[5] I worry when dissenters are told that they have turned against their people, that in refusing to blame racism for everything, they are blaming its victims. (*Somebody* must be to blame!) I worry when another scholar insists that black people who express doubt about the reconceptualization of affirmative action as diversity have been "domesticated" by the system[6]—another way, perhaps, of losing one's birthright. And I worry when I attend a convention of black professionals and watch as the moderator of a panel takes it upon himself to scold one of the panelists for not emulating the way black people talk "on the street"—the place, evidently, where the truly black learn a separate language.

Nevertheless, for me, the matter is uncomplicated. I value my identity as a black American, and cannot imagine existing without it. (*African-American,* on the other hand, I place in the same category as Léopold Sanghor's and Aimé Césaire's *negritude* and Kwame Nkrumah's *African personality*—a tantalizing clue to one's reaction to an identity rather than an identity itself.)[7] I value my unavoidable commonality with other black Americans. I value, in short, my group identity: How could I not? I have in common with other black

Americans a history of brutal oppression, passionate struggle, and magnificent triumph, a history I would not surrender or forget or have my children forget even if that option existed. Contemplation of that history and its lessons might lead me down paths different from those the traditional civil rights agenda prescribes, but the impact of this shared history is as significant in my life as in anyone else's. And I doubt that other dissenters, who have been through a great deal more trouble than I have, feel any different.

Activists who would silence the dissenters apparently believe, however, that group identity should be purchased at the price of thinking freely, that to be a black *dissenter* is to surrender one's right to the term *black*. This is the entire point of the epithet *Oreo* (black on the outside, white on the inside), and during the era of Black Power the point was very much a part of the debate. And the exclusion of the dissenter is not simply a verbal device. DuBois was forced from one position after another because powerful black leaders thought his views were harmful to the race. There was a moment when it appeared that Clarence Thomas, a black lawyer, might lose a judgeship because of his vigorous dissents from the mainstream civil rights program. Many black dissenters in the academic world can tell tales of the conferences from which they have been excluded and the panels to which they have not been invited because of their views. The dissenting black intellectual, in short, can expect ostracism; and the predictable effect of the ostracism is to discourage freedom of thought.

The silencers often respond to such arguments as this by saying, in effect, that it is nonsense to suppose that they have ostracized anybody. The black dissenters, they say, can always find an intellectual home because there are white institutions (and, in particular, white neoconservatives) everywhere waiting to welcome them. If anyone is threatened, say the critics, it is those who propound the views from which the others are dissenting, for they have no secure place in the white male world that it is their goal to subvert.

I am not prepared to say that there is nothing to this claim. One of the many complications of becoming known as a black intellectual who purveys dissenting views, no matter how small, on some aspects of the mainstream civil rights agenda, is that a new world of possibilities opens for those who are interested. For one thing, representatives of various organizations opposed to much larger chunks of the agenda come calling. I see no evidence, however, that the predominantly white educational institutions where much of the conflict takes place are more interested in black intellectuals who are dissenters than in black intellectuals who are more supportive of the traditional agenda. On the contrary, it is my impression that intellectuals and activists who press the various "different-voice" hypotheses are sought after at many of the nation's elite institutions and have little trouble finding publishers for their books or air time for their commentaries. From the comments of some of my colleagues both at Yale and at other institutions, however, I fear that many white intellectuals are likely to follow fashion—that is, to respond to the pressure or the arguments of the silencers—and therefore to join, often unthinkingly, in the ostracism of dissenters. (I remember vividly a white colleague's labored explanation of why it was *accurate* to refer to Clarence Pendleton as both an Uncle Tom and an Oreo, and another's tortured argument that black scholars, struggling to find their authentic voices, are likely to take longer than white ones to produce good work.)

Besides, even if the silencers are right, even if the ostracized dissenting intellectuals can find homes among white academics and policy makers of similar views, there is no reason to assume that this phenomenon makes the ostracism any less painful—unless one thinks that a home among white people of similar views is what the dissenter wants. I have often seen that desire *ascribed* to black dissenters, who are almost routinely dismissed as worrying about how their white colleagues will view them, but an ascription is not evidence. Such anecdotal evidence as I possess runs much the other way: the dissenters I know tend to be puzzled, frustrated, and deeply pained by their exclusion.

Clarence Thomas put it this way: "I don't like being con-

troversial and unpopular among members of my race. . . . I
hate it that other people of my race think, 'Here's this black
guy trashing everything that's supposed to be good for us.' "[8]
Few seem in any particular hurry to join the ranks of the
neoconservative movement (Thomas is in this case a bit of an
exception), a movement in which, as the writer Christopher
Hitchens recently put it, the people "one associates with affirmative action" are "noticeable by their scarcity, not to
mention absence."[9] Most dissenters surely crave acceptance
(unless too iconoclastic to crave it at all) from people of color
far more than they care for the adulation of people who are
white (and who may, from time to time, make common cause
with other people who are white and at whose clubs and homes
the dissenters would never be welcome). So the ostracism and
name calling hurts. And as any economist or lawyer or parent
knows, what hurts, discourages: all of us have met people who
have chosen *not* to dissent publicly—because of a fear not of
harming the race but of being ostracized.

It is difficult to imagine that the excluders don't know all
of this, don't in fact count on it; after all, if expelling people
from the race has no effect, it is hard to see why anyone would
bother doing it. Moreover, I suspect that the excluders are
sincere: they really do believe that there is an important sense
in which people of color who hold the wrong views have no
right to call themselves people of color. They really do believe
that the dissenters are traitors, Uncle Toms, merely biologically black, not bona fide representatives of their people.

Naturally, one can dismiss all of these *ad hominem* assaults as nonsense, and cold-hearted, shortsighted nonsense at
that. But something more than name calling is involved, especially today. A principal thesis of the contemporary diversity
movement, as I have explained in chapter 2, is that people of
color bring to bear a distinct and valuable perspective on the
problems generated by racism. The trouble is that some people
of color—for example, the Glenn Lourys, the Thomas Sowells,
the Shelby Steeles—offer arguments that are inconsistent with
what some advocates of diversity seem to think the unique
perspective should embrace. The short of the matter is that

there is an inexorable link between the notion that people of color have a special perspective and the idea that dissenters from the orthodoxy are more dangerous if their skins are not white. A diversity of opinion in our own intellectual community, particularly when some of that opinion dovetails with the views our intellectual leaders have set themselves to fight, is terribly subversive of the idea that we have all been marked by oppression in the same way. Sadly, the way out of the dilemma seems to be to say, in effect, that the dissenters are not saying what they really know to be true; they have betrayed the rest of us, sold out, and are now spreading the same vicious lies that our opponents do.

Besides, the idea of selling one's birthright for white acceptance works just as well the other way around. It would make as much sense to argue that the critical assertion that dissenting black intellectuals can find welcome among neoconservative whites reflects the critics' own status anxieties. Perhaps the critics have been seduced by the very dream of white acceptance that, in their rhetoric, guides the work of the dissenters. Indeed, the entire rhetorical construct of the contemporary diversity movement—*they don't listen to us!*—could be said to rest on the premise that what really counts is gaining the recognition of the white world. Such speculation might seem harsh, but it is no more harsh and no less logical than the same accusation directed against those who dissent. My point is that one cannot tell from the views that a black person expresses on the community's problems where his or her loyalties lie. If one could, it would be easy to conclude that nobody, except one who partakes of the dream of white acceptance, could possibly imagine that it would mean so much to someone else that he or she would bargain away a birthright in order to achieve it.

II

But perhaps I am being unfair. People of color are not alone in trying to silence those who disagree with some orthodoxy.

The rest of the society has not yet learned to cherish intellectual or political diversity. White dissenters, too, are often stifled; sometimes they are even punished. If two-thirds of the American people had their way, flag burners would go to prison. In an earlier era Communists, and scholars thought to be fellow travelers with Communists, were banned from the campuses, and even today they could not possibly be elected to serious public office in America. Nor are various subgroups more charitable. Pro-life women are routinely labeled right-wing and antifeminist, American Jews critical of Israeli policies in the occupied territories are often smeared as self-hating, and Christians who doubt that Scripture allows ordination of women are dismissed as misogynistic. The spectrum of permissible views in serious public political life is far narrower in the United States than in the democracies of Western Europe. If mainstream America is unwilling to tolerate the voices of dissent, why should we who are black be any different?

One reason we should be different is that in an era in which a third of black people still live in poverty, when the inner cities are besieged by drugs and crime, when nearly a quarter of our children are themselves having children,[10] we cannot afford the luxury of insisting, in the name of solidarity, that any of our problems has a single, unchallengeable answer. Certainly it makes no sense to alienate some of the best minds we have—minds that include the Sowells and the Lourys and the Wilsons and the Lesters. They dissent from the civil rights mainstream not because they do not care about the problems but because they have thought about the problems and the traditional solutions alike; and thinking of better answers is something we should not discourage. So, for example, when we are told—and some among the dissenters tell us frequently—that racial preferences tend to help those black people who least need the assistance and to make little or no difference in the lives of the growing black underclass, we ought to listen to the evidence, not bristle at the assertion. And if the evidence supports the assertion (and it does), we ought to admit it and perhaps rethink our own ideas.

This is why I suggested earlier that the anguished assaults on the black dissenters are shortsighted. The desperate effort to preserve racial preferences as the untouchable centerpiece of the struggle for justice rests on the assumption that once a strategy has been selected, it cannot be discarded. The criticism of black or white dissenters would matter little were racial preferences not considered so important. They have become, in our rhetoric at least, a sort of crutch on which our budding professionals must lean; to hear the most ardent advocates describe affirmative action, we as a people would not survive without it. (Many years back, as a law student awaiting the Supreme Court's decision in the *Bakke* case, I asked another black student a few years older than myself what we would do if the Court rejected "our" position. He replied, with considerable equanimity, "We got along fine before there was affirmative action and we'll get along fine after it's gone"—a wise answer, but one I found, at the time, infuriatingly aloof.)

Again, the history contains a bit of irony. I am constantly surprised at how many of today's college students seem unaware that there was ever a time when a substantial part of the black left opposed affirmative action programs. Then I remember that most of these young people were in grade school, or even busy being born, when the first widespread systems of benign preferences were adopted in the wake of the rioting of the late 1960s. To the black left, to the leaders of the Black Power movement, affirmative action represented an effort by a terrified white power structure to buy off the victims of racist oppression by offering the same old integrationist strategy in a new and unpersuasive guise. The white community, so the argument went, was holding out the promise of division and assimilation when what we needed most was solidarity and the separatism that solidarity entailed. By offering racial quotas, special financial aid packages, and other forms of preference, the radicals argued, the power structure was seeking to deny us our radical moment, to co-opt the best minds in the black community, the "talented tenth," who would, in DuBois's vision, lead black America to-

ward equality. By opening to them the rewards that corporate
capitalism bestows upon those at the top, the system would
skim off the cream while leaving essentially unchanged the situation of those at the bottom.

One reason today's students find this argument so bewil-
dering is undoubtedly that radicalism of the sort I remember
has all but vanished from the campus. Students may demonstrate against their law *schools,* demanding greater "diversity" in faculty appointments, but I think it unlikely that
many of them will demonstrate against their law *firms,* even
though their experience after graduation will bring them face
to face with what they doubtless already know: the law firms
offer far less diversity, by almost any measure, than do the
faculties that have taught them the law. The radicals of the
1960s would have considered the decision of many of the
brightest black students to enter the corporate world a betrayal of any number of ideals; they would also have predicted
it—in fact, they did—as the inevitable concomitant of affirmative action. The fear that the opportunities now available
might vanish is surely a reason the contemporary civil rights
movement insists on the programs; the fact that those opportunities now tempt into the economic mainstream many of the
brightest young black people (who would otherwise have been
marginalized and thus more easily radicalized) is precisely
why the black left once thought preferences a bad idea.

But what a shortsighted notion it is to imagine that we
who have survived so much will collapse if the crutch of preferences is removed! What a paradox it is to insist, in the interest of equality of opportunity, on programs that often
work to deny to those of us who are beneficiaries the opportunity to show what we can do! And how stifling it is when those
of us who choose to point out the paradox are told that we
should not be speaking as we are; and that if we do insist on
speaking, on explaining how preferences may do people of
color more harm than good, we are somehow betraying the
group. Evidently, we can show our loyalty in only two ways:
either we can pronounce the shibboleth correctly, extolling the
virtues of preferences and crying "racism" whenever white

people criticize them; or we can keep our views but remain silent, purchasing group identity at the price of surrendering our right to express ourselves freely. In such a world, it may be better to be called a traitor than a patriot.

III

The tendency to divide our community into patriots and traitors sometimes comes into conflict with the integrationist ideals that racial preferences are designed to serve. If our country continues its recent trend of electing relatively conservative presidents and relatively liberal Congresses, the conflicts are likely to be more frequent. As more and more people of color who are professionally successful move away from the left politics of student days and toward the center, or even the right, more and more consciously conservative people who are not white will join the ranks of presidential nominees for positions requiring Senate confirmation.

The nomination of a black conservative to a position of real power and influence creates a quandary for many black activists. On the one hand, they desire role models, to show the world what people of color can do; on the other, they sense that this particular role model will have "objectionable" political views. In the first year of the Bush administration, the dilemma arose twice.

The first episode involved the nomination of William Lucas, former Wayne County executive and unsuccessful candidate for governor of the State of Michigan, to serve as assistant attorney general for civil rights. The second was the nomination of Clarence Thomas, a former congressional aide serving as chair of the Equal Employment Opportunity Commission, to serve as a judge of the United States Court of Appeals for the District of Columbia Circuit. On a variety of issues both nominees held what in the relatively narrow American political spectrum are known as conservative positions. Both nominees were black and both were nominated for posts carrying considerable authority and visibility. The head of the

Justice Department's Civil Rights Division, in effect, runs a huge law office devoted to enforcing the nation's civil rights laws. The District of Columbia Circuit is probably the nation's most important appellate tribunal after the Supreme Court of the United States. In the end, the civil rights establishment made the difficult decision to oppose Lucas, whose nomination did not survive scrutiny in the Senate Judiciary Committee, and then chose to sit nervously on the sidelines on the Thomas nomination, which sailed through the Senate amid a general air of relief.

The opposition to Lucas was couched in terms of qualification: he lacked, the critics insisted, any experience in the civil rights law field. This was certainly true, although Lucas's relative inexperience hardly distinguished him from the incumbent under the Reagan administration, William Bradford Reynolds, or from the next Bush nominee, John Dunne. (Maybe that was the point.) The nomination's supporters in the Senate responded, in a conscious but unfortunate borrowing of the language of affirmative action, that Lucas deserved a chance to show what he could do.

Thomas, on the other hand, could not sensibly have been presented as unqualified for a judgeship, and perhaps that is the reason the opposition was finally muted: it could only have been cast in terms of politics. Thomas, after all, is widely regarded by movement conservatives as one of them. He has long been an opponent of racial preferences; and, when invited to give the Heritage Lectures, sponsored by the Heritage Foundation, a Washington, D.C., think tank often described as a haven for movement conservatives, Thomas proclaimed his allegiance to the movement in ringing terms. He has also been a consistent and vociferous critic of the pressures on black intellectuals to think the right way and to reach the right results, what I have described as the pressure to think black.

Several activist groups considered opposing his nomination. But in the end, they decided to let it go—not least, I suspect, because any number of white judges of far more solid conservative credentials had been confirmed without a murmur. To have battled against the Thomas nomination, especially after taking a pounding for the ultimately successful fight against Lucas, would have been reverse discrimination with a vengeance.

Some of Thomas's critics were concerned that he might be too inexperienced to be a judge, but these were in the minority. Many more were troubled by various of his actions during his tenure as chair of the Equal Employment Opportunity Commission and, earlier, as head of the Office of Civil Rights in the Department of Education. Doubters argued that he had cut back on civil rights enforcement, a contention Thomas has heatedly denied at every opportunity. Still, it is fascinating to note that the principal sin Clarence Thomas committed was evidently to combine a black skin with an unabashed conservatism, not simply in his politics but in his ready identification with the neoconservative movement—a movement, he charged in his Heritage Lecture, that has only uneasily embraced him. For his troubles Thomas has been called the usual names—an Uncle Tom, a traitor, and the rest—and he has said of his situation, "It is lonely, I mean really lonely."[11]

Lonely, really lonely. Some iconoclasts revel in it. Stanley Crouch, author of *Notes of a Hanging Judge* and another sometime critic of a variety of icons of contemporary black culture, has said that he is proud to be a traitor to the black nationalist movement of the late 1960s.[12] Others with a greater need for human contact will likely chafe at the enforced loneliness. Either way, that loneliness is precisely what the ostracism of the traitor is meant to accomplish. Better, the would-be dissenter is meant to conclude, to be a patriot.

IV

But I still do not like labels. I certainly do not want to be known as a traitor. I don't even want to be known as a dissenter. I want to ponder the problems facing black America and to engage in thoughtful, reflective dialogue about them. I want to live in a world in which the ideas themselves, rather than their purveyors, are the topic of debate. That world, however, is not this one. In this world, reasoned debate isn't easy. As Glenn Loury has noted: "Whites don't want to get called racists. Blacks don't want to be called disloyal. As a result, a genuine critical discourse where a lot of different ideas get put on the table and bandied about never happens."[13]

It is that discourse, however, that should be our goal. On the second day of the New Orleans African American summit in April 1989, Coretta Scott King lamented the conflicts within our community: "Today we have more of what we fought for. More African American elected officials, more educational opportunities, more access to public accommodation, yet we have less unity than we had during the civil rights movement."[14]

Exactly. We have less unity. We need more. Rather than bickering among ourselves, we should be working together to fight the many real enemies that are crushing our people: crime, drugs, inferior education and training, and real racism. We need to avoid the error of thinking, however, that unity means solidarity and that solidarity, in turn, means groupthink; we have to try to delight in our diversity and take the time to discuss our differences. And we must be very careful about how we define those who have the right to call themselves black, for our need for these free-thinking dissenters may prove to be greater than their need for us. The black conservatives, so-called, are quite comfortable in their tenured academic positions and other posts, which is, after all, what academic sinecures are for. Despite the name calling of their critics, they will not be silenced. Nor should they be. A central message of freedom for even hated and hateful speech—a message missed equally by those on the right who would ban flag burning and by those on the left who would ban racial epithets—also holds true in this case: silencing debate solves no problems; it simply limits the range of possible solutions.

Looking at the deep rift between the dissenters and the mainstream, I cannot help but think back on the Niagara

Movement, a forerunner of the NAACP, organized in 1905 by
DuBois and other opponents of Booker T. Washington in
order to provide a platform for their dissenting ideas and a
base for their burgeoning efforts to thwart Washington's as-
cendancy. Washington, whose insistence on industrial training for the black masses remained enormously popular in
white America and black America as well, still held most of
the black colleges and newspapers in a strangler's grip; the
Niagara Movement, as organized dissensus, was intended to
serve as a counterweight, and Washington spent a substantial
portion of his considerable influence in efforts to suppress it.

Matters have changed less than one might think; too
often, a challenge is still condemned as an attack on the group.
For the black intellectual who dares to dissent, the principal
difference between the first and the last decades of the twentieth century seems to be the identity of the one holding the
whip hand. "[T]he real issue," according to Clarence Thomas,
"is why, unlike other individuals in the country, black individuals are not entitled to have and express points of view
that differ from the collective hodge-podge of ideas that we
supposedly share because we are members of the same race."[15]
The answer, I think, is because of the mistaken view that dissent is more dangerous when the skin of the dissenter is black.

The ostracism of the dissenting intellectuals is an unhappy gift for our generation to bequeath to the next. But it
is all too possible that our legacy will be the lessons that the
right to train our minds, a right purchased at enormous cost
in blood, is only a right to learn to express politically proper
thoughts and, therefore, that the right to think and doubt and
criticize freely belongs to white people alone. For many in the
black community, it seems, the felt need for solidarity may
render dissent too costly.

I say "many" because it is my impression (anecdotal, to
be sure) that despite the name calling, despite the ostracism,
the ranks of the dissenters may be growing. Indeed, the members of the burgeoning young black middle class—the generation, ironically, that affirmative action produced—are moderately more likely than their parents' generation to call

themselves conservative and to vote Republican. (Indeed, the fervor of much of the angry response to the dissenters may be motivated by a perception of that very phenomenon.) But every political scientist, and, for that matter, every successful politician, understands that the organized group beats the disorganized group almost every time—even when the disorganized group is larger.

So perhaps the time has come for a latter-day Niagara, for a new manifesto in which we who are black and choose to dissent might proclaim, in much the same terms DuBois used, our right to think for ourselves. We must demand the right to comment on any subject, no matter how sacred to the orthodoxy. We must worship no authority as absolute, except for the authority of truth itself. We must do, in short, what intellectuals are supposed to do: turn our critical and analytical faculties to the problems that seem to us most important, and make up our own minds. We must say what we think. That, at least, is what I think—and I have a right to think.

V

I do not want to be misunderstood. The mainstream civil rights leaders have as much right to their views as the dissenters to theirs; and the dissenters, although far weaker in number and influence, have generally held their own in the name-calling derby. The tragedy in all of this is that so much on both sides is thoughtful and rich that what we need most is a time for talking with rather than at each other. Surveying the landscape, looking at the scattered, divided forces that should be working together to advance the community, I am reminded of the account in Thucydides of the way Alcibiades sealed, in the nick of time, the growing breach among the Athenians through his power of persuasion, convincing competing factions to swallow their enmity and work together to defeat the common enemy. "There was not another man in existence," Thucydides tells us, "who could have controlled the mob at that time."[16]

I wish sometimes for a latter-day Alcibiades, an orator so fluent and powerful that the deeply enraged forces on both sides will pause and listen. (Perhaps we had one, for a magical moment, in Martin Luther King, Jr. But he has been dead these two decades and more, and, for my students at least, he sometimes seems as much a part of ancient history as Alcibiades; besides, we must look forward, not back, to solve our problems.) But that is not the way the world works. "[T]here has always been a tendency among us," Roy Wilkins once wrote, "to carve one another up over questions of leadership."[17] Nevertheless, I continue to fantasize. I wish that for an instant the passions would be stilled, because then, finally, our mutually exclusive monologues might end and genuine dialogue might at last begin. Sometimes I even have childish daydreams: Thomas Sowell and Derrick Bell shaking hands across the conference table; Julius Lester and Jesse Jackson breaking bread together; Glenn Loury and Benjamin Hooks sitting down to thrash out their differences—not, perhaps, out of friendship but out of a deep and abiding mutual respect and a willingness to listen born of a shared love for our people and our troubled community.

As I said, all of this must sound very naive. But then, a few years ago, so did the idea that the Berlin Wall would come tumbling down or that Nelson Mandela would travel the world, a hero.

CHAPTER 7

Why "Black Conservative" Is Pejorative

L ike many other Americans of all colors, my wife and I watched a great deal of television during the visit of the African National Congress leader Nelson Mandela to the United States in the summer of 1990.* One morning, a prominent member of the American conservative movement (whose name I no longer recall) appeared on the C-SPAN cable network to press the following argument about South Africa: first, apartheid is an evil that must be destroyed (*Hear! Hear!* we are thinking); second, violence is not the right means for securing the overthrow of apartheid (*Ah, but what about the contras?* we are wondering); third, indiscriminate violence by the South African government also should be condemned *(But not the discriminate kind, evidently);* and fourth, the United States should resume direct military aid to the South African government *(Uh—whazzat?).*

My wife and I turned to each other in baffled fury. We are suburban, successful, middle-class black professionals, ac-

---

*I understand that Mandela is not the nominal head of the ANC, that he is instead the deputy president, but my description reflects the way he is perceived in much, perhaps most, of the world.

customed to wondering aloud whether some civil rights leaders preach "white racism" in an unnecessary and inflammatory way, but an enormous amount of our high-minded rhetoric goes *sphut* in the face of such nonsense. But in conservative and neoconservative circles, this is what all too often passes for reasoned argument. The conclusion—resumption of military aid—makes sense only if one supplies two key premises, both unspoken. First, that the United States should aid regimes—even ideologically totalitarian ones*—that are faced with Communist insurgencies; second, that the ANC is a Communist insurgency.

I am not sure either of these premises is correct, and, indeed, the second seems clearly an oversimplification. Even if both are granted for the sake of argument, however, the case for resuming military aid to the South African government makes sense only if one is willing to say that a Communist-dominated South Africa is worse than a racist-dominated one. Now, this might have been a plausible argument in a world in the grip of East-West competition, although it's always a little frightening to discover afresh the relative ease with which some public figures are able to dismiss the horror that is apartheid. More interesting to me at the moment is that for those in the conservative movement, who have their litmus tests just as those on the left do, the argument is politically correct. It is a shibboleth: those who are not able to pronounce it correctly need not seek membership. Consider the words of the Reverend Keith Butler of Detroit, a black minister who is evidently a movement conservative of some attainment, quoted by the conservative guru Paul Weyrich in *Conservative Digest:* "We agree on 90 percent of the issues," says the minister,

---

*A centerpiece of neoconservative thinking on foreign affairs has been the sensible distinction, popularized by Jeane Kirkpatrick, between authoritarian dictatorships (such as Chile under Augusto Pinochet), where what stands between the people and their freedom is a strongman and the self-interested coterie around him, and totalitarian dictatorships (such as Nazi Germany and the Soviet Union), where a pervasive ideology warps most aspects of social life. According to the thesis, lately in trouble because of the basically nonviolent collapse of communism in Eastern Europe, authoritarians might be trampled by the rush of events, whereas totalitarians must be overthrown by force. What has never been clear in this fascinating analysis is why the South African regime has always been classed as authoritarian rather than totalitarian.

"but because my position isn't identical to theirs on South Africa, I am somehow a traitor."[1]

There are, of course, black people who hold what is to movement conservatives the politically correct position on South Africa, but not many, not as many as the substantial numbers of black people who agree with movement positions on many other issues, particularly the so-called family values social issues. Some focus-group surveys conducted by conservative organizations have indicated, for example, that the proportion of black voters stating that they would support a Republican candidate tends to increase dramatically when they are told that the Republican is pro-life and the Democrat pro-choice, and that black voters are more concerned about crime than white voters are.[2] Indeed, apart from political issues relating directly to race, black Americans tend to be more conservative than the nation as a whole on a number of matters—at least as the words *liberal* and *conservative* are used in the relatively narrow spectrum of American opinion. On abortion, prayer in public schools, the role of women in society, the rights of criminal defendants, and a host of related matters, consistent survey results show black people significantly more likely than white ones to take what we tend to call the conservative position.[3] Indeed, in the particular case of school prayer, one study suggests that black people are twice as likely as whites to oppose the Supreme Court's decisions, and in the case of crime, as much as eight times more likely than white people to think that the courts are too soft on criminal defendants.[4]

Such results should scarcely be surprising. While other data point in other directions—for example, notwithstanding their general views on crime, black people are three times as likely as white people to oppose the death penalty[5]—a strong conservative strain runs through the black community. And yet the fact remains that the black conservative is an outsider, the word *conservative* itself considered an epithet by many in the black community. Even black people who hold many positions that are, in our discourse, labeled conservative are reluctant to accept the application of that label to themselves.

Shelby Steele, who says he voted for Jesse Jackson in 1988, has complained, "All I do now is spend my energy saying I'm not a conservative."[6]

I will admit that I share this reluctance. In a previous chapter, I related some of the correspondence I received following the publication of my *Wall Street Journal* essay raising questions about certain aspects of racial preferences. If I am to be honest, I must confess that the part of the criticism that really stung me—and that continues to sting as, increasingly, it is applied to me as I try to set out the costs of racial preferences—is that marvelously complex label *black neoconservative*. Not only black people seem to think it describes my views; a white colleague at Yale, on what evidence I have no idea, recently told a gathering of alumni that I am "quite conservative." Indeed, my friends and I share a variety of painful jokes that have in common the "fact" that I harbor "rightwing views." Actually, I don't harbor many, or at least I don't think I do.

Oh, I confess that there are aspects of what we call conservatism that attract me, particularly the belief in the importance of standards of excellence and of inculcating strong positive values. Like many conservatives, I am not always sure that a new government program is the answer to each social problem. And I suppose that I hold my share of what we are bold to call conservative positions. In my relentless contrarianism, I have expressed my doubts about affirmative action, at least as currently practiced, and I have mispronounced other left shibboleths as well: for example, by suggesting in print that a defensible moral vision supported the so-called Reagan doctrine in foreign affairs,* or by arguing in a *Harvard Law Review* symposium that the Bork hearings represented a threat to judicial independence.[7] Moreover, my constitutional law scholarship—the principal body of my academic work—

---

*This is as good a place as any to own up to and apologize for a geographical *faux pas* that has bedeviled me these past few years. In the essay about the Reagan doctrine, I inadvertently made a glowing reference to the controversial and ultimately unsuccessful intervention of United States Marines in Guatemala, when I meant to laud instead the 1965 intervention to enable free elections to be held in the Dominican Republic.

has consistently adhered to a vision of the original understanding as the basis for constitutional adjudication, a claim
that is practically anathema among serious legal theorists,
most of whom come from the left. But I am one of those un-
fashionable folk who believe that one's constitutional conclusions need not coincide precisely with one's political preferences—a lesson that must be relearned, I fear, by left and
right alike.

I hardly think that any of this makes me a conservative,
however, and I cannot imagine that the American right, in its
new or old varieties, would embrace me. The targets of my ire
are sufficiently varied that I often get the shibboleths of the
right wrong. Any movement conservative who learned my
views on, for example, taxes, would no doubt be just as quick
to brand me a "left-liberal," which has become the intellectually fashionable term for political derogation of almost anybody who is not a Republican. My parents raised me to believe
that paying taxes to the United States of America is a privilege, not a burden. As one who loves my country, I am sufficiently old-fashioned to consider it my patriotic duty in a democracy to pay taxes sufficient to support the programs that
the democratically elected legislature decides we ought to have
and, if I dislike the programs, to vote against my legislator on
that ground, not on the ground that I have been made to pay
taxes. As I read the rhetoric of the right, however, taxes (except for national defense) are one of the great evils of the
modern age. I consider this notion ludicrous. No nation with a
per capita gross national product as high as ours has effective
or nominal tax rates that are so low, but some of their econo-
mies are stronger than ours. The rest of the Western world
understands what America, with its emphasis on the short run
and the bottom line, too often forgets: the future is expensive.

This is particularly true with respect to education. Possibly we should try some of the popular neoconservative ideas,
such as voucher programs to allow parents to purchase educational services in the private market, forcing the public
schools to compete or collapse, although I admit to being
among those who fear that such programs might increase seg-

regation. In any event, something must be done about the educational disaster that has struck our inner cities. I believe strongly that it is an obligation of government to act forcefully (including spending much more money) to make us a far better educated society than we are. Indeed, it strikes me as shortsighted at best and oppressive at worst to oppose racial preferences and at the same time to try to make our financially strapped inner-city schools, which are nearly devoid of white students, do most of the job of training the next generation of black professionals without an influx of capital.

I hold other views, too, that would surely not be congenial to the right. In particular, I am perfectly willing to attack racial prejudice in arenas where the right evidently prefers to keep silent: for example, in the stark fact that capital juries, charged with meting out the death penalty, tend to value the lives of white murder victims far higher than the lives of black ones. (How many white people, in all the nation's long and violent history, have been executed for murdering black people? Answer: none. Yes, that's right, none— or, in the immortal words of Dan Rather, "zero, zip, zilch, nada.")

So I am where I like to be: difficult to pin down, hard to label. (Some tell me that makes me a moderate, but I hardly know what the term means. Many of my views would strike those in the middle as extreme: they are simply extreme in various directions.) Because I take such pleasure in the eclecticism of my political views, I am annoyed when critics (including my friends) try to stuff me into an intellectually stifling little box with a label on the front that reads "conservative" or "neoconservative" or anything of the like.

But the label sticks. Indeed, one of the more awkward side-effects of gaining a reputation as a dissenter on the desirability of a widespread system of racial preferences is the development of a concomitant assumption that one must be a dissenter on other aspects of the traditional civil rights agenda as well. Nowadays, scarcely a week goes by when I do not receive an invitation to comment about the latest controversy over faculty diversity, to serve on a panel about some aspect of law and race, to review (or perhaps provide a jacket quote for) a book about civil rights, or to involve myself in some other way in the intellectual end of the agonizing debate over the nature of racial justice.

I usually say no. Law and race, I explain, is not my principal area of scholarly expertise (but try me, I suggest, on intellectual property or law and religion or separation of powers), and besides (it is, I admit, somewhat harder to put this second point into polite language, so I often say it in so many words), I have no interest in serving as an exhibit. That is how one escapes from the box that predesignates one's scholarly interest.

Getting out of the box that preconceives one's political position is growing harder with each passing day. Two examples will suffice, both of them stemming from the *Wall Street Journal*'s publication of the essay on affirmative action to which I have alluded. Not long after the essay's publication, as I discussed in the last chapter, Clarence Thomas was nominated for a seat on the United States Court of Appeals for the District of Columbia Circuit. Thomas is usually described as a political conservative and his nomination was expected to provoke a furor. I received feelers from some of his proponents, who had read my essay and thought perhaps that since he and I both have objections to racial preferences, we must agree on lots of other things: Would I be interested in testifying on his behalf? I declined; I explained that while I have considerable admiration for what Clarence Thomas has achieved, I don't know him and have little expertise on the matters in dispute.*

Subsequently, legislation was introduced in the Congress to overturn a series of Supreme Court decisions widely

---

*Perhaps more surprising, but consistent with the notion of labeling, I had a telephone call from one of the groups trying to decide whether to oppose the Thomas nomination: If they decided to fight, would I be willing to testify against him? Bemused, I asked why the group had contacted me. The caller said that he had been told I had "some interest in affirmative action," which, he said flatly, "Thomas opposes." Evidently, as a black professor, I was supposed to be in favor of preferences and, by hypothesis, would want to oppose a judge who opposed them. (Did it matter that the judge was black?) I told the caller that I wasn't persuaded on that account alone, but that I like to keep an open mind and would be happy to look at the material he thought might convince me to testify, but the group decided not to fight the nomination and the material was never sent.

viewed—and, with minor exceptions, I think correctly
viewed—as too greatly burdening the plaintiff in an employment discrimination suit or too greatly restricting the remedial power of the court hearing the case. Again, the telephone
began to ring as the opponents of the legislation (that is, the
supporters of the decisions) tried to marshal their forces. One
Senator's legislative assistant wanted to know whether I
would be willing to testify against the legislation. I asked
what made him think of calling me. A little more cagey than
some who call, this gentleman said only that he had been given
my name. I suspected that he was trying to line up an opponent who happened to be a person of color, but some residuum
of the politesse inculcated in me by my parents restrained me
from asking. (Today I would probably be bolder.) Instead, I
told him essentially what I have told almost everybody else:
civil rights law is not my principal area of expertise. Besides,
I went on, the legislation seemed to me essentially correct and
the Court decisions essentially wrong, but if he would be so
kind as to send me materials, I would be happy to take a look
before making up my mind.

This response seemed to confound him: How could I possibly be a critic of one part of the contemporary civil rights
orthodoxy and not the rest? There is, it seems, no adequate
label for a black person of such complexity, and the lack of a
label throws people off stride. So I was not particularly surprised when, notwithstanding the legislative assistant's promise to send them, no materials were forthcoming. (Later, a
black journalist who interviewed me about affirmative action
admitted a similar perplexity: "I was a little surprised," he
said, "to hear you endorse the Civil Rights Act of 1990.")

But what is operating here is plain: the assumption that
if a person who is black dissents from the civil rights agenda
on the matter of racial preferences, he or she must dissent on
lots of other matters, too. Not only are dissenters presumed to
oppose the entire agenda; they are also supposed to want to
press those disagreements into policy at every opportunity, to
serve as exhibits. Glenn Loury, at his most sarcastic, has
grumbled that many white people look on black dissenters as

people who "will come riding in, battle-scarred, to say that it's O.K. to tell these runny-nosed kids who have tyrannized these white students to go to hell."[8] Nor is Loury exaggerating. When the black folks get out of hand, it seems, many white folks think that it is nice to have another black person to shut them down; and the assumption is that anyone who has criticized any part of the civil rights agenda is willing to do the job. It is as though white critics of the same agenda think that the *reason* some black people dissent is in order to get into squabbles with other black people, that shouting down or shutting up other black people is the dissenter's goal in life.

It's bad enough that there are white people who prefer to find black people to take the heat they are too timid or too shrewd to take themselves. What is more troubling is that white people who oppose this part or that of the civil rights agenda readily assume that when they have found a black person who has questioned *any* part, they have a ready (if not always entirely willing) heat-taker. Attitudes of this kind refuse to treat people as complex individuals. They refuse to look even slightly beyond the skin color of the critic. It is the problem of the box all over again: we have labels, not positions, and the labels, once affixed, are difficult to remove.

So I suppose I am stuck with my label, whether or not it makes sense. Evidently, I am now a "black conservative." No matter that I think it a scandal that we underfund education, especially in the inner city, as radically as we do. No matter that I think the death penalty is implemented in a race-conscious manner, offering scant protection to black folk, who, although capital juries seem to forget this, are also victims of murder from time to time. No matter that I think racial preferences, for all their serious problems, are generally constitutional. I have no choice in the matter. The label will stick.

But I must concede that there is more to my concern about being called "conservative" than my general aversion to the anti-intellectual force of labels. If labels there must be, this is one that will cause trouble. To black people, Clarence Thomas has noted, the word *conservative* is all too often inseparable from the word *racist.* And the Republican Party, as

Jack Kemp has pointed out, was "nowhere to be found" during the struggle to enact basic civil rights legislation.[9] For a successful professional who is black, then, a seemingly unshakable burden of guilt comes with the acceptance of the label *conservative,* as though to earn that label is already to have betrayed one's people. And it is the responsibility of movement conservatives, not of people who are black, to bring about the climate in which that burden can be shed.

II

The first point that must be made is that it is not easy even for those black people who want to be movement conservatives to find a comfortable niche. Black intellectuals who have, as I put it earlier, used the opportunities the civil rights movement made possible to train their minds and have come to positions on the right are not necessarily as welcome in the movement as their critics seem to think. I have already mentioned Keith Butler's lament about litmus tests. Paul Weyrich uses Butler's concern as evidence that movement conservatives will not attract many black converts until they grow more tolerant of differences, and I am sure he is right. Clarence Thomas, in his fascinating but generally overlooked Heritage Lecture, relates his experience as a newly minted movement conservative in the wake of the Reagan landslide:

> [T]here was the appearance within the conservative ranks that blacks were to be tolerated but not necessarily welcomed. There appeared to be a presumption, albeit rebuttable, that blacks could not be conservative. Interestingly, this was the flip side of the liberal assumption that we consistently challenged: that blacks were characteristically leftist in their thinking. As such, there was the constant pressure and apparent expectation that even blacks who were in the Administration and considered conservative publicly had to prove themselves daily. Hence, in challenging either positions or the emphases on policy matters, one had to be careful not to go so far as to lose his conservative credentials—or so it seemed. Certainly, pluralism or different

points of view on the merits of these issues was not encouraged or invited—especially from blacks. And, if advice was given, it was often ignored.

In fact, says Thomas of those early days, "it appeared often that our white counterparts actually hid from our advice."[10] And Lugenia Gordon, head of the Freedom Republicans, sometimes described as the only black-led Republican organization to survive the Reagan years, complained in 1988, "I think the Republican National Committee thinks we're like Limburger cheese. A little bit goes a long way."[11]

In other words, the black conservative is both frequently shunned by other conservatives and, at the same time, called upon day after day to prove that he or she is really in the right box with the right label, and really wants to be there, a notion that suggests little appreciation for freedom of thought. And there is more to Clarence Thomas's devastating critique:

> Needless to say, in this environment little or no effort was made to proselytize those blacks who were on the fence or who had not made up their minds about the conservative movement. In fact, it was already hard enough for those of us who were convinced and converted to survive. And, our treatment certainly offered no encouragement to prospective converts. It often seemed that to be accepted within the conservative ranks and to be treated with some degree of acceptance, a black was required to become a caricature of sorts, providing sideshows of anti-black quips and attacks. But there was more—much more—to our concerns than merely attacking previous policies and so-called black leaders. The future, not the past, was to be influenced.[12]

Thomas, of course, has long ago moved past all of this. He is now a lionized member of the movement. Still, the troubling question raised by all of these initiation rites is whether the conservative movement is truly interested, as many of its leading lights proclaim, in adding significant numbers of black people to its membership. I suspect that all too many black people, even those of relatively conservative views, when they envision sitting constantly in the company of movement conservatives, would shy away for much the same reason that William Douglas offered as explanation for his refusal to accompany Earl Warren on the former Chief Justice's regular visits to the all-white, all-male Bohemian Grove: "I knew I would chafe as a captive of an elitist group of men, most of whom I did not admire."[13]

III

Conservative is such a quiet word, but it evokes tremendous emotional responses in very different directions, according to who is asked. To be white and conservative is to be a part of the American mainstream. To be black and conservative is to be a part of the lunatic fringe. To be black and also a conservative, says Thomas Sowell, "is perhaps not considered as bizarre as being a transvestite, but it is certainly considered more strange than being a vegetarian or a birdwatcher."[14]

In America, the question of why so few black people are willing to call themselves conservatives largely reduces to the question of why so few black people are willing to vote Republican, for although there is by no means a perfect fit in voting patterns, in our national politics the Republican Party is seen as the party of the conservatives, the Democratic Party as the party of the liberals. (Remember them?) When he ran against Republican George Bush for president, Democrat Michael Dukakis received around 88 percent of the black vote; this was seen as a great Republican triumph, because Walter Mondale four years earlier had received something like 91 percent. Mondale, of course, was running against Ronald Reagan, the man who made the never fully explained choice to open his 1980 campaign in Philadelphia, Mississippi, where three civil rights workers had been massacred by white terrorists in the 1960s. Reagan went there to extoll the virtues of "states' rights," the old doctrine under which the South denied the right of the federal government to tell it how to treat its black folk. It is conceivable, if just barely, that neither candidate

Reagan nor his handlers were aware of any possible offense this old code phrase, in such a setting, might give to the millions of Americans who suffered horrible oppression under the states' rights regimes of slavery and Jim Crow; but if they didn't know, they should have known, and the fact that they didn't know, if it is a fact, would help explain why the vast majority of black Americans were suspicious of Reagan throughout his campaign and, indeed, throughout his presidency.

On matters that black people might take as indications of feelings toward them, Reagan as president made one error after another. He proposed tax exemptions for private segregation academies. He seemed to favor weakening the Voting Rights Act.* He vigorously opposed sanctions against South Africa, offering such bizarre arguments as the fact that some of the South African police who were slaughtering black people were also black. He went into communities like Charlotte, North Carolina, where school busing was enjoying a rare success, and railed against it. He opposed a holiday to celebrate the birth of Martin Luther King, Jr., and, in the course of a press conference, suggested offhandedly that it was too early to tell whether King was a patriotic American or a Communist dupe. The officials who ran his Justice Department often seemed to reserve their most stinging public rebukes for racial preferences.

George Bush, of course, has a better approval rating among black Americans than his predecessor—in fact, it is on the order of *three times* as high. (At one point during Reagan's presidency, the unemployment rate among black Americans was higher than his approval rating among them.)[15] As Fred Barnes noted in the *New Republic,* "Bush is helped enormously simply by the fact that he's not Reagan."[16] Whether this will translate into black support for the Republican Party is, of course, a different and far dicier matter. After

---

*To be technically correct, let me say that he first took no position on whether the act should be extended after it expired, and then opposed amendments to overturn Supreme Court decisions that made voting rights cases more difficult for the plaintiffs to win.

all, although Bush has appointed many black and Hispanic people to positions of prominence, the fact still remains, as *Time* magazine put it, that "[t]he most prominent black in the George Bush campaign was Willie Horton."[17] In the fall of 1988, it will be recalled, the nation's television screens were saturated with images of Horton, the black killer and rapist who committed despicable crimes after escaping from a Massachusetts work-release furlough program—the point, it seems, being to suggest that if Michael Dukakis were elected president, there might be a lot more Willie Hortons roaming the streets.

The *Time* comment notwithstanding, Roger Ailes, the Bush media wizard who has disclaimed any responsibility for the Horton ads, has insisted that only the media thought the commercials racist. (Lee Atwater, who ran the 1988 Bush campaign, said in 1990 shortly before he died that he was sorry for the emphasis on Horton.) Fred Barnes argues further that if so many black people thought the commercials bad, surely Bush's approval rating among black Americans would be lower than it is. Another way of looking at the data, and a sensible way, I think, is that the commercials *were* racially insensitive, terribly so, but few people think that Bush himself is a racist. On the contrary, unlike Reagan, Bush has gone to great pains to make himself and his administration available to the old and new leadership of the black community, and for that, surely, everyone commends him, or should.

One might respond, of course, that the constant criticism of Reagan as insensitive to black people was misleading and unfair. And it should be said that there were principled arguments available for every one of his objectionable positions. Perhaps the Internal Revenue Service should not be in the business of deciding which public policies to enforce through denial of tax-exempt status. Perhaps aspects of the Voting Rights Act designed to ensure that black people are elected, as against making sure that black people can vote, are misguided. Perhaps economic sanctions against South Africa are not the best route to majority rule. Perhaps school busing is wrong even when it works. Perhaps another public holiday was too expensive, or perhaps we needed a longer time before deciding whom to honor with one. And racial preferences certainly have their problems.

But in every case, Reagan chose the principled argument that went against what most black people thought was right. And in the case of the Philadelphia, Mississippi, speech that kicked off his first fall campaign, no principled explanation is available for the selection of venue, given the remarks that he chose to make. Moreover, it does a disservice to black people to suggest that the widespread suspicion of Reagan was due entirely or even mostly to distortions of his record by the civil rights leaders he persistently attacked. Black people are not that politically unsophisticated; they do not need others to tell them what to think. The support for tax exemptions for segregation academies in the *Bob Jones* case particularly rankled. I was living in Washington, D.C., at the time, saw it in the newspaper, and simply refused to believe it. They cannot possibly, I thought, be this stupid. The decision to side with Bob Jones, says Clarence Thomas, took the wind out of the sails of the drive to attract black people to the conservative movement, and his efforts to warn administration officials of this went for naught; for black conservatives seeking respectability in the black community, it was, Thomas says, "our death knell."[18]

The point is that the conservative movement has something more than an image problem. It is not merely that its record has been distorted by its enemies, although, to be sure, there is certainly some of that. The unhappy truth, which the conservative movement (and the Republican Party) must ultimately face if its members care about black support, is that there are *reasons* the movement has the poor image it does among black people. And rather than blaming the messenger (which neoconservatives like to accuse the left of doing, often with sound basis), the movement ought to take some time to look inward.

One reason is, to be sure, readily cured, if the movement's leadership but cares to do so. This is the perception of who is welcome in the movement and who is not. The conserva-

tive movement generally and the Republican Party in particular proudly and sensibly trumpet the achievements of black
conservatives who have succeeded, they insist, without any
special consideration on the basis of race. Indeed, the GOP
reserves many of its proudest huzzahs for the conservative
black candidates whom it has put up for high office in recent
years—a governorship, two Senate seats. But critics have
noted that the party puts up black candidates only for seats
that it expects to lose. Indeed, Alan Keyes, nominated at the
last minute for a race against the popular incumbent Senator
Paul Sarbanes in a Maryland so Democratic that the Republican Party can scarcely raise money there, was described as
being on a suicide mission. This tendency does not mean that
the party wants the candidates to lose, only that it seems to
see black candidates as a gamble when all else fails. Black
Republicans, as GOP strategist Edward Rollins admits, are
never nominated for the party's "safe" seats, of which there
are many.[19]

One path to gaining greater black confidence, then, would
be to nominate these qualified black conservatives for seats
they are likely to win.[20] The reason this would increase confidence is not because of a vision of fairness, but because a successful black candidate for high office would retain visibility,
probably on a national level, for a long time to come—as
Douglas Wilder, a Democrat and the first elected black governor in our history, clearly and deservedly does. "Nothing is
clearer," went an editorial in the *National Review* shortly
before the 1988 election, "than that the first black President
will be a fiscally and socially conservative Republican."[21]
Maybe so: but first the party has to get some of those fiscal
and social black conservatives into positions of national prominence.

It must be said, however, that the election of black conservatives to the state houses or to the Senate would go only a
short way toward solving the problems that drive even relatively conservative black folk away from the conservative
movement. A larger difficulty is that the movement is widely
viewed as actively hostile to the progress of black people.

The conservative strategy to remedy this perception has been to talk up the economy. The late Lee Atwater, former head of the Republican National Committee, argued that low taxes and low inflation are bound to benefit black families.[22] This, of course, is basically true, but one wants to be wary about pressing the point too far. A rising tide doesn't lift all boats, because some of the boats have holes—which, as a matter of fact, the social safety net does, too. I suspect that the emphasis on economic improvement is a strategy aimed principally at gaining the confidence of black yuppies, who do not in opinion surveys differ markedly on most issues from their white counterparts and who, surveys show, are significantly more likely to vote Republican than their parents are.[23] (There is an excellent chance that their grandparents, if they were allowed to vote, did vote Republican, as mine nearly always did on both sides of the family, for it was not until Barry Goldwater's nomination in 1964 that black support for the GOP evaporated.)[24] So far, the strategy has little to show for it; the promise of economic gains has not overcome the basic black fear of conservatism. The movement, then, must look elsewhere.

Paul Weyrich has suggested that the problem is simple: "Conservatives don't want to get their hands dirty." White conservatives, says Weyrich, do not appear in the inner cities except at election time. Once more, he quotes the Reverend Keith Butler:

> The difference between liberals and conservatives is that liberals never take anything for granted. They go into conservative strongholds and work the neighborhoods and eventually make gains. Conservatives stay away from liberal and Democratic strongholds and then wonder why they never get anywhere.[25]

The tendency among movement conservatives and Republican strategists is to write off the black community, to make few serious efforts to win black votes. Clarence Thomas says that to the Republican Party, black people have "just happened to represent an interest group not worth going after"—a proposition that is, he insists, a violation of basic conservative principles.[26] (One thinks inevitably of Barry Goldwater, who remarked back in 1961 that the GOP would not get the black vote in 1964 or 1968, and said "therefore we ought to go hunting where the ducks are.")[27] Come each election, Republican leaders talk boldly about the percentage of black votes they expect to receive, and when the election is over, they are left to explain why they did not come close to their expectations. Again, consider the perspective of Clarence Thomas in his Heritage Lecture:

> I am of the view that black Americans will move inexorably and naturally toward conservatism when we stop discouraging them; when they are treated as a diverse group with differing interests; and when conservatives stand up for what they believe in rather than stand against blacks.[28]

There is an important point here. Defenders of conservatism and the Republican Party—especially former high-ranking Justice Department officials such as Edwin Meese and William Bradford Reynolds—say that conservatism has gotten a bad rap on civil rights because of opposition to racial quotas. The movement, its defenders insist, is in favor of civil rights and strongly opposes the barriers that keep black people from competing fairly for jobs or college admission.

This may be; but as one who has attended many conferences at which these issues are debated, I can state with some confidence that movement conservatives, whatever their views on racism generally, reserve by far the greater part of their vehemence for affirmative action programs—not, incidentally, on the issue of quotas alone but on the considerably broader matter of racial consciousness. Indeed, the casual listener might be excused for supposing that opposition to affirmative action is the sum total of the movement's interest in civil rights. To be sure, racial discrimination is always condemned in words, but affirmative action is always condemned in spirited argument and, before conservative audiences, often to thunderous applause that somehow does not greet the throwaway lines about traditional antiblack racism. If black Americans read hostility in all this, it is not because the message is distorted; it is because the positive message is not being presented. Clarence Thomas complains that the movement does too little to tell black people what it is "for." But it has been the conservative movement's own disturbing choice to emphasize what it dislikes, rather than what it likes, about the civil rights orthodoxy.

The emphases here take on considerable importance. Again, Weyrich quotes the Reverend Keith Butler: "The black community is the one place where the federal government is actually popular." And Butler goes on to say this:

> You also have to realize that conservatives cannot always be seen as the group wanting to take away—especially in education. We have kids who have the capability of learning but have no hope of getting a higher education. If conservatives and Republicans want to make inroads here, they had better be willing to offer solutions.[29]

They do offer solutions, of course, sometimes quite elaborate ones, but it isn't clear that the solutions make much difference to the black voters. Clarence Thomas has this to say about the problem:

> [G]adget ideas such as enterprise zones are [not] of any consequence when blacks who live in blighted areas know that crime, not lack of tax credits, is the problem. Blacks are not stupid. And no matter how good an idea or proposal is, no one is going to give up the comfort of the leftist status quo as long as they view conservatives as antagonistic to their interest, and conservatives do little or nothing to dispel the perception. If blacks hate or fear conservatives, nothing we say will be heard.[30]

Exactly. If nobody is willing to listen, then it doesn't really matter what one says. And when the conservative movement speaks, very few black people are prepared to listen.

I V

And this leads, finally, to the modern conservative movement's principal difficulty in gaining black converts: for many, perhaps most, black Americans, the word *conservative* is synonymous with the word *racist*. Conservatives are seen as the people who want to hold us back. This is not, as some would have it, a simple-minded reaction to a historical memory of the "old guard" conservatives who were actively hostile to the cause of racial justice. Nor is it a simple matter of misperception, a favored but ultimately insulting explanation for the problem. (I remember bristling every time President Reagan or his defenders would answer a question about his horribly low standing among black voters in the polls by suggesting that the voters had been misled about his record, as though black voters are manifestly more stupid than the white voters who apparently managed to understand his record just fine.) Nor is it, finally, a problem of emphasis, or lack of good candidates, or lack of good ideas.

Part of the problem is programmatic. The Civil Rights Act of 1990, which I have already mentioned, provides an example of the problem. President Bush, after first insisting that there was no need to overturn any of the Supreme Court decisions the bill was designed to reverse—decisions that everyone agreed made it more difficult for plaintiffs to prevail in employment discrimination cases—finally decided to veto the legislation on the ground that it was a "quota bill." Mindless racial quotas should be as repugnant to black observers as to white ones, but the fact that there is something bad in the legislation is not always the end of the story. In the first place, the claim that the bill would promote the use of numerical hiring quotas was almost certainly a misreading, and it is difficult to imagine that the current Supreme Court would read even ambiguous language in a way that would encourage racial quotas. But assume that the president was correct, and that the only way of overturning the objectionable decisions was to accept a bill that included a provision of which the

president viscerally disapproved, a provision that would encourage racial quotas. One might reasonably ask why the bill
could not nevertheless be treated like other legislation, where
sometimes, in order to get the bill he wants, the president
must accept provisions he would prefer not to have—as happens, for instance, whenever there are budget negotiations
and the final resolution includes what are charmingly called
"revenue enhancers." If the bill is important enough, the
president signs it, swallowing the bad medicine with the good.

So why not the Civil Rights Act of 1990? The obvious
answer is that the president, and perhaps his party, did not
consider reversing the decisions a sufficiently important goal.
No matter what the theoretical justification for that position—and certainly justifications exist—my concern here is
with the message Republicans send. The net result of the
brouhaha over the Civil Rights Act of 1990 is that a Republican president has pronounced himself more concerned about
avoiding any hint of racial quotas than about easing some of
the new procedural burdens the Court has placed in the path
of employment discrimination plaintiffs. This comparative
judgment sends a message that black Americans can hardly be
expected to miss.

Then there is the Racial Justice Act of 1990, which was
designed to make it easier for defendants in capital cases to
show racial bias in their sentencing. This legislation, too, was
aimed at ameliorating the effect of a Supreme Court decision,
and this legislation, too, was opposed by the Bush administration. The fear, one Justice Department official explained in a
letter to the *New York Times,* was that the bill would establish
a quota system (that word again) for death sentences.[31]
Maybe so; but what one wants to see, very badly, is an acknowledgment that the many surveys indicating racial disparities in capital sentencing raise some concern other than the
quota question. Even if one has little sympathy with vicious
killers trying to get off on technicalities, what about sympathy
for potential murder *victims* whom the law is supposed to protect? After all, if one honestly believes that the death penalty
is a deterrent to murder, then the stark fact that a black per-

son who kills a white person is twenty-two times as likely to be
sentenced to death as a black person who kills a black person,[32] must show that fewer murders of black people than of
white people are being deterred. And the fact that in the long,
violent history of the United States, no white person has ever
been executed for the murder of a black person ought to gen-
erate at least a few words of sympathy rather than more mut-
terings about quotas. Playing every game by racial counting
is indeed a misguided notion, and it may be that the data have
reasonable explanations; but the development of the science of
statistics is one of the most important scientific advances of
the century, and we blink at reality to pretend that *nothing*
lies behind any statistical disparities.

But put programs to one side. There are any number of
largely symbolic steps through which the conservative movement and the GOP could send a more encouraging message to
the black people who worry about both. For example, during
the controversy over the Supreme Court's decision protecting
as free speech the burning of the American flag, I was moved
to wonder about the display of the Confederate flag (and I
was not alone). At a county fair in rural Connecticut not long
ago I saw for sale a huge Confederate flag, emblazoned with
the ungrammatical slogan IF THE SOUTH COULD OF WON THE
WAR, WE WOULD OF HAD IT MADE. My first, foolish instinct was
to steer my five-year-old daughter away from it, lest she ask
for an explanation. (My wife, wiser in these matters than I,
always opts to explain, on the sensible ground that today is
always the best time to learn.) What I wonder, though, is this:
If burning the American flag is an insult to those who have
died to protect it, what message does the open display of the
flag of the Confederacy (which is also a part of the flag of a
couple of states) send to the hundreds of thousands of Americans who died at the hands of those fighting under it—or the
many millions of black folk who perished at the hand of the
slave system that the Confederate flag recalls? Many black
people shudder whenever a car or truck with a Confederate
flag decal passes or approaches us on the road—I know I do;
and while my own view is that Confederate flag waving, like

American flag burning, is protected by the First Amendment, I suspect that millions of black people would have felt encouraged, even embraced, had some of the conservatives who insisted that the second was not protected speech said something equally strong about the first.

But public posturing is only a part of it. There is something else at work here, something simple and sad, something the Republicans, and movement conservatives, have to acknowledge if they want to get anywhere in the black community. The something else is that the Republican Party is now what the Dixiecrat "Party" once was: a natural and evidently comfortable home for white racism in the United States. When I refer to racism, I am not using the word as it is too often used nowadays, as a term for describing anybody who opposes some part of the traditional civil rights agenda. My reference, rather, is to true racists, people who really *do* mean black people ill. I emphatically am not suggesting that most or even many Republicans are racists; my suggestion, rather, is that true racists are far more likely to be and talk and vote Republican and conservative than Democratic and liberal.

It will do no good for the right to bristle at this truth. It is not necessarily even a criticism, at least not yet; it is rather an observation, a bald statement of political reality, in the same way that it states political reality to say that when doctrinaire Marxist-Leninists bother to vote for mainstream candidates, they will almost certainly vote for liberal Democrats rather than conservative Republicans. This is a genuine problem, and efforts to sweep it under the rug, or to treat those who raise it as rabble-rousers, will move matters no closer to a solution.

Consider once more Ronald Reagan's "states' rights" speech in Philadelphia, Mississippi. It may be true, as Reagan's staff quickly explained, that all he had in mind was to return to the states the administration of certain federal programs. But to any real racists who may have been lurking in the audience, the vision of getting the federal government off the backs of the people could not but have been attractive, for racists are one group on whose back the government has often, and with reason, been. In the South, where politics are often so terribly polarized that it is fair to say that city mayors are either black Democrats or white Republicans, it is more common than it should be for Republican candidates to run campaigns full of code words, all the while playing up the black support for their Democratic opponents.

The writer John B. Judis has referred to the problem as "court[ing] the backlash vote." He adds, "In their campaigns, most Republicans in the South assume and attempt to exploit a racially divided electorate."[33] In 1986, the Republican National Committee launched an ill-fated "ballot-integrity" campaign directed, according to an internal memorandum, at "keep[ing] the black vote down." The campaign, which Clarence Thomas called "pretty disgusting," backfired and, as *National Review* lamented, "may have cost the party its Senate majority."[34] In the wake of all of this, and if, as news reports suggest, racial preferences are to become an important campaign issue for the GOP in the 1990s, one can only hope that a repeat of the carefully coded but racially charged Jesse Helms campaign of 1990 is avoided.

Helms, locked in a close Senate race with a black opponent, ran commercials suggesting to voters ("reminding" them is no doubt how his supporters would put it) that white people were losing jobs to less qualified minority candidates. The news media, I think, made an error in attributing most of the late surge of votes this brought in to racism. The campaign might be better described as tapping the fear and resentment that are inevitable results of difficult economic times—the backlash vote. It is hard to imagine, however, that Helms did not realize that *some* of those who would flock to him would be casting backlash votes.

It was the backlash vote, of course, that gave us the specter of David Duke—a former head of one of the branches of the Ku Klux Klan, an admitted admirer of Hitler's *Mein Kampf,* and the founder and president of the National Association for the Advancement of White People—as a serious political candidate, most recently for the United States Senate, a race in which he ran as an independent and yet garnered over

40 percent of the vote. Earlier, when he had run for state office as a Republican, national Republican officials, from the
president on down, rightly rushed to repudiate him and, to
their credit, even taped commercials opposing his candidacy
and denying that he is a real Republican. (Although some
analysts credited those commercials with helping rather than
hurting Duke, I think it is vitally important that the commercials were made.) But what is more interesting and more troubling about David Duke is his insistence that he belongs in the
Republican Party and that he is a conservative.

Lately, conservatives have paid more attention to the
problem, although sometimes with more gentleness than perhaps is warranted. An editorial in the *National Review* pointed
out that as bad a reputation on civil rights as the Republican
Party might have among black voters, its reputation is in a
sense equally bad among white racists. Equally bad or equally
good, depending on one's point of view, but the argument in
the editorial is that the same misinformation about the Republican Party makes racists feel welcome and black people
feel unwelcome.[35] If this is so, then the GOP must do more
than it has to make clear that white racists are neither wanted
nor welcome.

The same prescription applies to the conservative movement generally. A good deal of conservative rhetoric, from the
ringing condemnations of affirmative action to the repeated attacks on welfare cheaters to the fervent opposition to federal
regulation, dovetails nicely with the program of those who
mean black people ill. When such surging rhetoric is reserved
for attacking the orthodox civil rights agenda, it is hardly any
wonder that racists feel welcome. As Clarence Thomas points
out in his Heritage Lecture, the trouble is that while the
movement is very good at articulating the negatives about
programs that most black people see as good for the black
community, it has not been nearly as good at articulating a
positive program to replace what it wants to take away. I do
not mean that no positive program exists; I mean that the positive program is presented as an afterthought, and rarely to
conservative audiences, who evidently would rather listen to

condemnations of affirmative action than engage in serious discussion on what should replace it. (The latest fashionable comparison is between racial preferences and apartheid[36]— stronger language, as far as I can tell, than is used to describe any contemporary discrimination *against* people of color.) The positive program is never presented with anything approaching the rhetorical vehemence with which the negative program is pressed—a point of which black listeners can hardly be unaware.

So the problem is simple to understand, if difficult to remedy. *Conservative* is a dirty word in the black community because the conservative movement is frightening to many black people. It is frightening not because it is hostile to black people, which it is not; it is frightening, rather, because it is far better at explaining what is wrong with civil rights than what is right with them; because it seems far more comfortable standing against black people when it thinks they are wrong than standing with black people when it thinks they are right; and because it willingly, if not perhaps happily, accepts as members people who *are* racist and who *are* hostile. It is frightening, as Clarence Thomas puts it, because it seems always to take its most important public stands against black people rather than with them. Evidently, even those of us who are merely biologically black are able to figure that one out.

CHAPTER 8

Silencing Doubt

O n the campuses, of course, there are no black conservatives. Oh, there are neoconservative intellectuals with black skin, but, as we have already established, they lack any claim to blackness other than the biological. They have forgotten their roots. They may look black, but they are not, we might say, the black people who matter.

And what about people who are white? Well, they are free to challenge what part of the diversity movement they wish, as long as they are willing to take the consequences: it may not be easy to discover, late in one's career, that one is a eurocentric heterosexist right-winger (as professors who raise questions about the diversity movement risk being labeled). Unfortunately, the conversational habit that affirmative action has become has given rise to a new grammar of race—and woebetide anyone who uses the words incorrectly!

Consider, for example, the *Dictionary of Cautionary Words and Phrases,* published in 1989 by the Multicultural Management Program at the University of Missouri School of Journalism. The *Dictionary,* one of those well-intentioned ideas that goes a bit too far, lists "offensive," "derogatory," and "objectionable" words that journalists, the authors hope, will avoid. Under the term "qualified minorities," we are warned: "Do not use in stories about affirmative action. Unnecessary description that indicates minorities are generally unqualified."[1] Evidently, although news reporters are allowed to discuss affirmative action, asking the qualification question is off-limits. (Oddly, they are not told to avoid "unqualified minorities," or even "qualified minorities" if the term crops up in stories that are not about affirmative action. Perhaps James Watt's famous gaffe, describing an advisory committee as comprising "a black, two Jews, and a cripple," was not as horrible as many of us thought. After all, he ended with "and we have talent.") The new grammar of race is constructed in a way that George Orwell would have appreciated, because its rules make some ideas impossible to express—unless, of course, one wants to be called a racist.

Intellectuals chafe under these rules. Richard Herrnstein, the controversial Harvard psychologist, has complained that some ideas are treated in the way obscenity once was: simply not to be discussed in polite society, and certainly not among people who are smart. (Herrnstein's provocative example is the possibility that the median black applicant generally *is* less qualified than the median white applicant for most educational or employment opportunities.)[2] The columnist Russell Baker has called racism the new communism—the implication being that just as in the 1950s, when one had only to cry "Communist!" in order to shut opponents up, and possibly get them fired, as we enter the 1990s, the cry "Racist!" serves the same function.

It is not difficult to understand how these conversational rules have evolved. Assertions of racial inferiority (and code words carrying the same message) have throughout history been the source of tremendous pain and oppression. Racism has been horror made real, centuries of nightmare; and the nation's racist legacy, whatever its implications for policy, lives on in racial memory. No wonder, then, that those of us who are black are often a bit skittish about the free expression of ideas that seem to us likely, should they triumph, to lead us back into the pit of racial subjugation.

On campuses across the country there is a move afoot to make the expression of racist sentiments a punishable offense. Although some advocates of what is usually referred to as "hate speech" or "racial harassment" rules evidently would like to place the entire debate over affirmative action off-limits,[3] the movement is not fired principally by a fear of the qualification question; its motive force is largely other fears, some of them far more legitimate. It has never been easy to be black in a white world, but, as one black student at Yale recently put it, one hopes while pursuing an education to spend some time outside the real world. Unfortunately, matters do not work quite that way. The 1980s saw a sharp upswing in racially charged incidents on college campuses, ranging from the defacing of posters with racial caricatures and epithets, to the delivery of anonymous hate messages, to harassment and intimidation, to physical assaults.[4]

My sympathies generally run toward freedom, and I would oppose efforts to regulate racism that is reflected in simple speech, even when the racist views are insulting, offensive, or painful. For example, I would fight, forcefully if unhappily, for the right of students to express the view (in the classroom or in the dining hall or on wall posters, signed or unsigned) that black people display a tendency toward criminality or are intellectually inferior. Cruel and insupportable such views might be, but they are plainly speech. Consequently, I am left cold by the widely quoted words of a black Stanford undergraduate during a debate over the adoption of a code of conduct to restrict what might be said about students of color: "What we are proposing is not completely in line with the First Amendment. I'm not sure it should be. We at Stanford are trying to set a standard different from what society at large is trying to accomplish."[5] My sentiments are more in line with those expressed by former State Department official Alan Keyes: "To think that I [as a black person] will . . . be told that white folks have the moral character to shrug off insults, and I do not. . . . That is the most insidious, the most insulting, the most racist statement of all!"[6]

But my blood is set to boiling and my commitment to

freedom is stretched when I discover that many of those who agree with me about speech seem to think that the offensive remarks are not even worthy of condemnation. Many critics of what is sometimes called the "p.c." (politically correct) movement lavish vitriol on the regulators, but are oddly restrained when discussing the students whose comments lead to all the righteous p.c. fury. Apologists for racism—what else is there to call them?—continue to insist that nothing is involved in any of these incidents except free speech and, it seems, good clean adolescent sport. For example, when a small group of Asian-American students at the University of Connecticut was surrounded by a number of white students who called them "Oriental faggots" and sang "we all live in a yellow submarine," other white students assured the victims that the perpetrators were "just drunk, trying to have some fun."[7]

Right.

My empathy lies with the victims, and when I hear such nonsense, sometimes offered by the very people who would like to make flag desecration a criminal offense, I think of the black student at another school who was cornered in his dormitory room by white students wearing sheets that covered their faces and carrying a noose, for the purpose, they announced, of lynching him. I think of one of my law students who, as an undergraduate, returned to her room to find the door painted bright red and emblazoned with the words, "NIGGER BITCH, THIS IS YOUR BLOOD." And then there are the ten black students at the Yale Law School who recently found in their mailboxes notes from a group calling itself with rare honesty Yale Students for Racism, notes that announced the commission of a crime against another student by two black males and concluded, "Now you know why we call you niggers."

If terrorizing people this way is good clean fun, then Bernhard Goetz must have had a grand old time in that subway car, joshing and kidding around with the four black youths who were, in the polite euphemism of the street, hassling him for money. Back in 1987, it will be recalled, Mr. Goetz was acquitted of charges that he had attempted murder

by rising angrily from his subway bench and shooting down
the four "hasslers." His defense attorney made his client's
fear and rage the centerpiece of his case, and the jury accepted Goetz's story that he felt in fear of being beaten or
worse. Fair enough. A large chunk of the public, most of
whom never set foot inside the courtroom and therefore had
little information on which to judge, also accepted Goetz's
story, even before the trial took place. His claim to have been
first frightened and then enraged resonated with a frightened,
enraged public that decided long before the verdict came in
that Goetz was telling the truth.

Students of color who want to make the same claim,
being frightened of those who harass them, seem to have a
harder time making their feelings real to the listener. There is
little resonance: How can one be scared of a bunch of adoles-
cents having good clean fun?

Again, consider the Goetz case. Because the shooter was
white and the hasslers black, the racial imagery of the case
was stark, but Mr. Goetz's defenders insisted that race had
nothing to do with their decision to tilt, as it were, to his side.
Maybe, had the shooter been black and the hasslers white, a
substantial portion of the public might nevertheless have ral-
lied to the shooter's defense before trial, just as Mr. Goetz's
defenders insist. One cannot sensibly add, however, "assuming the other facts to be the same." The other facts could not
possibly have been the same were the skin colors reversed, for
America, however noble its aspirations, sees skin color. Blackness can threaten simply by appearing unexpectedly: in a
wealthy white suburb in the middle of the day, on a darkened
sidewalk in the middle of the night, on the other side of the
peephole in the door when no one is expected.[8]

Thus when Barry Slotnick, Goetz's defense attorney,
kept inviting the jury (and, by extension, the public) to imagine the atmosphere in the subway car, he conjured, whether he
planned to or not, an image of innocent whiteness surrounded
by threatening blackness. Emotive power would be lost were
one to conjure instead an image of "innocent blackness" surrounded by "threatening whiteness," for that is not a part of

most (white) people's experience—which might help explain why, when white students on college campuses surround students of color and chant racist slogans, there is a rush to insist that no threat is involved, that the white students are only indulging the adolescent's need for good clean fun, and fun that is protected by the First Amendment at that. For many black people, however, our history has taught well that an unexpected whiteness can be threatening too. But this threat, I suspect, is a bit harder for most Americans to envision. I shudder to think about how the criminal justice system will respond the first time a black student who is subject to such harassment reaches for a weapon. I suspect that we will not see the Goetz case revisited; the unfortunate black kid is not likely to be called a hero by white people who will not understand why he felt so threatened.

It is important for us to build a bridge of understanding that will help white people to see. There is a John Wayne movie in which Wayne says to the bad guys something like, "Wherever you go, always look over your shoulder, because one day I'm gonna be back there, right behind you." For many people of color, this line captures precisely the fear of racist violence. Of course, it is true that most racially charged incidents on campus are "harmless" in the sense that the students who are the perpetrators do not intend any physical harm. But that is small consolation to the victims, who have no way to be sure; indeed, the fact that they cannot be sure that no harm is intended is presumably a part of the appeal for the perpetrators. It isn't much fun to scare somebody who knows you aren't serious about it.

II

Consider once more the Yale Law School incident I just described. The note that the students received was passed in a context in which it could only be perceived as threatening: an anonymous leaflet, directed at particular individuals, hinting darkly at group responsibility for the crimes of some of the group's members.* It is conceivable, if just barely, that a free speech justification could be constructed for the leaflet; although, had it threatened harm to the recipients explicitly, as the students think it did implicitly (I think they are right), the free speech defense would be much weaker, although not, perhaps, wholly implausible. I mention the incident, however, to make another point. Had a similar anonymous notice been posted on the law school's walls, or had the notes in the mailboxes been signed, I would be more inclined to treat it as an exercise in protected, if vile, speech, and would oppose any efforts to expose the perpetrators or even to remove the offending posters. On a university campus, perhaps more than anyplace else, unfettered debate is essential.

But the facts of the Yale incident taken as a whole tend to transform it from one of speech to one of harassment and, more important, to one of intimidation. If I were among the students who found the letter in my mailbox, I suppose I might be looking over my shoulder from time to time. I might even feel, as the legal scholar Patricia Williams has written on a different subject, "so manipulated that I cannot remember my own name . . . so lost and angry that I can't speak a civil word to the people who love me best."[9] I might feel very suddenly the crushing burden of lingering white racism resting on my two lonely shoulders.

Maybe Alan Keyes is right. Maybe the students should have dropped the leaflets in the trash and not given them another thought. Many of us might prefer to imagine students of color full of a kind of noble stoicism—sticks and stones and all that—but threatening letters are not easy to ignore. One might want to argue, of course, over what counts as a threat, or what the recipient should appropriately view as one, but then we are back in the subway car, second-guessing Bernhard Goetz.

Still, even if it is true that such racial incidents are on the upsurge, we must be careful about what lessons to draw

---

*At this writing, despite considerable investigation of the Yale Law School incident, no perpetrator has been found.

from the fact. The power to regulate must always be used
deftly, because it is in the nature of regulatory movements to
demand more, and after a while, legitimate needs and illegitimate wants can get tangled up. That is what is happening on
many campuses, where the perfectly sensible desire to protect
students from harassment and intimidation has led to the
crafting of detailed codes concerning language that can and
can't be used. Were the stakes not so high, on both sides, the
idea of a code of verbal conduct would seem quaint, almost
Victorian in its presumption.

The schools, of course, have an obligation to protect their
students from physical harm and intimidation, and spurious
First Amendment claims should not detract from that task.
There is, however, a sharp line between attacking or in-
timidating particular individuals and offering comments that
many will find offensive. Some colleges and universities, in
their rush to regulate those things that make life unpleasant,
have unfortunately crossed the line, adopting codes that
would punish, for example, "demeaning epithets" and "generalized" racist and sexist remarks. These categories are rarely
defined in detail, although the University of Michigan's code,
later struck down by a federal court as violating the First
Amendment rights of students,[10] offered as a tantalizing example of punishable conduct the case of a "male student" re-
marking "in class" that "Women just aren't as good in this
field as men" (evidently a female student would be free to
make such a claim). Very often, these codes are written in
language easily broad enough to cover—that is, to forbid—the
speech of students who want to argue that other students, admitted because of explicit racial preferences, are less capable
than students who were admitted without them. Many students, and not a few professors, have argued that the codes
should be adopted with that idea in mind.

A lot of blood has been spilled defending the opposite
idea, that speech should be free even if it hurts. Still, the sentiment to tilt the other way, away from "harmful" speech,
runs deep in the American character. The authors of the Constitution, many of whom were involved in the passage of the

Alien and Sedition Acts, which sharply limited freedom to criticize the government, would have been impressed by the cleverness of these new rules; so would the reactionary Supreme Court from the early years of the twentieth century, which sustained a number of efforts to punish speech the government didn't like.

Today's proponents of limits on what is sometimes called "hate speech" are perfectly aware that they are opening themselves to unflattering historical comparisons, but once again, the diversity movement comes to their rescue. It turns out that speech is objectionable only when it will have the effect of diminishing the learning environment for those whose backgrounds of oppression make them especially sensitive to the threatening nuance that lurks behind racist sentiment masquerading as serious intellectual discourse.[11]

One major analytical problem with the codes has been well put by Ira Glasser of the American Civil Liberties Union. If it is true that the campuses are hotbeds of racism, Glasser muses, then why would anyone concerned about racism want to put in the hands of campus authorities the power to decide what words can and cannot be used?[12] To imagine that an essentially racist authority would wield so extraordinary a power only in the ways that its designers envision is sheer fantasy.*

Moreover, there is something disturbing about the amount of emotional and intellectual energy that sharp and talented people of color have put into crafting and negotiating and debating these codes. With all of the problems facing people of color who are not fortunate enough to live the relatively sheltered lives of those on college campuses, there is tragedy in the occasional tendency of those who are luckier to turn inward, ever inward, worrying more about what other stu-

---

*A similar fantasy led the radical right and the feminist left into their uneasy alliance to stop exploitative pornography, a high-minded effort that exploded into the Mapplethorpe trial, and led the designers of Marxist-Leninist political *praxis* to assume that the state could be trusted with the power to regulate nearly all areas of individual life, a fantasy recently demolished by popular demand. The theory, in both cases, was that the state would use its new-found power wisely and in furtherance of the general good, but matters did not quite work out that way.

dents are saying or thinking than about what to do about education or health or physical safety for those who are serving
life sentences in the violent prisons that so many of our inner
cities have become. I am not suggesting that we should necessarily allow racial slurs to run off our backs; I do think we
should try to be choosy about which ones we let get under our
skins. For we live in a world sufficiently full of cruel and insensitive and racist thought that people whose skins are thin
as well as dark will end up spending all their time thinking
only of themselves.

And besides—let's be honest here—much of what students of color must face on campus today is horrible, but,
when one considers the obstacles facing their parents and
grandparents, much more of it is relatively petty. Is it really
necessary to run unhappily to some white authority figure to
complain that a racist white student thinks black students are
stupid? Lots of white people think black people are stupid.
They are stupid themselves for thinking so, but regulation
will not make them smarter.

I suspect that many of those who fought and died to
make it possible for today's students of color to have the opportunities they do would have been alarmed at the idea that
this much energy would not go into learning, but into making
sure no one says anything to suggest doubt about our abilities. I am quite sure that the answers our grandparents would
have given is that our response must be to work hard enough
to make ourselves, very simply, too good to ignore.

Our task, it seems to me, is less to regulate that foolish
white student's right to express foolish and dangerous ideas
than to prove those ideas wrong. One might reply, of course,
that the white student might one day try to put his or her
racist ideas into practice, but shutting the student up now will
not stop *that;* it will, however, teach the value of controlling
the regulatory apparatus when there is speech out there that
one doesn't like.

It is not my purpose to dismiss concern over all racist
comments intended to intimidate; as a black person, not only
do I want to see other black people protected; I am also natu-

rally sensitive to the possibility that the next victim might be me. Racism and sexism are still alive in American society; some say they are even on the increase, although I would want both a clear definition and a proffer of evidence before accepting that claim. But whether declining or growing, they are both insidious and distorting forces in American political and social life. The Yale letters, although defended in the press as free speech, seem to me quite close to the sort of racist intimidation from which a school ought to protect its students. But the problem for which the school is responsible is the intimidation, not the racism. It is our responsibility—the responsibility of people who are black—to battle against genuine racist intimidation without allowing ourselves to be intimidated, or even affected, by everything that is racially offensive.

True, I would rather have students of color comfortable than uncomfortable as they make their way through the academic world. When students of color complain that the expression of racially denigrating sentiments makes it more difficult for them to concentrate on their work, they are stating a simple truth. The widespread expression of openly racist opinions is bound to make campuses less hospitable places for students of color, and I would not want to think that the apologists for the "fun-loving" racist students want things that way. So I dearly wish that some of those on the right who spend their rhetorical efforts attacking what they call the forces of p.c. would craft equally eloquent essays explaining to the white students who make the objectionable remarks the evil of what they are doing, for they are silencing students of color every bit as forcefully as the p.c. movement is silencing racists. Both forms of silencing are wrong, but it would be preposterous to suggest that they are morally equivalent.

Still, what the proponents of anti-harassment codes seek is not only a threat to freedom of expression; it is also a way of screening out hard truths about the way many white people look at the rest of us. When the students who advocate these limits of speech escape to the real world, they will find confirmation of what they already know: lots of people who have lots of doubts about what they can do, and many will not be afraid to say so.

Again, I do not want to be misunderstood. The battle against racism must be never-ceasing, but we must pick our fights carefully. And I worry about the automatic transformation of all doubters or dissenters or critics into racists. We have only so much energy to spend battling the real or imagined predations of others; we have to spend some of it on equipping ourselves for our careers. It frustrates me to see all of this energy spent fighting battles that often seem ill chosen or unwinnable; and yet, at the same time, I am fairly certain that were I sitting where my students are, I would be making most of the same arguments they do, in much the same way, and, perhaps, for much the same reason. In *Balm in Gilead,* Sarah Lawrence Lightfoot's moving biography of her mother, Margaret, we are told what it was like to grow up in a relatively privileged black family in racist, segregated Vicksburg, Mississippi: "One of Margaret's worlds—the black community—felt abundant and rewarding. The other—the white world—was recognized as dehumanizing but experienced as largely irrelevant." And the reason Margaret could rise above the slights of the white world was simple: "She did not feel the daily assaults of exclusion because she did not want to be part of it."[13]

I think that our difficulty—the difficulty for black students across the country, the difficulty for black professionals like myself—is that we are not in Margaret's situation. If the white world is dehumanizing, that *is* relevant to us. We feel its daily assaults because, whatever our protestations, we *do* want to be part of that world. That is why we made the choice to go to college and, for many of us, to professional school. The day is gone when large numbers of black students see themselves as the vanguard of a revolution; what students want now, and with reason, is a piece of the action. So do I. If you want to get on the inside, the racial slights and offensive comments of insiders are bound to hurt a little more. They build up a barrier, at the very moment when we are being assured on all sides that the opportunities are all there for those of us who will go out and seize them. The truth is that more and more opportunities *are* there, the civil rights movement has won them—which is precisely why the comments hurt, for they are ungentle reminders that there are many people who would prefer to see those opportunities disappear. So what all of us must keep in mind is that the racist comments will not hurt us nearly as much as they would if we wanted to get in but weren't allowed.

Our parents and their parents fought to breach the barrier, faced far worse than we must, and won the fight. To honor them, perhaps, we must alter slightly the terms on which Margaret lived; we must strive not to feel the daily assaults even though we *do* want to be a part of the world that generates them—perhaps *because* we want to be a part of that world. We have little time to spend chasing down racists and punishing their speech. The barriers are starting to come down, opportunities are opening up, and there is work to be done.

III

Words do wound, and wounds do fester. But behind the words are the ideas that the words symbolize, and the ideas are always more dangerous than the words. Consider what is perhaps the best example of what on campus has come to be thought of as racist scholarship: the assertion that the concept of a measurable general intelligence (denoted g) is real and is determined predominantly by inheritance, and that black folks tend to have less g than white folks do. The classic instance of this position would be the once-fashionable psychological and anthropological theories of the innate intellectual inferiority of black people.

These theories, given much of their modern intellectual content by Cyril Burt and Arthur Jensen, were adopted and popularized in the 1960s by the late William Shockley, who had won the Nobel Prize in physics back in the 1950s for his pioneering work on the transistor but who became a public figure only as a result of the IQ controversy. After many years in and out of private industry, he at last settled into an academic position at Stanford University. There he began to branch out, moving away from the field of electrical engineering where he had made vitally important scientific contributions and musing instead (the reason was never clear, and doesn't matter) on the relationship among intelligence, inheritance, and race. What he finally decided was that the mean intelligence of black people is significantly below that of white people, and that this result is so heavily influenced by genetic inheritance that it is folly to imagine that environmental factors can do much to change it.

It is important, in any discussion of Shockley, to distinguish what is common ground among psychologists—that a substantial amount of the average measured aptitude differences between the black and the white populations cannot currently be explained—from the thesis that the explanation for the difference resides in the different average genetic endowment of the white and the black populations. Put simply, Shockley's thesis was that white people on average score higher on intelligence tests because, on average, they are more intelligent, and they are more intelligent because they are born that way. This theory continues to have academic adherents, albeit fewer than it once did, perhaps because it has not stood up to the evidence or perhaps because, as Richard Herrnstein has recently suggested, it is the social science equivalent of obscenity.

But Shockley was engaged in more than an academic exercise. He also had a policy proposal, which he described as a thought experiment. Shockley was worried about the possibility of "retrogressive evolution through the disproportionate reproduction of the genetically disadvantaged."[14] To avoid this threat, he proposed that parents who scored below 100 on IQ tests be paid by the government not to reproduce. The lower the scores, the higher the payment: $1,000 per IQ point would do, he said, for a "thinking exercise." This way, only the most intelligent parents would bear children, and—as long as one grants the inheritability of g—the nation's mean intelligence would rise. True, black people would receive a grossly disproportionate share of the cash payments for declining to bear children, but that, according to Shockley, was simply the luck of the draw. In fact, he argued, black people would be better off under his proposal:

> To fail to use a potentially effective means of diagnosis for fear of being called a racist is irresponsible. It may also be a great injustice to black Americans themselves. If those Negroes with the fewest Caucasian genes are in fact the most prolific and also the least intelligent, then genetic enslavement will be the destiny of their next generation. The consequences may be extremes of racism and agony for both blacks and whites.[15]

To many of his critics, Shockley's ideas did not bear discussion. This was not because they were bad science—most of the loudest critics lacked the training and, I suppose, the dispassion to determine that—but because they were perceived to be dangerous. They were, in fact, routinely described as genocidal. That danger, in turn, made them bad science, in the political, not the scientific, sense. It also made them unworthy of debate.

Similarly, I take it that many of today's critics of campus racism would have little trouble concluding that Shockley's view is the sort that should be excluded from campus discourse. A literal reading of the codes of conduct adopted by some schools to control racial harassment would strongly suggest that expressing support for the idea of innate black intellectual inferiority is *already* forbidden. (I note in passing, however, that Mari Matsuda, one of the most thoughtful academic critics of racist speech, has argued that such views as Shockley's should *not* be excluded, as long as there is plausible scientific support for them—a welcome voice of reason in a rather discordant chorus of fury.)[16] Certainly the critics of this vision were right during the 1970s, and are right now, to insist that the theory of innate intellectual inferiority is a terribly harmful idea, and they are right, too, to say that there are racists in the world who are willing to seize on it to further oppressive designs. But no amount of danger can make the idea wrong; no matter how wicked a weapon it might appear, a hydrogen bomb will explode all the same. Similarly, no amount of danger *to black people* can make the idea racist; it is quite likely that racists would endorse it, but that does not make everyone who endorses it a racist. If Shockley and the latter-day theorists who agree with him are wrong, it is not because their ideas are frightening.

Back when Shockley's views were creating a small sensation in the academic universe, those colleges that gave him a platform were hotly criticized, and he was prevented from debating or even speaking at others. Evidently the marketplace of ideas, then as now, had little space for ideas considered particularly pernicious. I was an undergraduate at Stanford when Shockley was there, and although I rarely dared say so, I sometimes found myself wondering how much of the fear of debate was really a fear that this admittedly brilliant Nobel Laureate might make a convincing case. I, too, wanted his ideas to be false, but I wanted them to be *shown* to be false. Eventually, the spectacle of politically correct people fleeing from confrontation with Shockley became depressing.

Stanford finally gave Shockley his platform. A debate was arranged in the main campus auditorium. In addition to Shockley, the speakers included a rabble-rousing psychologist who happened to be black and a world-renowned geneticist who happened to be white. The audience was largely black and noticeably nervous. I was there and I was nervous too. Shockley proceeded to make mincemeat of the psychologist, to the dismay of the audience, who seemed to be rooting for the polemical view. (Among the claims by the psychologist was the assertion that Shockley harbored secret fears of black superiority. A good part of the audience went wild with pleasure over this point, as it did over his thinly veiled threat to discuss some personal problem that a member of Shockley's family had evidently suffered.)

But the geneticist in his turn made mincemeat of Shockley's arguments—such utter mincemeat, in fact, that I began to wonder what all the talk of dangerousness was about.

Shockley came across as bitter and hostile and rather befud-
dled, a sad old man who as a geneticist probably made a pretty
good physicist. It was then that I began to perceive the possibility that justice, even in the sense of winning the battle
against racism, would come only through confronting the
truth. (I recognize that this must seem terribly obvious, and
in retrospect, it strikes me as even banal; but, arrogant undergraduate that I was, I thought at the time that I had reached
an epiphany.) The point is not that Shockley's arguments
were correct—they were nonsense[17]—but rather that the decision to dismiss them, if indeed they were to be dismissed,
should have been made on the ground of scientific error, not
on the ground of racist effect. Put otherwise, the mere fact
that his theories were unattractive should have had no bearing
on whether they were accepted as true.

   Moreover, if his theories had turned out to have more
scientific merit than they did, that would have been the beginning, not the end, of policy debate. I am reminded of an essay
by the historian Loren Graham discussing a hypothetical geneticist in Nazi Germany who must decide whether to reveal
publicly his discovery that Tay-Sachs disease, a genetic dis-
order, is more common among Jews than other population
groups. He knows that going public will simply play into the
hands of those who are seeking to prove the inferiority of the
Jewish "race." In those circumstances, says Graham, whether
to publish and to whom to send reprints "become moral acts
. . . because of the possible impact in that particular political
setting of this purely scientific (not technological) finding."[18]
The clear implication is that the hypothetical geneticist ought
not publish the fruits of his research.

   Maybe, maybe not; in either case, there is an unmentioned second step. Once the researcher has made the decision
to publish the research, the rest of the scientific community,
and the political community as well, must decide how to respond. Here, as with Shockley, it is not enough to cry, "Look
at the damage you are doing!"—for once the idea is out, it can
hardly be withdrawn. Moreover (as students in my courses on
law and science argue whenever we discuss Graham's hypo-

thetical), it probably stretches an otherwise interesting point
to suggest that on Graham's facts, at least, the researcher
could make matters any worse by publishing; for the regime
was determined to have its Holocaust and hardly could have
been affected either way.

The possibility that the consequences of a piece of knowledge might be reasonably foreseeable does not alter the plain
truth that there is a distinction between information and policy. The short of the matter is that the problem represented
by Shockley was captured only dimly by the cry that his views
were racist; the real fear was that his views might have racist
consequences, because real racists in the world might use them
to defend racist policies. But if that was the problem, then the
enemy was not Shockley or his views but racism itself, and the
fight to suppress his views was poorly chosen and ultimately
irrelevant. For if those who would use power for racial oppression really have so firm a hold on the levers that allow
them to make policy—as they did in Nazi Germany—then
they will make their policies with or without scientific support.

I V

The charge that the word *racism* is overused has become so
commonplace that it is virtually a cliché; Shelby Steele has
recently devoted much of a fascinating book to attacking the
overuse of the word,[19] and the defenders of the traditional literary canon—the set of works that are, in Matthew Arnold's
much-quoted, much-criticized, and much-misunderstood dic-
tum, "the best that is known and thought in the world"—have
had a field day mocking the way the word is used by critics of
conventional humanities courses. It would be nice to dismiss
the cliché as a canard, except for the embarrassing fact that it
happens to be true. In the eyes of some black activists, the
prosecution of Marion Barry, the mayor of Washington,
D.C., on drug charges was racist; according to others, criticizing Jesse Jackson for his entanglement with Louis Farra-

khan, the anti-Semitic leader of the Nation of Islam, was racist; indeed, some activists even say that calling Farrakhan anti-Semitic is racist. With so many false cries of racism around, it is hardly any wonder that the *true* examples of racism—for example, the thoroughly documented tendency of sentencing juries in capital cases to value the lives of white murder victims far more highly than the lives of black ones—tend to be drowned in the sea of less compelling complaints.

Campuses are no exception. There is all too much real racism around—it is hard, although some foolish people have unfortunately tried, to dismiss as hazing pranks with no racial content several incidents in which white students have donned bedsheets and told black students they are members of the Ku Klux Klan ready to lynch them—but it is often lost amid cries that one classroom comment or another is racist or sexist. A couple of years ago, a group of students at Yale Law School asked the administration to keep a list of wrongful classroom comments, and any number of students have complained that the law school provides no formal mechanism for students who are offended by a professor's words to challenge them. (Challenging the professor in class is not a useful option, the students explain, because of intimidation, which is about as tautological, in the strict sense, as a claim can be.)

Russell Baker, as I noted earlier, has proposed that racism has become in the 1990s what communism was in the 1950s, and I very much fear that he is right. We have reached a point where the accusation of racism is treated as a conclusion of fact; and the fact is thought sufficient to warrant punishment, perhaps even dismissal. Tenured professors are expected to go to considerable rhetorical lengths to prove that they are not racist, heterosexist, or Eurocentric. Classroom "insensitivity"—that is, in the professor's choice of words—is something that schools are told they ought to be monitoring, and even correcting when matters get out of hand.

I admit that there are days when my heart is with those who want to force racists from every position of authority in any institution. Racism is, after all, a force of great evil and misery in the world, a denial of the human spirit. The word *racism* conjures visions of slave auctions, lynchings, Bull Connor's dogs, relocation camps for Japanese-Americans, P. W. Botha's riot police. But one of the troubling aspects of being an intellectual is that my head does not always follow my heart, and I sense trouble ahead if the argument for excluding racists is accepted too blithely. The trouble is that communism, to take only the most obvious example, is also a force of evil and misery in the world, and if one added up all the people murdered or oppressed in this century because of racism and all the people murdered or oppressed in this century because of communism, it is by no means obvious which way the balance would be struck between these two great forces for destruction of the human spirit. Certainly there is good reason to think that as much damage as racism has lately done, communism has done even more; but I would not suppose that we should on that account drum Communists out of academia. And if the horror of communism does not mean that we should shunt Communists away from our faculties, I do not see how the horror of racism can mean that we should bar racists.

Another possible explanation for treating racists differently is that racists will treat their students differently, in accordance with the professor's particular definition of race. Given the chance to be a professor, a racist might use students as a foil for racist hostility, or perhaps treat them in accord with some stereotyped notion of black folk. I would certainly agree that the teacher who gives a student a higher grade because of skin color has no place in academia, although I think I would make the same argument about teachers who punish students for disagreeing with them or who reward them for their fealty—sins not unknown in academia, and by no means restricted to professors of any particular political persuasion. And besides, racism is not the only ideology that might lead a professor to treat students differently according to criteria that ought to be irrelevant. Should we examine politics? What, for example, should be a school's response when a candidate is a believer in the old Leninist doctrine of entryism, moving into institutions in order to subvert them?

I have never believed that rhetorical questions are valid forms of argument, and I do not expect what we call in the law slippery-slope arguments to do our thinking for us. So let me put the intellectual difficulties to one side and simply say that I think that if a professor is genuinely racist in the sense of bearing enmity toward students of color, that predisposition is so likely to interfere with pedagogy that it would be irresponsible (as well as pedagogically foolish) to allow the professor to indulge it. And however one might evaluate the threat to America and its liberties actually posed by communism at the height of the cold war, the threat posed by racism has, for people of color, always been more than hypothetical. Whatever the case with those of other troubling predispositions—and they are troubling—I am quite clear that real racists, people who bear ill will to some of their students, shouldn't be hired.

But not everybody who is called a real racist is a real racist, and if we don't recover the distinction between ideas that are racist and ideas that are uncomfortable, we risk losing far more than the exploration of ideas that our refusal to be serious will discourage. We risk, too, losing the moral high ground from which real racism can be condemned. Whom do we rally to our side to battle the real racism of the white supremacist movement when many of those who should be standing with us are said to be racists because they have criticized Jesse Jackson? Who will be convinced that only juror assumptions about race can explain racial disparities in capital sentencing if our natural allies in academia stand accused of racism themselves, for the sin of questioning the wisdom of diversity in the sense of representation?

The equivalences that the grammar of preferences forces upon us are ultimately absurd. No matter how cleverly the case is put by smart theorists who know their way around an argument—and it *is* put, cleverly and frequently—opposition to affirmative action cannot be transformed into the same animal as support for segregation. The differences are of kind, not of degree, or if they are differences in degree, they are sufficiently vast that they ought to be treated as differences in kind. The alternative is moral disaster: for if everyone is equally guilty, then everyone is equally innocent.

V

My more mature and far wiser colleagues tell me that these things are cyclical, that the occasional upsurge in student activism is natural, perhaps even desirable, to shake us all from our academic complacency. I suppose there is something to this. It is easy for a tenured professor to hide away in an academic sinecure, gradually losing all connection with the world beyond the ivy-covered walls. Perhaps being shaken up is not a bad thing—now and then. I'm not sure that a *continuing* revolution is much to be desired, but intermittent ones might serve the valuable purpose of making all of us rethink our ideas. Not necessarily to change them—that isn't the point—but to think about them more deeply than before.

Moreover, at the risk of offending students whom I know to be very sincere, there is the occasional smattering of trendiness in the intellectual fashions that are presented as revolutionary. And there are always those who will follow fashion. Not many of the New Left activists of the 1960s are members of the rather fragmented left of the 1990s, and indeed, some of them are at the core of the fragmenting neoconservative movement. Many more have moved on to well-paying professional sinecures where they work much too hard to worry about revolutionary precepts. Over time, people do seem to move toward the center.

Still, that tentative assurance doesn't make the current wave of racist and sexist hunting any easier to live through, especially, I suppose, for its targets. What am I to say to my flabbergasted colleague who was informed by a student that it is racist to make explicit mention of any "minority group" in class? Or to the unhappy professor who was told that it is sexist to use the word *date* to describe what I suppose we might call instead a voluntary temporary nocturnal association of a romantic nature between two individuals with differing secondary sexual characteristics? Or to another who was accused of racial insensitivity for referring to Watts as a ghetto—the student accuser evidently committing the popular semantic confusion of *ghetto* with *slum?* And what, for that matter, am I to say to my students, whose anguish and frustration are evident when they raise such protests?

I have no answers, at least not yet. Still, I am reasonably sanguine—not to say cynical—about the future. Capitalism will co-opt most of the current activists, because that is what capitalism does best. Liberalism will learn from them, absorbing what is valuable in their ideas and discarding what is not, because that is what liberalism does best. And, God willing, something over a decade from now, my own children, rebelling angrily on college campuses, will be lamenting the demise of "real" student radicalism—you know, the kind they had back in the 1980s and 1990s.

PART III

On Solidarity and Reconciliation

How did it happen that we quarreled?
We two who loved each other so!
　　　　　　　—*Jessie Fauset,*
　　　　　　　　Words! Words!

CHAPTER 9

The Special Perspective

Traitors/patriots, dissenters/loyalists, neoconservatives/left-radicals: it is past time, surely, for black people to put an end to these efforts to divide us. Our task is to reconcile and, having done so, to work toward building a reconciled solidarity, a coalition built not on our agreement on a program, not on our willingness to profess a particular viewpoint, but on our shared love of our people and our culture. For although the diversity movement has many faults, and although those faults can lead down unhappy paths, it nevertheless possesses an underlying theme that seems to me unexceptionable.

I have in mind the notion that people of color are marked and tied together by a shared history and, to a lesser extent, by a shared present of racial oppression. We cannot shrug off this history the way a snake sheds its skin, and we shouldn't want to. I want my children to grow up in a world in which they are confident that nothing is closed to them, and I frankly believe that virtually nothing will be; but I do not want them ever to forget that generations of our people have suffered and sacrificed to build that world, and that the forces that would hold them back, while put to rout (no, one *can't* fairly draw parallels between the Reagan era, whatever its many problems, and the years of slavery and Jim Crow), still lurk in the shadows, looking for chances and occasionally taking them, and will continue to do so for as much of the future as my children and their children are likely to see. I want them to understand their rich culture and glorious history, and I want to steel them against the many forces that will seek to deny and distort both.

So, yes, a history of oppression (but also of triumph) is our shared legacy, and a certain uneasy vigilance is our responsibility to our progeny. Black people, says Alice Walker, can be "middle class in money and position, but they cannot afford to be middle class in complacency."[1] These aspects of our situation undoubtedly combine to produce a predictable, if not always unique, perspective on any number of issues, explaining everything from why black people in such overwhelming numbers vote Democratic to why opinion surveys show black people far less supportive of the death penalty than white people are.

If one wants a further example, consider the case of William Coleman, a lion of the corporate bar, a wealthy partner in one of the nation's most exclusive law firms, tailored and elegant, a Republican to his fingertips. Coleman, who is black, was an avowed supporter of President Reagan, but nevertheless felt compelled to testify—indeed, in effect to lead the charge, for his was by far the most effective testimony—against the nomination of Robert Bork as an Associate Justice of the Supreme Court. Opening his prepared statement, Coleman (who had been courted by both sides) explained his decision to oppose the nomination:

> I have tried very hard to avoid this controversy. The Supreme Court has played such an important role in ending so many of the horribly racially discriminatory practices that existed when I first came to the bar. As one who has benefitted so greatly from this country's difficult but steady march towards a free, fair and open society, the handwriting on the wall— *"mene mene tekel upharsin"* ["thou art weighed in the balances and found wanting"]—would condemn my failure to testify against Judge Bork.[2]

I do not mean to suggest that Coleman's blackness created
some compulsion to oppose the nomination; Bork certainly
had his black supporters. (I took no position on the nomination, although I did find much of the campaign against Bork,
excepting the reasoned and stirring testimony of Coleman and
some others, a triumph of rhetorical excess.)[3] But the example
of Coleman's own explanation for his decision emphasizes the
main point: our shared history of oppression might affect us
in different ways, but affect us it does.

So, again, I do not deny that the shared history that
helps define us makes black people different from white people. My quarrel with the diversity forces is that it is far from
evident to me how any of this translates into a single, genuine,
preferred black perspective, a voice that is specially to be
valued, to be sought out for celebration when other voices are
not. We are by no means the only group in society that has
suffered and drawn a perspective from its suffering, and different groups will define hierarchies of suffering in sharply
different ways. Other than the fact that it makes our lives
(and arguments) easier, there is no *a priori* reason to prefer
our vision of suffering to any other. Perhaps we should be
looking for commonalities of suffering rather than parading
our uniqueness. But the unhappy truth is that too much has
been allowed for too long to turn on whether or not the suffering of black people is unique.

To see why this must be so, consider the matter the other
way around: if all people who have suffered have suffered in
essentially similar ways, then it is difficult to explain why the
law should treat some sufferers differently than others. Perhaps others who have suffered the predations of racial oppression might be admitted to share in the uniqueness—but no one
else. Special treatment for everyone, after all, means special
treatment for no one. Everything from minority set-aside programs to diversity to good old-fashioned political solidarity
rests in some way on the claim of uniqueness. Thus it ought to
be unsurprising that many black people find the notion of
commonality of suffering profoundly threatening. If we lose
our claim to have suffered in ways that are unique in history

(so the fear must run), then how much else of our hard-won political ground will we have to surrender?

The claim that the suffering of black folk is unique grounds much of the current civil rights agenda. We were dragged here unwillingly on slave ships, our culture has been forcibly abolished, our education prohibited in one century and inferior in the next, our general unfitness for the ordinary occupations of life drummed into us relentlessly for centuries, so that we have very nearly been destroyed as a people. We are society's victims. Consequently, racial preferences and other special programs are described as payment for a debt that society owes us, and whether society pays out of guilt or out of simple justice, pay it must, because we have been wronged like no people before.*

To expunge the debt, the society must recognize our claim on a share of such scarce resources as jobs with real prospects of advancement and education in the most selective programs of the best professional schools. The underlying assumption is that the problems the rest of the world has caused are problems the rest of the world must solve. Life may be unfair and, in the words of the aphorism, tests may measure the results, but according to the argument from difference, those are only interim results; the world that has caused the unfairness must come back later and adjust the scores.

The claim of uniqueness takes the majority's historical insistence on the difference between black and white and tries to make it work the other way. Once upon a time, the nation justified its oppression of us on the ground that we were different than they. It is easier to make it a crime to teach a black person to read once you are prepared to concede that it is not possible to do so. Well, fine, the argument concludes: you treated us as different then; you will choke on those dif-

---

*Sometimes this proposition takes on bizarre proportions. As an undergraduate, I was part of a group of black students who went to complain to a history professor who had made the suggestion in a lecture that slavery in Brazil was far harsher than slavery in the United States. Quite apart from the point that he was of course exactly right, it is plain that politics was driving our evaluation of the facts: he had to be wrong because it was inconvenient for him to be right. To his credit, he did not apologize for insensitivity, as faculty members today seem to do all the time; instead, he told us some things that we should read.

ferences now. And in the era of affirmative-action-as-diversity, the idea of celebrating the things that make us different is more than a rallying cry. It is also a critique of accepted understandings, a demand for a share in the interpretation of the world. It says we matter. Our oppression makes our world different from yours and our voice different from yours. Those differences matter.

Again, this is in a sense unexceptionable; history *does* make black people different from white people. But it is both wrong and dangerous to insist that it makes us different in some predictable, correctly black way. And, for reasons I shall explain, it is also wrong, and potentially quite dangerous as well, to insist that our differentness is to be more valued than anybody else's.

II

The idea of difference, and its importance, has been worked out more fully by feminist scholars than by those propounding what might be called the racial critique. Most prominent is perhaps the hugely controversial work of the psychologist Carol Gilligan, who contends that from early childhood, males and females evidence markedly different forms of moral reasoning.[4] Gilligan has her critics, including psychologists who have questioned her methodology or conducted independent studies that they describe as throwing doubt on her results.[5] Other critics are fearful of the uses to which their opponents might put the notion that there is some fundamental distinction between the way men and women analyze problems.[6]

A vision similar to Gilligan's was long ago seized upon by scholars asserting the "point of view" of the putatively oppressed black community. Although much of the analysis of the significance of difference requires considerable erudition to be understood, the underlying proposition manifests a rough-and-ready common sense that probably reflects the day-to-day experience of vast numbers of people in our "us and them" society.

The difference approach proposes, for example, that writers who are white and writers who are not are on opposite sides of an unbridgeable chasm, that their experiences of reality diverge so sharply that beyond a certain, limited point, a shared understanding is virtually impossible. Black (and other nonwhite) writers are said to have different voices from white ones, to think and speak and, of course, write in a way that reflects their backgrounds. They see some things—those related to their oppression, those related to their culture— more sharply than others possibly can. A just society, then, according to this approach, would take account of that difference rather than seek to silence it.

This vision of difference presupposes the existence of what is often called the "black experience," a uniquely black reality that has shaped in similar ways the lives of all people who are black. The black experience, it is said, cannot possibly be fathomed by anyone who is white. A classic statement of this proposition is in Stokely Carmichael and Charles Hamilton's 1967 book *Black Power:*

> Our point is that no matter how "liberal" a white person might be, he cannot ultimately escape the overpowering influence— on himself and on black people—of his whiteness in a racist society.
>
> Liberal whites often say that they are tired of being told "you can't understand what it is to be black." They claim to recognize and acknowledge this. Yet the same liberals will often turn around and tell black people that they should ally themselves with those who can't understand, who share a sense of superiority based on whiteness.[7]

Plainly, this idea has the advantage of silencing critics. The three magic words, "You can't understand," free the object of criticism from the need to seek a dialogue with those who disagree; the fact of oppression becomes its own authority.

Like the claim of gender difference, the claim of racial difference has its critics. They challenge, for example, the premise of a monolithic black experience that has shaped all black people in ways that make them more like one another than like people who are white.[8] The idea of difference, more-over, carries a very real risk of stigmatizing and perhaps even "ghettoizing" black intellectuals. If they—white intellectu-als—can't do what we—black intellectuals—do, then perhaps we can't do what they do, either. Harold Cruse must have been painfully aware of this possibility over two decades ago when he wrote in *The Crisis of the Negro Intellectual:*

> Even at this advanced stage in Negro history, the Negro intel-lectual is a retarded child whose thinking processes are still geared to piddling intellectual civil writism [*sic*] and racial in-tegrationism. This is all he knows. In the meantime, he plays second and third fiddle to white intellectuals in all the estab-lishments—Left, Center, and Right. The white intellectuals in these establishments do not recognize the Negro intellectual as a man who can speak both for himself and for the best interests of the nation, but only as someone who must be spoken for and on behalf of.[9]

Small wonder that black intellectuals might be seen this way, if our claim is that we speak, in effect, in a language that oth-ers cannot hope to understand.

Besides, there is something vaguely derisive in the con-clusion that those of us who are black intellectuals are stuck with doing things in one way, forever marked by race. Ed-ward Shils, writing at about the same time as Cruse, surely recognized this when he observed:

> [M]embers of the various communities in the major areas of intellectual life evaluate intellectual performance with little or no reference to nationality, religion, race, political party, or class. An African novelist wants to be judged as a novelist, not an African; a Japanese mathematician would regard it as an affront if an analysis of his accomplishment referred to his pig-mentation; a British physicist would find it ridiculous if a judgment on his research referred to his being "white."[10]

This was obviously a hope, not a statement of fact, and as hopes go, it was a good one. But Shils's closing prediction—that "primordial attachment to color . . . will survive but not so strongly as to deflect the intellect and imagination from their appropriate activities"[11]—is precisely what theorists of difference deny. And in that denial, they implicitly condemn all scholars of color to a narrow and unhappy path, writing mostly for one another rather than for a universal audience, and never able to aspire to a higher goal than, for example, best *black* economist.*

Theorists who believe that difference means a common perspective face a further and more fundamental difficulty. Without a good deal of sidestepping and rhetorical excess, they are unable to account for the work of such prominent black critics of racial preferences and other aspects of the civil rights orthodoxy as Glenn Loury, Thomas Sowell, and Shelby Steele. Has the black experience touched them? Does it touch their work? Ah, well, perhaps they have surrendered to the racist society, sold out. In any event, the problem must be with them, the dissenters, and not with the theory that the black experience has shaped us all in similar ways. The notion that reasonable minds, even reasonable black minds, might differ over some part of the dominant civil rights agenda is treated by theorists of difference as worse than absurd—why, it isn't even worth mentioning!

The diversity theorists will very likely have similar trouble accounting for the work of Julius Lester, who is nobody's conservative, neo- or otherwise, but nevertheless is evidently a critic of difference, and on grounds that are quite instructive. In 1988, as I discussed earlier, Lester published *Lovesong,* a fine book in which he chronicled his evolution from a rather chic and trendy spokesman for the black separatist movement in the 1960s to his recent conversion to Judaism—and, along the way, his estrangement from the remnants of the movement he had once helped lead. His narrative is a statement of the universality of human experience—including the suffering and oppression that are said by scholars of difference to be

---

*In a story that might be apocryphal, but is too good to pass up, it is said that Thomas Sowell hung up on a member of Ronald Reagan's staff who telephoned him shortly after the 1980 election to inform him that the new president wanted Sowell to be his first black cabinet member.[12]

crucial to creating the different voices in which different communities speak. But for Julius Lester, different communities speak *to* one another, and there are messages for those prepared to listen.

Thus, although he wonders as he prepares a seder whether "a Gentile can understand Judaism and Jewishness," his conclusion is a rejection of the idea that the uniqueness of black experience makes white understanding impossible:

> The thought is as repugnant to me as when blacks tell whites they cannot know what it is to be black. It is a statement that negates literature, art and music, nullifies the realm of the imaginative and says it is impossible for human beings to reach out from one loneliness to another and assuage both. If that were true, I would not see aspects of myself in haiku and the poems of Sappho, the music of Bach and the watercolors of Winslow Homer.[13]

The point of this passage, and a good one, is surely not that the scholars of difference are wholly wrong, but that the experiences that make us different do not make us unable to understand or appreciate one another. Jack Greenberg *can* successfully teach a course on law and race, and can even describe a part of the perspective of people of color. Jonathan Pryce, a white actor whose award-winning performance in a nonwhite role nearly led to the cancellation of the Broadway musical *Miss Saigon, can* successfully and authentically portray a Eurasian on the stage. Daniel Lewis James *can* learn what it is like to live in a barrio and write about it. As Felix Gutierrez, then a professor at the University of Southern California, said of the James incident: "You don't have to be a Latino to write on the Latino experience, and Latinos should not write only on that. There's nothing to stop an Anglo from writing authentically about it if he spends the time. That's the key, get to know us."[14]

Get to know us. Why not? For those who care to, it isn't that hard. People of color are not mysterious; our world is not impenetrable. But we do have background and experiences and visions that it is important to share, not as cartoon characters who are all alike, not as representatives of our people but simply as people ourselves. Difference, in short, is a bridgeable chasm. It is bridged when we "reach out from one loneliness to another," not in anger, not in frustration, not in hatred, but in love; not lifting the world up by its ears but touching it on its human heart.

Still, in order to be useful, the bridge must finally be built not simply in the mind of the observer but in the world; the decision might begin with emotion, but it must end with will. This, surely, is what the theologian David Tracy had in mind when he noted that "[e]mpathy is much too romantic a category to comprehend this necessary movement . . . from otherness, to possibility, to similarity-in-difference."[15] Bridging the chasm is a choice, and not always an easy one. But it is not enough just to look at the one who is different, the lonely, suffering other, and say, "Gee, that's too bad" or "Gee, I understand." For Lester, as for Tracy, the triumph over difference is finally a social act as well as a spiritual one.

Armed with the notion of difference as a chasm to be bridged, one can readily imagine an impressive panoply of lines that might be blurred or crossed by a world willing to proclaim, "We love you because you are different; we love your differentness; we value it; we want to learn from it." The continuing struggle to mend the division between black and white in the United States is only one such border crossing. The gay and lesbian rights movement and efforts to empower the homeless are plainly others. Difference ought to have a human face, and people should talk to each other.

There are borders to be crossed, fences to be mended, bridges to be built within our community as well as outside, for we who are black fairly sparkle with an internal diversity that the rest of the world, so often stuck in its obsession with stereotypes, seems to ignore. We should not make the same mistake ourselves; we should love and value *us,* black people in all of our diversity: rich, poor, gay, straight, religious, secular, left, right. For it is none of these distinctions that define our blackness; what defines us, rather, is the society's attitude toward us—all of us are black before we are anything else—

and our attitude toward ourselves, toward our culture, toward one another. We are defined by the choices we make.

In my other life as a scholar of the Constitution, I am fond
of quoting a metaphor from the late Alexander Bickel, and it
seems appropriate to repeat it here. In *The Morality of Consent,*
published in 1975 just after his death, Bickel warned the courts
not to ignore popular response to their decisions. The public reaction, Bickel argued, is an important part of an "endlessly re-
newed educational conversation" between the judges and the
public that must choose whether to obey their edicts. For Bickel,
a lasting and insistent chorus of protest was evidence that something was wrong, that perhaps the judges had made an error.
Thus he added the stern admonition that the dialogue he envisioned "is a conversation, not a monologue."[16]

We who are black, rather than establishing a hierarchy of
"correct" or "more valuable" black views, should adopt the same
model. We should be having a conversation, not a monologue,
and certainly not this bitter argument. We should talk to each
other rather than at each other. We should make our shared love
for our people the center of our belief, and use that shared center
as a model for the possibility of a solidarity that does not seek to
impose a vision of the right way to be black.

The task that faces us, then, long before we can insist
that the rest of the world shop for our perspective(s) in the
market, is to build a reconciled solidarity, a world in which an
appreciation of our differences, the attitudes and visions that
make black people unlike one another, is the focus of our efforts to re-create ourselves and our society. And who knows?
Our ability to love one another, whatever our politics and
policies, might finally serve as a model for the larger white
society which, in the rhetoric of diversity but also in fundamental fairness, is called upon to do the same thing.

III

The diversity movement is correct in insisting that the rest of
the world—including the academic and professional world,

but the larger nation as well—share in our own celebration of the aspects of our culture that mark us as special. But the point of appreciating difference is, or ought to be, that *everybody* is special. Every individual has a unique history, and so does every group. That wonderful truth is not something that should drive us apart, as racists have for too long tried to use it; it is, rather, something that should draw us together.

This much strikes me as both valuable and incontrovertible. The trouble with the diversity movement is that it goes on to insist that our specialness in effect *adds value* to us in a way that the specialness of other people does not. (If this is not true, then there is no reason for a university to search for excellent scholars who can tell our story, as the movement insists it should.) It is by taking this additional step, I think, that the diversity movement makes its analytical error, and the error, although subtle, is ultimately of sufficient import to make the theory unworkable. For there is no logical connection between the proposition that we are special people and the proposition that our voices are uniquely to be valued. The world is full of special people and all of their voices are unique.

The diversity movement proposes, however, that there are important reasons to value and search out people who can speak of *our* story, the most important among them being the fact of our oppression at the hands of people who are white. And it is that oppression that the cherishing of the special, excluded voice is meant to overcome.

But the supposition that it is white oppression of us, and our suffering under that oppression, that makes our perspective more to be valued, seems to me a rejection of the idea that recognizing difference can be a binding force, a form of love. There shouldn't be any hierarchy of suffering, not because no one person or group has any subjective sense of having suffered more than anyone else, and not because there are no moral standpoints from which to judge it, but because to make the fact of suffering the badge of authority defeats the purpose of valuing diversity. To try to impose a hierarchy— to say, in effect, "We have suffered more than you have, and you are not allowed to disagree"—is to make a potentially bitter contest of what ought to be a solemn and shared understanding.

This becomes a matter of practical importance when critics of affirmative action cite the experiences of other ethnic groups who have also been oppressed but who have, it is said, succeeded without the use of explicit preferences.[17] The responses from advocates fall into two categories: No, you are wrong, the other groups did benefit from preferences of some informal sort;[18] or, Yes, but that experience is not relevant because they have not suffered as we have. The second category seems to be the very tidy way in which the diversity movement steers away from a very slippery slope.

But the strategy of deciding who has suffered more entails considerable risk. To illustrate, I will borrow another story from Julius Lester, a story with no relation to the diversity movement, but one that many black people should find chillingly familiar nevertheless. Lester's most controversial thesis is his suggestion that the black community, or at least its leadership, is awash in anti-Semitic sentiment. It is tempting to dismiss his claim as lacking empirical support, as merely anecdotal, as a product of his understandable anger at his own treatment at the hands of the Afro-American Studies Department at the University of Massachusetts at Amherst, which I described in chapter 5. And yet there is a plausibility to Lester's suggestion that our community has some problems. Louis Farrakhan, who calls himself a man of God while weaving into his admirable gospel of self-reliance and self-esteem a stark and unmistakable thread of hate, does draw huge and enthusiastic audiences and sometimes his audience seems to be outnumbered by his apologists. Still, I believe (and also hope) that there is considerably less black anti-Semitism than Lester supposes, and in any case—and this is not to excuse any of us—in any case, the problem of black anti-Semitism is surely dwarfed by the problem of white anti-Semitism.[19]

But this is not the place to address that rather complex issue. I raise Lester's claim only as background to a story I wish to borrow from *Lovesong.* Lester describes a scene in which one of his colleagues, on reading an essay Lester wrote about black anti-Semitism, becomes apoplectic, and screams: "You think I haven't studied the Holocaust? Well, I have, goddamit! I don't see a damned thing about it that's unique. I think black folks have been through more hell than a Jew in Auschwitz could imagine."[20] Lester, by his own account, becomes so angry in return that he tells his colleague never to speak to him again.

There are many layers to the tragedy in that small story. The worst, probably, is the way his colleague insists on making suffering a competition. The argument is quite commonly made, and by no means by black people alone, that the Holocaust is not unique, that it is no worse in its way than, for example, the slaughter of the Hutu by the Tutsi or the Armenian genocide. But that is the same trap. The horror of the Holocaust does not lie in its uniqueness; the horror does not even need an explanation. It is plain on the face of history. The same can be said of the centuries of oppression of black folk in the Western world: the horror does not need an explanation. It is plain on the face of history. This does not mean that the oppressions are the same, but neither does it mean that they are different. Humanity has proved itself capable of perpetrating any number of horrors; and to those who suffer from them, each is unique. The error comes in assuming that it matters which one is the most horrible.

Is it anti-Semitic to criticize Jews for refusing to let the world forget the Holocaust? I would rather put the question another way: Why would anyone criticize Jews for refusing to let the world forget the Holocaust? God knows, we who are black ought never to let the world forget the African slave trade. Our responsibility is what Lester says it is: to share in the suffering of others. Thus, we who are black should also refuse to let the world forget the Holocaust; and we should insist that Jews join us in refusing to let the world forget the slave trade. Alliances among people traditionally despised are natural and important, and with good reason: had black people been present in Europe in significant numbers, Hitler would have had another project besides making the continent *judenrein,* for he despised us as well.*

This brings me back to the diversity movement, which does indeed seem to propose that we ought to make a contest of suffering, that we ought to value people of color specially because of the special nature of the oppression in our history. For a school to refuse to hire a scholar because she chooses to embrace a history of suffering would be a terrible wrong; but for a school to say that its faculty will be incomplete *unless* it hires one is to repeat, albeit on a smaller canvas, the wrong of Lester's colleague. For nothing about value or authority ought to turn on who has suffered more.

Our suffering might have marked us and it is surely a fact of history that we must never forget, but it is not a symbol of special worth. In the words of the philosopher Judith Shklar, "Victimhood happens to us: it is not a quality."[22] Besides, even were one to concede the unique value of the perspective that our suffering or even injury brings, there is an almost quaint sentimentality in the idea that the only shared inheritance from our past is a positive one. After all, when a taxi driver in New York City explains in the *Times* that he refuses to pick up black males as passengers because (according to a widely shared bit of suspicious data) black men are responsible for 85 percent of crimes against cabbies,[23] he also is making an assumption about the characteristics we share. The label that the driver proposes for our boxes may be more damaging than the one offered by the theorists of diversity, but that is a consequentialist judgment; there is no reason *in logic* that he cannot be as right as they.

There is a point here that is often overlooked in discussions about racial stereotyping. The popular image of stereotyping holds that an irrationally skewed reasoning process guides it. Gordon Allport, for example, in *The Nature of Prejudice* (1955), insisted that racial prejudice is "an antipathy based upon a faulty and inflexible generalization."[24] This ar-

*Early in 1942, Hitler told associates: "My feelings against Americanism are feelings of hatred and deep repugnance. . . . Everything about the behavior of American society reveals that it's half Judaized and the other half Negrified."[21]

gument suggests that the problem with racial stereotypes is overinclusivity, a judgment less normative than empirical. Racial stereotyping is bad, in this view, because it is irrational, and therein lies the difficulty: "Don't use them *because* they don't work" carries the same normative message as "Don't use them *if* they don't work." The implication is that there might lurk somewhere a set of better, more accurate stereotypes that should not be dismissed as involving "prejudice" because they are rational.

It is dangerous to suggest that racial categorizations, even negative ones, might be acceptable as long as a case can be made for rational fit between ends and means. If the result of a categorization is oppressive, the reality of that result has little to do with the rationality of the racialist categorizations that might have been involved in bringing it about. In those areas of human endeavor the law simply cannot reach with any practical effect—most areas of life traditionally, if suspiciously, considered private—virtually anyone who makes a judgment about anyone else that rests on race will believe the judgment to be a rational one.

In this sense, the diversity movement runs into the trouble that has bedeviled every effort to define the special shared characteristics that would justify preferential treatment for people of color. The peculiar language forced upon us by programs that treat people as members of groups and assign characteristics on the basis of that membership has an ugly mirror image, for it is as easy to assign negative characteristics as positive ones. Preferential treatment comes in two kinds, the kind we like and the kind we hate.[25] Both kinds have roots in the idea that race is a useful proxy for other information: in the early days of affirmative action, a proxy for disadvantage; today, a proxy for the ability to tell the story of the oppressed; and, to the taxi driver, a proxy for a high potential for criminality. That is why there has always been something unsettling about the advocacy of a continuation of racial consciousness in the name of eradicating it. The one thing that every version of racial preferences has in common, by definition, is an explicit consciousness of race; the programs *insist* that an employer or college or professional school take note of the race of an individual applicant. That might be a way to ensure minority representation or diversity or better opportunities or compensation for disadvantage, but it has little to do with getting people to stop thinking of others in racial terms.

There is a surface innocence to all of this, and certainly systems of racial preferences are not intended to denigrate either those permitted to benefit from them or those who are excluded. But although those who are excluded are plainly not victims of a system of racial subjugation, such as the one that long oppressed people of color, they are just as plainly victims of racial discrimination, an entirely distinct wrong, but not a trivial one. The backlash against racial preferences is not trivial, either, and explaining it away as racism is just another way of silencing critics without debating them—and another sign that we are losing the moral high ground, for there was a time when the civil rights movement had no reluctance to debate. We must learn once more to love and cherish individuals for who they are, not for what they represent; and, having learned it once more ourselves, we can once more teach it to a doubting world.

CHAPTER 10

Special But Equal

I went to college a year too late to be part of what we used to call The Movement. The last massive antiwar demonstration at Stanford occurred in the spring just before my matriculation as thousands of students massed and marched along El Camino Real where it runs close to the campus. I read the headlines as I leafed through the heavy bound volumes of back issues at the offices of the *Stanford Daily,* the student newspaper, and I writhed with envy. I had missed so much! During my four years, students occupied no buildings, blocked no thoroughfares, and disrupted no classes. (There was a candlelight vigil to protest proposed changes in the school's financial aid policies, but that hardly counts.) Some of the old radical hands still hung around the campus, people who had lived on the fringes of the Venceremos Brigade and nurtured fond memories of tear gas cannisters fired by blue-helmeted police officers—in the parlance, "pigs" who needed to be "offed." (Some of these old hands were members of the faculty.) The old radicals complained that all my generation wanted was to get good grades and get a good job.

Perhaps we did, but many of us chafed at this blow to our self-images. I had spent my high school years literally in the shadow of Cornell University (our house was across a ravine from the campus, and Ithaca High School sprawled in the valley below), where SDS marched, it seemed, incessantly, and black students had just a few years earlier waved unloaded guns in the air as they marched into the sunlight (posing, to be sure, at the request of the news photographers), ending a takeover of the student union. Stanford, from the tales that I had heard, would surely be full of the same radical certainty: the people united would *never* be defeated.

Perhaps it was just as well for my self-image that I turned out to be wrong, for I was even then too much the loner (and, perhaps, too much the egotist) to see myself as simply one of the indefatigably united people. I had little interest in marching, really, and I did not want to be led. My consciously chosen (but often poorly informed) leftish stances were of a reflective and scholarly nature. So I fashioned a world where words would be my weapons, not realizing, or perhaps not wishing to believe, that I was guilty of the unholy sin of armchair radicalism. I wrote papers for my history courses about how Truman's racism led to the dropping of the atomic bombs on Hiroshima and Nagasaki. I encouraged the *Stanford Daily,* where I was for three years a member of the editorial board, to tweak the noses of the power structure by running editorials, for example, applauding student takeovers that occurred at Brown University and Spelman College (since we had none of our own); or chiding the United Nations General Assembly for adopting its "Zionism Is Racism" resolution, but only on the ground that the resolution would do more harm than good for the Palestinian cause (wiser heads prevailed, fortunately, and that editorial was pulled from the paper before it ran); and of course, dumping on Henry Kissinger, whatever he might be doing in a given week.

And for three years the *Daily* provided me space for a signed column, sometimes biweekly, sometimes weekly, sometimes semiweekly—we were not particularly well organized. From this pulpit I did my best to outrage the establishment on as many issues as possible, for a contrarian desire to shock, far more than reasoned ideology, was the nature of what I was bold to call my radicalism. Many of my columns were about race, most took positions on the left, but in my zeal to outrage, I attacked the darlings of the left as well as of the right, including a critique of what I considered Judge Sirica's inquisitorial tactics at the Watergate trial and, one of my favorites, a very controversial column entitled "The White Movement's Burden," in which I criticized the Stanford's radical left movement for trying to co-opt the various demands pressed upon the university by organizations representing students of color. As I read over my columns today, I blush at the boyish, and sometimes insensitive, enthusiasm of my untutored politics. (Although I was quite proud then, and still am today, of a series of columns criticizing the well-financed effort to bring back the Indian as the nickname and mascot of Stanford's sports teams. "Ethnic stereotypes," I wrote, "are inherently racist." We won that one.)

Given this contrarian, establishment-baiting background, I suppose I should have been less stunned than I was when I read late in 1990 that one of ten black New Yorkers surveyed agreed that the AIDS virus was "deliberately created in a laboratory to infect black people," and an additional 19 percent agreed that it might possibly be true.[1] But I was shocked and disappointed all the same, as much by the fear of my own irrelevance as by anything else. Here I am, arguing for an end to our divisions and for a world in which we who are black proclaim ourselves willing to face any standard, and I learn that nearly one of three black New Yorkers is willing to entertain seriously the preposterous and dangerous notion that AIDS is just another part of what black residents of Washington, D.C., have come to call simply "The Plan"—as in, "Yeah, they got Barry, that's another step in The Plan."

Back in the mid-1970s when I was in college, I suppose I might have agreed, or at least claimed to; certainly, I would have tried to concoct some plausible explanation for the survey results. Today, however, I can only shake my head, depressed by the realization that any argument calling for black people to stand proudly on our own achievements runs up against the widespread fear that white people will not give us a fair shake. I might propose the development of a cadre of black professionals too good to ignore, but there are plenty of black people who are certain that white employers are capable of finding ways to ignore any black person, no matter how good.

The fact that there is racism even in the professional labor market, however, only strengthens the case for committing ourselves to excellence. That way, even if some racists refuse to believe the evidence of the résumés before them, more rational employers will hire the excellent and available lawyers and investment bankers and architects who are people of color and, over time, drive the discriminating employers out of business.[2] A generation ago, this might have been nothing more than a naive economist's model, but today, with the increasing penetration of the professions, even at very high levels, by people who are not white, the scenario seems entirely plausible.

This is not to suggest that the racism problem will go away anytime soon. Racism has declared its presence in many millions of lives with stunning force and pervasiveness. Racism has an existential reality that has defied most attempts to discover its sources and explain its power. And if forced to offer an evaluation, even a potential source, I suppose that I must cast my lot with the elderly black woman who wrote in 1942: "Prejudice is one of the Devil's trump cards to increase misery, heartbreak, and unhappiness in this nether world, and he has succeeded admirably."[3] It might be, as more and more black professionals are insisting, that we are better off making our way in the corporate world without racial preferences, but the price of this particular liberty is likely to be our eternal vigilance: for we must continue to watch for signs of racism, which might erupt with virulence at any time. At the same time, we must be cautious about what we decide to call racism, what we decide to call racial discrimination, and what we must take as signs of life's unfairness with which we must deal in other ways.*

---

*In other work I have drawn a distinction between *racialism,* which involves using race as a proxy for other characteristics, positive or negative, and *racism,* which is the difference that the most damaging racialist distinctions make in the real world.[4]

II

There are aspects of our situation that do not reflect racism, at least on the part of anyone now living. It is a tragic fact that on almost every measure of socioeconomic achievement, the black community lags far behind the white community, and much of the explanation lies in the nation's racist legacy. But it is also true that if one disaggregates the statistics, the black professional class acquits itself rather well. Indeed, it is a well-known phenomenon that the more nonracial factors one holds constant (age, education, marital status, and the like), the smaller the gap between white and black. So one of the things that we must in our vigilance avoid is the easy generalization from statistical disparities. In this sense, the perfectly respectable use of statistics to assist in making out a *prima facie* case of employment discrimination has led to a conversational habit in which the mere existence of a disparity is said to be evidence that racial discrimination has occurred, rather than what it often is, evidence that discrimination of some other kind has a racially differential impact.

To take the purest example, the fact that no black person who has run for president of the United States has ever been elected, and that black people are therefore historically underrepresented in the presidency, provides no evidence of racial animus among the voters who make the selections. One might believe that voters are racially motivated, and the belief might even reflect reality, but one cannot assume the truth of the belief simply because of the statistics.

A good example of the misunderstanding of statistics occurred in 1988, when members of the Michigan legislature argued that they could tell from the numbers that the Detroit Symphony Orchestra was not doing all that it could to attract black classical musicians. Only discrimination, it seems, was a permissible explanation for the fact that the orchestra employed only one full-time black performer. Never mind that an entirely blind screening process was used to hire musicians; never mind that out of 5,000 orchestra-bound musicians at the nation's twenty-five top conservatories, only 100 were black, of whom a normal distribution would predict that perhaps a fifth—twenty—were good enough to play in a major orchestra.[5] The Detroit Symphony might have been the most racist institution in the world or the most racially benevolent one, but the statistics do not hold the answer.

Differential impact is not the same as discrimination that the law ought to forbid. Every policy has a differential impact on some group, and with a bit of work the group can nearly always be identified. But to conclude too quickly that whatever has a differential impact on black people ought to be forbidden—that, always, it is the world, not we, that must change—is to make a terrible mistake, not only in policy analysis but also in morality. To be sure, there are times when we should force the world to change for our benefit; but there are also times when we must recognize that the world will not change, and must, to avoid the differential impact that is so troubling, change ourselves.

This, I think, is where the New York branch of the National Association for the Advancement of Colored People made a sad error when, in 1986, it endorsed the Tobacco Institute's semantically correct but morally ridiculous position that ordinances that limit or forbid smoking in public places constitute discrimination against black people. The theory would be cute, were it not so dangerous: black people are significantly more likely than white people to smoke, so if one forbids smoking, one is barring black people at a higher rate than one is barring white people. Said Hazel Dukes, president of the New York NAACP, and a member of the Committee for Common Courtesy, created by the tobacco industry to fight against the ordinances, "[F]ines for anybody caught smoking someplace off limits would hurt minorities more."[6]

Well, yes: literally, this is correct. At the time of the New York debate, 39.6 percent of black men as against 31.6 percent of white men, and 31 percent of black women as against 28.1 percent of white women, were cigarette smokers.[7] So punishing their conduct does have a differential impact on black people, just as restricting the availability of any other drug to which black people are disproportionately addicted has a differential impact on black people. This is not commonly thought to be an argument against prohibiting the possession of crack.* Something on the order of 40,000 black people a year die of smoking-related diseases, a figure that dwarfs the tragically large number (perhaps 8,000) who are, for example, gunned down in what we like to call drug-related violence. The point is that these 40,000 black people who smoke themselves to death are also dying of drug addiction, only less violently. A law that limits the ability of all people to smoke actually has a *favorable* differential impact on black people, for if there is less opportunity to smoke, perhaps fewer of us will die of that particular addiction.

What is fascinating, and often overlooked, about the opposition of so many influential black New Yorkers to the smoking restrictions is that much of the opposition evidently had a basis not in any particular feeling about these laws but in a suspicion of white officialdom in general, and white health officials in particular.† Wilbert Tatum, the fiery and controversial publisher of the *Amsterdam News,* New York's principal black-owned newspaper, called health officials who claimed that the ordinances would help black people "a bunch of hypocritical bastards." He added: "When government, when Koch, when Reagan, and when other 'good government' organizations—the AMA—start making attempts to 'help' black people, I get scared."[9]

The implication of such comments is that the goal of improving the health of black Americans is a smokescreen, that the diabolical public health authorities are actually pursuing another goal, one that is inimical to people who are black. This

---

*Sometimes, however, uncommon things happen. In December 1990, a judge in Minnesota held unconstitutional a law punishing the possession of crack more severely than the possession of the same amount of powder cocaine. The law, the judge explained, discriminates against drug users who are black.[8]
†This suspicion does not evidently extend to the tobacco companies themselves, whose enormous contributions to the coffers of civil rights organizations are legendary and are accepted without murmur. Unlike some other critics of the industry, I see little problem with the groups' accepting the money. If our people are to die disproportionately from addiction to this legal drug, we might as well take our share of the profits, so that some tiny portion of what we pay is actually put to some good use.

flavor of mistrust is perhaps the single most notable feature of white-black relations in America: for many millions of black folk, white people in general, and white people with power in particular, are simply not to be trusted. They cannot possibly, so the story goes, want what is best for us. They are only in it (whatever "it" happens to be) to pursue the interests of their own race, an interest that means domination of ours. Exactly *why* white people in power want to keep us down is rarely specified, but racism has never needed a rational motivation; indeed, following a talk I gave about affirmative action one student argued that all of the literature showing racial discrimination to be economically inefficient is beside the point because people who are racists are not acting in a rational manner. (This position, ironically, sweeps aside the traditional left argument that racism is a rational means for pursuing economic advantage.)

This attitude of mistrust, the vision of powerful white people as always "out to get us," probably helps explain the terrible stranglehold that the idea of differential-impact-as-racial-discrimination has on the imagination of so many smart and sincere people who are black (and not a few who are white): if on any particular social or economic measure black people as a group do not do as well as white people as a group, the reason must be—*must* be—that someone has designed things that way. Or is acting, even now, to make things come out that way. Or at least is happy that things are coming out that way.

Our sensitivity to this possibility has provided an opportunity for shameless exploitation. Since the antismoking ordinance brouhaha in New York City, interest groups from beverage bottlers battling recycling legislation to the National Rifle Association have used a variety of specious arguments about discrimination and mistrust of white authority to gather black support for their positions.[10] And the argument pressed by the interest groups is always the same: the legislation in question is being urged by a bunch of elitist white do-gooders who care little that black people will bear a disproportionate share of the costs. (Including the cost of the bottle return bill, criticized in Washington, D.C., as a regressive tax). The argument plays nicely in the inner city where mistrust of white power is sufficiently ingrained that other competing centers of white power can play on it for their own benefit—and, very often, to our detriment.

III

One can hardly ask black people to take the blame for their continuing mistrust of white people. It is relatively easy for me, a middle-class professional living in the suburbs, to say that I see no secret conspiracy holding us back. And looking at the opportunities that have opened over the past two decades, one might think it should be easy for anybody. But one would be wrong. Even if racist oppression has been largely removed and replaced with problems of class, poor and working-class black folk, who look around and see white people who seem consistently more successful than themselves, can scarcely be expected to appreciate the distinction. No wonder, then, that so many black people, maybe most, simply do not trust white people to be fair. Every bad thing that happens to a person who is black also happens *because* the person is black. The white folks are everywhere, and they have done it all to us; indeed, one might think that they have nothing better to do than sit around and think up ways to make us hurt. Back in the 1950s, the *Amsterdam News* published a cartoon in which two black men, out hunting, had been treed by a bear. One is saying to the other something like, "If we get out of this alive, I'm calling the NAACP, because I know the white folks arranged this somehow."

This attitude, I think, helps explain the strong suspicion on the part of many black people that Marion Barry, the flamboyant mayor of Washington, D.C., was treated unfairly by the federal government that spared few resources, and fewer tricks, to catch him in the act of using a dangerous drug. For many black people, the Barry trial stands as evidence that the white establishment will not tolerate powerful and popular black politicians. The prosecutors, and Barry's critics, respond that he was simply a high official who used drugs and that it was the prosecutor's responsibility to try to convict him, without regard to his race.

Both sides have valid points. Whether the prosecutors were out to get Marion Barry or not, they used means—his ex-girlfriend, the lure with intimations of sex; the decision to let him ingest the drug, at obvious risk to his health; and so on—that go far beyond what one expects a democratic government to do in uncovering criminals. At the same time, none of this excuses the fact that the mayor of Washington, D.C., was a crack user and, like other crack users, was lending financial support to a cruel, vicious empire that is enticing our children into self-destruction and slaughtering them in the streets. I cannot say whether the prosecutors were out to get Marion Barry or not; I do think Marion Barry (along with such other mysteriously popular miscreants as Oliver North and Michael Milken) deserved to be gotten.

And the getting was, in a sense, inevitable, for Barry, by seeming to flaunt the inability of prosecutors to catch him, was in effect flouting their authority: he was, à la Gary Hart, daring them to catch him in the act. One needs no racial explanation for supposing that an attitude of this kind is likely to move a prosecutor in the way a quieter defiance might not; anybody, white or black, who dares the prosecutor to catch him had better do a very careful job of watching his back. As Judge William Hastie once noted, discussing the prosecution of Angela Davis, "there are certain types of offenses against society against which the public authorities are going to move vigorously regardless of whether the culprit is black or politically unpopular."[11] (Davis, unlike Barry, was acquitted, and that result for some reason led her to indict the American criminal justice system, although one might suppose that a system that acquits a politically unpopular defendant is actually a pretty good one.)

Still, the rumor of a concerted effort to "get" black elected officials persists, an element in the conversational background of many political discussions among black people. In

Washington, D.C., the rumor has long carried a peculiar credibility because of a sense that the nation and its government are restless with the idea of black rule—in particular, *uppity* black rule—of the nation's capital. In Washington, as I have already noted, this conspiracy is called simply The Plan. The rumor of The Plan rises above a mutter whenever a popular black politician gets in legal or ethical difficulties. The notion of The Plan is routinely dismissed as an absurdity by prosecutors and journalists and, I suspect, by nearly everyone who is white.

But not by nearly everyone who is black. One 1990 survey of black New Yorkers, in fact, found 32 percent agreeing that "the government deliberately singles out and investigates black elected officials in order to discredit them in a way it doesn't do with white officials," and another 45 percent conceding that this might be true.[12] This view may be wrong, but it is not perhaps as implausible as it first appears: after all, J. Edgar Hoover's notorious COINTELPRO operation was explicitly aimed at, among other targets, the black civil rights leadership, which was to be "neutered." And besides, once one concedes that racism continues to bedevil our nation—a concession that it seems rather foolish to dispute—one can hardly avoid taking the further step of suggesting that the fact of election to public office is no evidence of anybody's freedom from the racist taint. Moreover, when one looks at the world through the eyes of the vast numbers of black people with little hope, whose principal contacts with white society are with what they view as a suspicious and hostile commercial or governmental bureaucracy, it hardly takes a vivid imagination to suppose that things have worked out badly for black Americans because that is the way somebody planned it. In short, the vision of The Plan is not ridiculous.

It is, however, almost certainly wrong, not least because it is not as clear as it was a few decades ago that striking down a black leadership that is no longer particularly dangerous to those who hold the levers of authority is in the interest of whatever white power structure sits around and dreams up these things. There is no current revolutionary threat of the sort that Hoover, in his late-career madness, thought he saw, and there is no longer any practical reason for white power to act as though there is one. Capitalism has made its peace with the civil rights movement. Dynamic, successful black entrepreneurs and consumers are far more important to the American economy than a helpless, oppressed *lumpenproletariat;* this is the reason corporate America has always found many forms of affirmative action quite attractive. The old left theories about capitalism's need for a pool of cheap, unskilled labor are simply irrelevant in the complex labor and consumer-goods markets of the late twentieth century. Anyway, a plan of the scope envisioned by the conspiracy theorists takes enormous effort, and there is no particular motive to explain why anyone would bother. Not to put too fine a point on it, we are, I fear, no longer worth the candle.

One might respond, of course, that even if market discipline makes conspiracies of this kind difficult for corporate America to launch, politicians respond to a different set of incentives. So even if powerful capitalist interests have nothing to gain by attacking the leadership of the black community, white politicians, seeking to please racist constituencies, might still be on the attack. But even if the idea of The Plan contains a grain of truth—if, for example, the image of successful black people so galls white Americans that they will often act, irrationally but eagerly, to suppress such uppity folk— that is no reason to excuse the behavior of black elected officials who commit offenses for which, by hypothesis, white officials go unpunished. On the contrary: if we really believe our enemies are using our leaders' behavior to hold us down, our *practical* solution (whatever our polemical stance might be) must surely be to insist that our leaders be more pure than Caesar's wife.

Perhaps it isn't fair to hold our political leaders to so high a standard; after all, as some believers in The Plan have pointed out, in the days when other ethnic groups controlled local political machinery, the corruption that today so outrages the voters was accepted as a matter of course. But crying out for our turn at unethical government is not a strategy likely to win many rhetorical battles. Far better to learn to live in today's ethical climate than to hand over our leadership on a platter.

The assertion that white people are out to get black people occurs in other contexts, too; in particular, it is a ready response to those who argue as I do that we should want to be judged by the same standards as everyone else. This argument about medical school admission is typical: "It is a sad irony . . . that when the door is finally opened to the minority student, the standards for entrance are raised."[13] No matter what one might think about affirmative action in colleges and professional schools, however, the evidence suggests that even in the absence of extra points awarded when the decision is made to hire, truly excellent people of color, standing on their own achievements and nothing more, are not likely to go begging for jobs. For elite academic employers, law firms, corporations, and other powerful institutions, race continues to add value in the hiring process. The value is often reflected, as values in a market generally are, by the price paid.

In Arizona, a white law professor has filed an employment discrimination suit against his university because another professor, much junior to himself, is being paid a much higher salary. The lawsuit charges that the school is paying more to the second professor because he is a Native American. Whether or not this is true and, if true, whether or not it is fair, are less interesting for my present purposes than the perception: it has become something of a commonplace that highly qualified people of color are the subjects of bidding wars among otherwise sedate professional institutions; the predictable result of the bidding, so the rumor runs, is that truly excellent professionals who happen not to be white often end up earning more than white professionals of similar intellectual attainment. One study of university faculties concludes that when one corrects for the number of years in the teaching profession, the quality of the program that yielded the doctoral degree, and the rate of publication, the top professors who are not white earn *more* than their similarly situated white colleagues.[14] A friend of mine who is a partner in one of the nation's largest and most prestigious law firms told me, after a moment's reflection, that his firm would be willing to pay a bit extra to get an outstanding attorney who happened to be black if other firms, motivated by skin color, had bid up the price. That is, he explained, simply the way the market works.

This trend, if it exists, is indeed an example of market forces in action—a point that must confound those critics who claim that the market is racist. But left to itself, the market isn't racist at all, and if highly qualified minority scholars or lawyers or doctors are a more valuable commodity than white ones, a free market will naturally bid up their price. That is what markets do (at least in the absence of regulation) when valuable commodities are in short supply; outstanding professionals who are members of desirable minority groups are expensive for the same reason that gold or diamonds are expensive. And that is evidently the result that the market currently produces, at least at the top end. Such results, of course, tell only a small part of a much larger story. But as any number of supporters of diversity will point out on many other subjects, the market is only fair, not just.

If the apparent market behavior is the result of the bidding war over the small supply of truly excellent black professionals, then as affirmative action swells those ranks, the price should drop and the alleged differences should disappear. In the meantime, opponents of quotas or the lower standards that some forms of racial preferences entail who nevertheless stress the importance of recruitment of highly qualified members of previously excluded groups would seem to have little option but to accept as a transitional situation the possibility of slightly higher race-specific salaries. That, after all, is how one recruits when there is competition. This is a point on which Derrick Bell, in his controversial protest at Harvard, was absolutely right. To refuse to meet the competition is in effect to refuse to recruit; and if the pool of truly excellent black professionals is as small as the critics of preferences insist that it is, then with or without affirmative action, the re-

firmative action, the recruiting wars for that tiny but talented group should logically be brisk.

IV

My hope for a future in which we who are black will be content with a world in which we are called on to meet the same standards as everybody else should not be confused with the vision of a color-blind society that enjoys such political currency. The notion of a wholly neutral assessment is, at its core, as empty and misleading as the idea that all black people (or all white people) are the same. As the Harvard law professor Martha Minow has put the point, "Because our language is shared and our categories communally invented, any word I use to describe your uniqueness draws you into the classes of people sharing your traits."[15] No matter how A might describe B, the process of categorization continues; at best, the role for law, as for moral suasion, is to try to prod people to favor some generalizations over others. The question for advocates of affirmative action, then, remains what it has always been: Is it a good thing, is it a *safe* thing, to encourage white America to continue to think in racial terms? And people who insist on color blindness must face the analogous question: Is it a good thing, it is a *safe* thing, to deny the differences among people, and among our many subcultures, that make our nation the wonderfully heterogeneous land it is?

I have no illusion that we can (and, I think, no desire that we should) move toward a world in which nobody notices that anybody is different from anybody else, for that would be a world made dull and (literally) colorless, a world in which no subculture could celebrate itself or call upon the larger culture to share, even for a moment, its ethnic pride. I do not even want to insist that the ideal government would at all times and at all places be entirely blind to color, because that stance would make it impossible for the state to play a role in celebrating those same achievements. What is needed, rather, is the development of a better grammar of race, a way through which we can at once take account of it and not punish it.

And a sensible way to start, so it seems to me, is to say that with all the various instances in which race might be relevant, either to the government or to individuals, it will not be used as an indicator of merit—no one will be more valued than anyone else because of skin color. The corollary is that everyone's merit would therefore be judged by the same tests, and if the tests in question are unfair (truly unfair, in the sense I have already described, and not just exclusionary), then they will be swept away *and replaced with something else.*

It is that last step, I think, that is often missed in debates over qualifications for admission or employment. No matter how bad one might think current standards are, some standard will be used, either explicitly or implicitly. My argument is that the standard should be explicit, and that once it is selected, everyone should be required to meet it.

And yet, in a nation with the turbulent racial history of this one, one must wonder: Somewhere along the way, has there been an error of analysis? Were the nationalists right—is this path to the profession simply a lure to get us to give up on true freedom? Mario Baeza, a member of New York's legal elite who also happens to be black, has put the dilemma this way: "You go to law school, you study like crazy, *and* you have to continually wonder, Am I adopting a way of thinking that could be used to enslave me?"[16] This possibility lies very near the core of the diversity movement, which counsels people of color against what is usually termed surrender of their identity in the cause of success. The same possibility, albeit put in far less sophisticated terms, motivates those black children who tell other kids that studying and even going to class is acting white. Why else, the nationalists demanded back in the 1960s, would whitey have made the opportunity of higher education available? Clearly, the power structure has something in mind, and whatever it is, as Wilbert Tatum suggested of the antismoking ordinance, cannot possibly be good for people who are black.

All of which returns us to the matter of academic and professional standards. There, too, it is whispered (and sometimes shouted) that people of color are victims of a plan—of the centuries of affirmative action favoring white males, for example, or at least of the virulent societal racism that has held us in a subordinate status. When one challenges racial preferences on the ground that they sometimes result in the admission or employment of people not as good (as well prepared, as professionally capable) as some who are turned away, or even on the ground that preferences call into question the legitimate achievements of very smart and very capable people of color, the modern vision of affirmative action quickly turns the challenge back on itself: the standards by which these judgments are made, the standards that black people are often less able than white people to meet, are said to lack objectivity, to import cultural bias, or simply to be racist. The idea that even if all of this is true, we should aim to meet and beat them anyway—that we should put ourselves beyond criticism on this ground, as well as on the ground of our leaders' conduct—is quickly dismissed as irrelevant, or as a smokescreen, or as naive, or even as thinking white.

But what it really is, is thinking like a professional. To rise to the pinnacle of professional success, a black person must function in an integrated world, but to do so is no more a betrayal of one's birthright than it is for white people to do the same thing. As Mario Baeza has put it, resolving his own dilemma, "I'm integrated, but I've never tried to be white. That's not what I aspire to in life."[17]

The professional world is competitive, now more than ever, and has little time or space for argument over what should count as standards of achievement. In the professions, unlike the campuses, there is a market test: one either performs well enough to justify one's compensation or one does not. And it is because successful professionals know this, I think, that many of them have grown impatient with the argument over affirmative action for hiring and advancement in their fields. "I've made it because I'm good," said the corporate executive whom I quoted in chapter 1, and that, at bottom, is what all professionals, black or white, must believe in order to succeed.

Making it because one is good is not a conceit that we develop in order to live in white America. It is, rather, the outcome of a deliberate decision to try to live in a world that encourages and rewards excellence. In "The Duty of the Intellectual," the thought-provoking essay that opens his fine book *Pathos of Power,* the renowned psychologist Kenneth Clark makes the following observation:

> An unfinished task of our society—probably one that must be clearly identified, defined, and justified by intellectuals—is to learn to differentiate between democratic philosophy, goals, and methods and stable standards of excellence. Literalistic egalitarianism, appropriate and relevant to problems of political and social life, cannot be permitted to invade and dominate the crucial areas of the intellect, aesthetics, and ethics.[18]

Clark's is straightforward and sensible: a commitment to an inclusionary politics bears no necessary relation to a judgment about what is good and right and what is bad and wrong. Affirmative action, diversity, cultural pluralism, and the like are all simply words or, too often, slogans; what matters is the understanding of society that they signify. For whatever one might want to call the effort to broaden opportunities for groups that have been kept out of the mainstream of American life, it seems to me quite clear—indeed, it seems to be common rhetorical ground among all sides in the affirmative action dispute, but bears repeating—that progress should never come at the price of pretending that nobody is ever better than anybody else at anything.

One must be very careful about the leveling that is implicit in the conversational habit that affirmative action has become. Elite educational institutions, after all, owe their existence in part to a belief that some people are smarter and more likely to achieve.[19] This, I take it, is just the reason that people of color are beating so hard on the doors to get in. So I wince when I hear supporters of preferences talk blithely of tossing out the window standards of excellence—for college entry, grading, hiring, or promotion—that might actually be rational. Sometimes the argument is that the standards are the playthings of white males, manipulated by this amorphous set for their own advantage. Sometimes the argument is that standards are not possible. Sometimes the argument is that meritocracy is itself a bad idea.

My own view is that the traditional justification for accepting a concept of merit is correct: standards of excellence are a requisite of civilization. To say instead that excellence cannot be judged is to say that excellence is not possible. To say that excellence is not possible is to say, really, that nothing is better than anything else. And if nothing is better than anything else, then the entire project of human progress is a joke. But it isn't a joke. There is such a thing as excellence; there is such a thing as civilization. We live in a world of brilliant scientific discoveries, remarkable acts of moral and spiritual courage, profound literary achievements, and outstanding professional performances. We live in a world that cares about excellence, needs it, and should not be afraid to judge it.

I do not mean to suggest that every standard that is defended as a requisite of civilization deserves that description, and some of what has been defended on that ground is repulsive. Separation of the races was once described as such a requisite, and in many corners of this troubled globe ethnic separation is still described that way. Moreover, our nation has insisted, in the name of meritocracy, on a good deal of cruel and senseless discrimination. The ideal of merit as the route to reward should not be confused with the very different proposition that the society in which we live today is one that gives out rewards that way. Similarly, not every standard accepted in *our* society is necessary for civilization in *every* society. Even the most confirmed cultural absolutist can hardly come away from such a book as Jomo Kenyatta's *Facing Mount Kenya* without conceding that others may have customs that work for them and not for us, and that forcing them to be like us would likely destroy perfectly moral, if somewhat different, cultures. Indeed, as any number of psychologists and anthropologists have pointed out, even the standards of things we often imagine to be measurable do not travel well. Intellect provides a fine example. There are people in other cultures who adapt extremely well to complicated tasks necessary to their survival who could not perform tasks of similar complexity here; and there are many of us who have adapted to complicated tasks here who could not perform tasks of similar complexity there.

Excellence and diversity, it must be emphasized, are not enemies; the professional success of generations of professionals who are not white gives the lie to this old canard. But most of that success has been enjoyed by individuals who have, as members of other excluded ethnic groups have, met whatever standards for success a profession has established. And if these professionally accomplished individuals happen to have been beneficiaries of affirmative action, then they have plainly made the most of their opportunity to show that they are able to meet the same standards as everyone else.

V

To think about the future is also to reflect on the past. If we as a people were not defeated by slavery and Jim Crow, we will not be beaten by the demise of affirmative action. Before there were any racial preferences, before there was a federal antidiscrimination law with any teeth, our achievements were already on the rise: our middle class was growing, as was our rate of college matriculation—both of them at higher rates than in the years since. Black professionals, in short, should not do much worse without affirmative action than we are doing with it, and, thrown on our own resources and knowing that we have no choice but to meet the same tests as everybody else, we may do better.

We must be about the business of defining a future in which we can be fair to ourselves and demand opportunities without falling into the trap of letting others tell us that our horizons are limited, that we cannot make it without assistance. I recall the historian Vincent Harding's discussion of black reaction to the Emancipation Proclamation and the prospect of a constitutional amendment banning slavery. These were fine as far as they went, says Harding, but "white definitions of black people's freedom had never been sufficient." Therefore, "the black community was not idly waiting for answers and clarifications from others." Instead, black people were "working toward their own answers, attempting in their own wisdom, through their own vision and prayer, to come to terms with this new stage of the struggle."[20]

The likely demise, or severe restriction, of racial preferences will also present for us a new stage of struggle, and we should treat it as an opportunity, not a burden. It is our chance to make ourselves free of the assumptions that too often underlie affirmative action, assumptions about our intellectual incapacity and other competitive deficiencies. It is our chance to prove to a doubting, indifferent world that our future as a people is in our hands.

My own faith is that we can, and will, survive in a world free of preferences. They are a convenience, true, but in their current form, as I have explained, they can also be an insult or, worse, counterproductive. Besides, the battle to preserve affirmative action will be won, if at all, only at an enormous cost—and after all of our political capital has been spent, the fight may well be lost anyway. Moreover, for all that it has assisted the black middle class, affirmative action has done nothing at all for the true victims of racism. We can talk all we want about diversity, about the need to bring into the corridors of power the excluded viewpoint of the oppressed, but that is not the same as bringing into the corridors of power the oppressed themselves.

To continue to make affirmative action the centerpiece of our strategy for the future will also have another cost, however: the continuing collapse of solidarity in our community. When white people criticize affirmative action, the response is anger. When black people criticize it, the response is bewilderment, pain, and, in the end, open hostility. In the difficult years ahead, we cannot afford the luxury of letting our squabble over preferences, which help mostly those who can best survive without them, interfere with the needed dialogue on what to do next. And the cost in solidarity might be greater than some would imagine, for it is my sense (admittedly anecdotal) that among successful black professionals, there is a growing uneasiness with any forms of affirmative action that allow black people to meet different standards than other people. As one black director of an investment banking firm put it, "I feel that if we're all on a level playing field, we'll be stronger."[21]

The ranks of dissenters, as I say, are swelling. I even suspect that I know why: it's a variant on the "Schelling effect," a well-understood phenomenon in the study of how integrated schools become resegregated. The Schelling effect is an elegant model of a complex phenomenon. Imagine a spectrum of white students, each with a slightly different tolerance for integration. As the first black students arrive in a formerly segregated school, the white students with the smallest tolerance for integration leave the school. This increases the proportion of black students, which means that the white students with the next smallest tolerance for integration leave. This once more increases the proportion of black students, and the white students with the next smallest tolerance for integration leave the school. This goes on until the only white students left are those who either cannot leave or possess an infinite tolerance for integration—not likely a substantial number.

I suspect that what is happening now, as more and more members of the affirmative action generation clamor for the chance to get beyond it, is a sort of reverse Schelling effect. What happens is that the black students and professionals with the smallest tolerance for being the beneficiaries of preferences insist on their right to exit, which leaves those with the next smallest tolerance wondering why they are staying aboard, and so on. We are very far from the point at which we might say that successful black people themselves have forced a move away from some forms of affirmative action in the professional world, but I think a critical mass may soon emerge, producing what the integration literature calls the tipping point.

And one way or another, the tipping point will be reached. It might be reached because in a time of economic stress, even the white professionals who have tolerated racial preferences will turn on them, leaving them almost devoid of political support outside the black community. Or the tipping point might be reached because we, the professionals who are people of color, decide to say that we have had enough— enough of stereotyping, enough of different standards, enough of the best black syndrome. We can decide that the time has come to phase affirmative action out of our strategy for professional advancement. In either case, I think the end of affirmative action is near. And it is always best to have the ark built before the deluge.

More of our future is in our hands than we often seem to think, not because we live in a world that is free of racism (we certainly don't) but because we remain what we have always been: a great people, held down for a very long time, but with the burning light of greatness refusing to go out. Yes, it is possible that white people will help us to be what we know we can, but it is also possible that they will not; and it is likely that they will not help us as much as we might think just. If white people do less for us than we think they should, there are really only two solutions: we can complain about it, or we can help ourselves. And we already know from the proverbs which path the Lord favors.

CHAPTER 11

Racial Solidarity and the Black Intellectual

Many years ago, before becoming the celebrated literary figure she is today, Alice Walker wrote a small essay entitled "The Civil Rights Movement: What Good Was It?" There she concluded that if the civil rights movement gave us "nothing else, it gave us each other forever."[1] The civil rights movement taught us our need for one another. It did not, perhaps, make us family, but at least, one hopes, it made us friends. This, perhaps, is why the historian Clayborne Carson has tried to rename the civil rights movement, calling it instead the "black freedom struggle." The movement, according to Carson, was not really about changing white America but about changing black America. At its core, the struggle was not about rights but about *us.* The struggle for freedom was a struggle of self-transformation, and whether racism grows or recedes, evolves or deteriorates, the fact that the movement happened means that racism can never again affect us with quite the same virulence.

Each other, forever: to gaze into one another's faces and read there a commonality, something shared. Call it experience. Or history. Whatever it is called, this, surely, is the bright and valuable side of racial solidarity. Not an identity of perspective, not an isomorphic mapping of one person's experience and personality onto another, but a shred of recognition, of familiarity; a common knowledge, a common history of woeful oppression and glorious triumph. A common transformation from a people that has been victimized to a people that has taken its fate into its hands. If this is what is meant by solidarity, it is an aspect of our coloredness to be cheered.

Solidarity, to be sure, can have its grimmer side. To be an intellectual is often to chafe at the burden of our groupness; for the task of the intellectual is to think freely, and solidarity all too often carries with it the expectation that one will act or speak or even think in a particular way, the way the group demands. The difficulty becomes particularly acute when some members of the group, purporting to speak for it, take it upon themselves to decide who is and who is not a member in good standing, basing that judgment on whether, in the leader's view, the intellectual has helped the group or harmed it.

Not surprisingly, there is a growing perception among black intellectuals that racial solidarity is less a solution to a problem than a problem in itself. The pre-eminent spokesman for this point of view is Shelby Steele. "As a middle-class black," Steele has written, "I have often felt myself *contriving* to be black." He has tried to conform his words and actions to his image of the black way to be. But now Steele has had enough of all that; he is ready to do away with solidarity. The time has come for black people to stop thinking of themselves as a group, Steele warns, because "[t]he collective black identity fogs up the sacred line between the individual and the collective." He adds:

To retrieve our individuality and find opportunity, blacks today must—consciously or unconsciously—disregard the prevailing victim-focused black identity. Though it espouses black pride, it is actually a repressive identity that generates a victimized self-image, curbs individualism and initiative, diminishes our sense of possibility, and contributes to our demoralization and inertia. It is a skin that needs shedding.[2]

What Steele describes—the "victim-focused black identity"—is certainly a real phenomenon, and one worth abandoning, but there is more to racial solidarity and more to black pride than the effort to make everybody think the same way. Loving our people and loving our culture does not require any restriction on what black people can think or say or do or be. Besides, even were it a good idea to surrender the idea of solidarity, one wonders how this miracle could be accomplished in a nation that, as Steele himself affirms, is hopelessly mired in race consciousness.

Oh, I know what Steele means. I know the frustration, even anguish, that comes from the simple-minded assumption that one who is truly black must prove himself or herself by pronouncing the shibboleths correctly. A single example of my frustration is found regularly in my mailbox. Because teachers at American law schools are racially identifiable (we are listed that way in an official guidebook), I frequently receive letters from a variety of organizations that begin with something like "Dear Minority Colleague" and go on to treat me as though I already agree with the organization's goals and strategies. And each time I receive such a letter, I begin reading in anger and end in sadness, for while it is true that I *sometimes* agree, no one, least of all other people of color, ought to assume they know my positions when all they really know is the color of my skin. Surely the minimum obligation of black people to one another is to accord the respect that comes from acknowledging that we fairly sparkle with a diversity of outlook that the larger society, in its mindless racialism, often fails to recognize.

That awful word *minority* is reason enough for displeasure. I understand why everybody uses it: the grammar of race is not adequately developed to provide alternative formulations for certain notions that one might want to convey. Sometimes I use the word myself, even in this book, and certainly in conversation, although it is not a word I like. Quite apart from the wonderful old black nationalist response— "I'm not a minority anything because I'm not less than anybody"—the word carries unsettling implications of perma

nence, for when used by activists (and by scholars and journalists and politicians, too), *minority* is a reference to group
identity, not a transitional measurement of relative group
size. *Minority* refers not to how many we are, we who are a
part of one or another of the minority communities, but to
how we are. And this *how we are* is evidently meant to be a
universal: how we *always* are, or are supposed to be. (I recall
the splendid irony of a "Doonesbury" comic strip in which
Uncle Duke states as one of his qualifications for the ambassa-
dorship to China his outstanding record of working with
minorities.) Yet even this would not be so bad if the word did
not carry with it as well all the baggage of our nation's woeful
history of mistreating its "minorities." By being addressed as
a "minority" anything, I am in effect being put into a set, told
who I am, what my history is, how I must act, and what views
I must endorse. And that I find inimical to the intellectual life
I wish to lead.

Still, I cannot let the matter rest there, on the strength of
a word like *inimical*. I am angered by the assumption that
skin color is the key to politics, as I am angered when skin
color is taken to indicate lack of intellectual ability or potential for criminality or aesthetic preferences or anything else.
The labelers know nothing of me and what I think or believe
or want or hope. I am not, for them, a human being, a free
thinker with ideas of his own. I am a name on a list, a "minority" law professor, and therefore presumptively in agreement
with an entire strategy for solving the "special problems"
that I and people like me (that is, people of like color) are said
to face.

The trouble is that too many critics seem to think that
the only way to get out of the box is to shed the second skin
that solidarity drapes over us. It is not clear to me, however,
that the problem is solidarity as such; no intellectual is
harmed, I think, by a conscious decision to identify with an
ethnic group. That identification, moreover, is tremendously
important, not only (as I have earlier argued) for the sake of
defining personality but also because affection for the group
itself is what finally gives meaning to racial pride. It does not

strike me as either plausible or desirable for intellectuals to say, in effect, "We put behind us all that we are. We have no interest in our backgrounds, in our communities and cultures that gave us birth." Besides, to put the matter bluntly, our people need us. The better trained our minds, the more we have to contribute to the debate over the best way of alleviating the crisis in which the black community finds itself—if, that is, debate is allowed. And our obligation to our history, and thus to our community, while it should not be a force for silencing, should not be mere lip service either. We need solidarity. We need unity, not in the sense of groupthink but in the sense of group love. Few ethnic groups, perhaps none, have made substantial socioeconomic progress without the aid of at least a temporary ideology of solidarity.

But why this puzzling effort to untangle self-reliance from solidarity? It may be true, as Steele and others have suggested, that the situation of black people will change in some significant way once black people begin thinking of themselves as individuals who are responsible for their own acts and achievements rather than as members of a victimized group. I have already argued (see chapter 9) that far too much has been allowed to turn for too long not only on our "groupness" but on the idea that our problems aren't really ours, but someone else's: the government's, white people's, history's. Such rhetoric is infectious: just look at campus debate, and the transformation of white males into evil oppressors. So, yes, to recapture the lost focus on black people as individuals who must achieve, if at all, through personal effort is a laudable goal, and if this means an abandonment of the contemporary versions of affirmative action, perhaps the time has come.

But do we really want to do this while abandoning any notion of groupness? The nationalists of an earlier day thought not; indeed, the idea of a lone black person adrift in a sea of white racism provided rich polemical territory for such theorists as Stokely Carmichael and Robert Allen, as well as some very fine imagery for such novelists as Ralph Ellison and Richard Wright. If today's professionals are to dismiss the old images of the need for solidarity as the outdated fears of an earlier and less fortunate generation, then one must posit a society in which there is relatively little overt racism, and not much more of the covert sort; in fact, one must imagine that even unconscious bias is evaporating. Many of today's black dissenters seem to argue that we do, in fact, live in such a world; I confess that I am less certain.

The dissenters are, however, at least partly right. Our horizons are not unlimited (whose are?), but there are more and more opportunities out there, waiting to be seized. It is inexcusable that so many black children and young adults refuse—there is often no other word—to take advantage of the opportunities for which their ancestors fought and sometimes died. Even worse, there exists among many young people in the inner city,* and sometimes elsewhere as well, an ethic suggesting that academic achievement is a betrayal of the group. (See chapter 5.)

But one wants to be wary of pushing the point too far. For even if, as Shelby Steele suggests, there are few effective barriers to advancement for the talented, there may be barriers to the acquisition of talent, and the barriers increasingly run along class lines. Although there are magnificent stories of poor children who have, by dint of individual effort, pulled themselves into the middle class, the truth is that socioeconomic status of parents is strongly correlated with success in school. There are many explanations for the data—the currently prevailing theory is that child-rearing practices likely to lead to academic achievement are less common in lower-income homes—but whatever the explanation, the data make plain that the social and economic conditions in which so many black children live are a principal barrier to the next generation's advancement.

Thus, although racist oppression might no longer be an important barrier, what might be described as racist indiffer-

---

*William Julius Wilson, whose work brought the term into widespread use, has recently urged social theorists to avoid the word *underclass* because of the baggage it has come to carry in contemporary debate. Wilson's suggested alternative is "ghetto poor"—overlooking, probably on purpose, the baggage that the perfectly good word *ghetto* has unfortunately come to carry in contemporary debate.

ence still rears its ugly head. As I have explained earlier (see chapter 4), considerable social science evidence demonstrates, for example, that such preschool programs as Head Start improve learning ability, especially in mathematics, and that the degree of learning for all students rises as school environments grow safer and more stable. These things, of course, cost money, and our society too often seems unwilling to spend what is needed. Perhaps this refusal isn't racism—the word *is* overused—but it isn't exactly a helping hand.

Very well, sometimes the society ignores the needs of the worst off among us. Is it clear (so Steele might ask) that we have in the notion of groupness some effective weapon for forcing the society to do otherwise? Maybe not. Steele and others are surely right to suggest that the time has long passed when the cry of racism is likely to accomplish much in the way of enacting positive new policies; the era of playing on our history of oppression, the fact of our victimization, to urge or shame or coerce the assistance of the larger white society is surely over. I do not mean to suggest that there are not among us those who believe that the time is ripe, only that the one thing their efforts seem unlikely to produce is concrete result.

Thomas Sowell, in *Ethnic America* (1981), has argued that if one looks at black people as an immigrant community, and traces the postimmigration history not from the era of slavery but from the time of the Great Migration to the cities of the North, it turns out that although we had a lot farther to climb, we have made about as much progress, socially and economically, as other immigrant groups have in similar periods of time. This vision, to be sure, has its critics; I mention it here to raise the possibility that if Sowell is right, an ideology of solidarity becomes even more pressing a need, for other immigrant groups relied on it heavily—solidarity, once more, not in the sense of collective coercion but rather in the sense of taking the progress of the group as a lodestar by which to measure our own achievements. Solidarity, then, means not, as the diversity movement would have it, embracing some special perspective gained from our history of oppression; nor

need it mean, as it did for some of the immigrant groups Sowell discusses, suppressing dissent; it means, rather, embracing our people themselves, in all their wild and frustrating
variety.

Embracing our people does not mean suspending judgment, a point that was brought home to me recently when certain bona fide representatives of the people, the ruthlessly oppressed victims of white racism, chose to settle a business
dispute ("turf battle," I believe, is the jargon) by firing semi-
automatic weapons at one another as well as at various bystanders including my daughter, my wife's parents, my niece
and nephew, their father, and myself. By the purest good fortune, none of us was struck by a bullet, although not all the
bystanders were so lucky. No degree of sensitivity to oppression should render these young drug dealers less culpable for
their choices.

We can believe that crime has causes and that people
aren't born bad, and we can demand of our government serious policies, even if they are expensive, to ameliorate some of
those causes. But we must never do ourselves or our people
the disservice of confusing the idea of causation with a mindless determinism in which individuals hold no responsibility
for their own actions and the larger society in all of its mani-
festations is always and everywhere to blame. After all, most
people of color, no matter how horrible their life circumstances, refuse to turn to lives of predation. We should not be
proud of our society for creating a world in which they are
tempted, but we should not confuse the temptations of an unequal society with the coercions of a racially determined one.

We must never lose the capacity for judgment, especially
the capacity to judge ourselves and our people. We can and
should celebrate those among us who achieve, whether in the
arts or in the professions, whether on the athletic field or the
floor of the state house, whether publicly fighting for our children or privately nurturing them; but we must not pretend
that they are the only black people who make choices. Standards of morality matter no less than standards of excellence.
There are black people who commit heinous crimes, and not all

of them are driven by hunger and neglect. Not all of them turn to crime because they are victims of racist social policy. Nor are they, in Huey Newton's evocative but finally unsatisfying phrase, simply "illegitimate capitalists" who lack the education or the power to steal and maim in ways that the law allows. We are not automatons. To understand all may indeed be to forgive all, but no civilization can survive when the capacity for understanding is allowed to supersede the capacity for judgment. Otherwise, at the end of the line lies a pile of garbage: Hitler wasn't evil, just insane.

II

But judgment is not inconsistent with solidarity, not in the positive, loving, embracing sense of the word. And professional attainment is not inconsistent with it, either. To be middle class, financially secure, suburbanite, need not mean, if one is black, to be fully assimilated. It *does* make a difference when I decide whether to move into a neighborhood that I see other black people there. It *does* make a difference to me that my children have black playmates, that they regularly interact with black adults other than their own parents. It *does* make a difference to me that I not be the only black, the first black, the best black. Alice Walker is right: the civil rights movement's greatest gift to my generation, and to generations to come, is not simply the opportunity to set goals that were denied, often by law, to our parents and theirs but also—and perhaps more important—the brimming confidence that solidarity breeds. Not solidarity in the sense of groupness, but solidarity in the sense of valuing one another. Solidarity in the sense of rooting for *us*—the way many of our parents and theirs did for Marian Anderson and Jackie Robinson and Martin Luther King, Jr.

This perspective is not richer than anyone else's; it is not better than anyone else's; it is not more valuable than anyone else's. But it is ours. It marks us as special and sets us apart. It is as good a definition as there is of what constitutes culture; we can both be angry at and take solace from our shared history. It is this shared history that makes us a people. That does not mean that the institutions that make our system go— the universities, the corporations—must go out and shop for our perspective in the marketplace. It does mean that our perspective is unique. It does not mean that we are all the same.

This point is ultimately definitional: it is necessary to take a moment to say who "we" are—who the black people are who share this tragic yet glorious history. Deciding who we are requires, first, an act of naming and, second, the pouring of content into (or the discovery of the content already existing in) the name that we choose. As the psychiatrist Price M. Cobbs has written, the evolution in what we call ourselves, from colored, to Negro, to black, and now, for some, to African-American, "highlight[s] profound shifts in the psyche of a group of people struggling mightily to define themselves rather than be defined by others."[3] And while it is possible (and, sadly, many have tried) to define our blackness by how we think, there is considerably more at stake than victory of one side or the other's vision of the right way to enhance the economic and political position of our people. We must have an identity in order to exist.

Consider the following proposition, penned by the philosopher Anthony Appiah in considering W. E. B. DuBois's vision of race: "[A] vast human family might contain people joined not by biology but by an act of choice."[4] Imagine that race might serve as a proxy for choice, or perhaps as a matter of choice. People, in this vision, might be black because they have chosen to be. I do not mean this in the sense in which I fear that Derrick Bell meant his comment about professors who look black and think white; I have in mind no exogenous standard of racial choice. What I envision, rather, is the possibility that each of us might make a choice about which racial group we prefer to join. A Yale colleague is fond of suggesting that white people who think that affirmative action unfairly favors black people should be free to switch races, provided always that they are willing to accept the burdens of blackness along with its benefits.

But, of course, this is not the way race is treated. Its assignment *is* exogenous, and it has nothing to do with the acts or intentions of the assignee. The society does it, and almost always with a reason in mind. One might quibble with the reason for a particular racial assignment, but there is no authority to which one can appeal to have the assignment changed (although it was at one time, and for all I know still is, actionable libel in many states to call a white person black). Whether the cause is segregation or affirmative action, there is a *point* to racial categorizations, and this is what social theorists mean when they say that race is socially constructed. Few biologists or anthropologists any longer think that the concept of race as it is used in America, as a synonym for color, has scientific significance, and indeed, the effort to define racial categories has been inexorably bound up throughout the history of science with the effort to prove that some of those categories are inferior to others.

But the social significance of race is considerable, even if often illogical. To take just one rarely spoken yet intellectually meaty question, is there any reason *in logic* to label children of racially mixed marriages black rather than white? The answer, of course, is that while society doubtless has its reasons, none of them are logical, a point that even the most ardent advocates of racial preferences would presumably concede. But the assignment does not change on this basis. Anthony Appiah, in the essay I have previously mentioned, takes up the question of DuBois's own racial identity. DuBois, after all, was prone to describe himself not simply as a Negro but in more complex terms. I once came across a passage in which DuBois said of himself: "I am, in blood, about one half or more Negro, and the rest French and Dutch, but thank God, no Anglo-Saxon." Appiah continues as follows:

> Consider, for example, DuBois himself. As the descendant of Dutch ancestors, why doesn't his relation to the history of Holland in the fourteenth century (which he shares with all people of Dutch descent) make him a member of the Teutonic race? The answer is straightforward: the Dutch were not Negroes;

DuBois is. But it follows from this that the history of Africa is part of the common history of Afro-Americans not simply because Afro-Americans descended from various peoples who played a part in African history but rather because African history is the history of people of the same race.[5]

That, perhaps, is, or ought to be, the final word on solidarity. Solidarity should ideally be a choice, a decision one makes to claim a people, a culture, a history as one's own. In race-obsessed America, however, even the requirement of solidarity turns out to be in some sense exogenous; it exists because others have defined for us the concept of race. If we wish to live in this society, moreover, we are not free to redefine it. Solidarity is required of us simply because we are "people of the same race."

III

Being accepted by one's peers as an academic, a professor, a scholar, does no more to eliminate racism than does any other form of professional success. In the wonderfully evocative scene that opens Toni Morrison's beautiful novel *Song of Solomon,* a black insurance agent commits suicide by leaping from the top of the lily-white hospital that dominates the unnamed Michigan community where most of the action takes place. It is not immediately clear whether the man expects to die: he seems to believe that he will be able to fly. The symbolism is no less powerful for being obvious—the more so when we learn later on that once upon a time, back before the Great Migration, there were black people who *could* fly. In the face of this knowledge, the suicide, if it is a suicide, seems more tragic still. The insurance agent, in his professional success in white America, unfortunately lives in a time when black people who used to fly have quite forgotten how it is done. He has (literally) climbed to the highest level of what appears to be the principal bastion of racism in his community—the segregated hospital—but somehow cannot survive in that rarefied air the same way that the white folks do. When he spreads his wings and leaps from the cupola, he is just as dead as any other nigger.

The law school classmate who laid out for me the facts of systemic racism (see chapter 4) doubtless would have described the scene as reflecting today's reality; the experience of racism was said then, as it often is now, to hold all of black people back. This is the point of Malcolm X's comment that a black man with a Ph.D. is still a nigger to a white man. The message is that there is one similarity that cuts across all the differences—social, economic, political—that divide people of color, and that is the reality of racism. We might have our beautiful wings, but we still can't fly.

Today's truth, I think, is somewhat more complex. Shelby Steele suggests that racism is receding, and he is partly correct. It still lurks in shadowy corners, but it is no longer the all-encompassing force it once was, and it no longer holds the entire black race in desperate thrall. What Steele misses is that racism, in its many modern varieties, continues to operate with awesome force in the lives of many of the worst off members of our community. But he is right to suggest the existence of a burgeoning well-educated black middle class, what one might view as the middle class that affirmative action was designed to create—a group of people for whom racism, although still perhaps a problem, really *is* receding. It is from this group that today's dissenting intellectuals tend to be drawn. Many have achieved substantial professional success. And whether they have relearned an old skill or developed a new one is beside the point: when the most talented of today's black intellectuals leap from the cupola and spread their wings, they are not likely to fall.

No wonder, in such an atmosphere, that there is dissent from the vision of a community incapable of significant advance without the aid of white beneficence. But even though we now have room to fly, we must not be careless, for it is easy, once up in the air, to grow arrogant, like Icarus, and fly close to the sun, melt our wings, and plunge dizzily and fatally from the heavens. The black intellectual, even if dissenting, must never lose sight of the solid ground below. Dissenters must always remember the sacrifices that were made to permit us to do the things we can do. It is easy to be smug, to be sure that we in our academic niches, with our libraries and our computers, have found the right answers. It is easy to set up our own tentative conclusions as the new shibboleths, and then to thunder our own condemnations at "the so-called black leadership" when it dares, on what we might consider thinner evidence, to disagree. So very, very easy, and so horribly misguided.

It is vital that those of us who choose to dissent, especially in my relatively privileged generation, do so without any self-righteousness. Unlike the civil rights leadership so often excoriated in the dissenting rhetoric, most of us in the rising generation of black intellectuals have never had to face Bull Connor's dogs, spend time in Southern jails for our beliefs, or sleep with one ear cocked for the sound of breaking glass that will mean someone has tossed a brick or a bomb through a window. John Jacob, president of the National Urban League, has put it this way:

> We have now raised a generation of young people who've never known poverty, who've never lived in our "segregated" communities, who went—by America's definition—to the finest schools and who have come to believe that their achievement is predicated on the fact that they are smart.[6]

Precisely. The ranks of the dissenters are thicker among black people who are younger and more professionally successful, but it is easy to forget how the opportunities to achieve because of smarts alone were purchased. During the 1950s and 1960s, when many among us were yet short of intellectual maturity, the civil rights movement waged a heroic and often desperate struggle against one of the greatest evils this nation has ever perpetrated—and it won. If not for the sacrifices of those leaders and their fallen comrades, few of us who now choose to dissent would have had the opportunities that have brought us to where we are today. So even in dissent, we should ever be respectful; the leadership of the traditional civil rights movement deserves our salutation and our love, not the back of our collective hand.

At the same time, the civil rights leadership, rather than dismissing prominent dissenters because we have not suffered, should recognize that we have lived in the world they have struggled to build. The undeniable truth that the opportunities for which so many fought and died have not become available to everyone does not mean that they have not become available to anyone. Those of us who have had the chance to train our minds have done what I assume we were supposed to do: used the education that the civil rights movement made available to learn to think for ourselves. Sometimes we have come out on the dissenting side. If our dissent is painful, that is an unhappy fact, and one that should grieve us; but it should ultimately be irrelevant to any assessment of our arguments. The dissents we offer should stand or fall on their merits, not on the basis of our race. Certainly our position should not be privileged simply because we are black; and certainly the position of the leaders of the traditional civil rights movement should not be privileged simply because they are black. Similarly, our views should not be privileged simply because of the opportunities we have had, but the views of the leaders of the traditional civil rights movement should not be privileged simply because they have suffered.

The goal, on both sides, should be open and robust dialogue. A loving solidarity need not stifle dissent or debate; on the contrary, it strikes me that a true love for our people must be open to the possibility that some preferred solutions are wrong, that there might be another, better path.

The role of the leader is to articulate on our behalf, the role of the activist to organize us, and these are roles that our community needs. The role of the intellectual, however, is to stand apart, to support what seems sensible and criticize freely what seems wrong. If we can begin to build a new tradition of tolerance of dissent, then it is yet possible that all of us, those who take the orthodoxy as correct and those who believe they have found a better way, can begin to work together rather than against each other to help to move the race.

If, on the other hand, we persist in our squabbling, we should at least bear in mind that the argument, for all its bitterness, is mostly among those black people who have attained a degree of success; the subject under debate is how best to bring other black people along. Because the principal battleground is affirmative action, which benefits mainly those least in need of society's aid, there may be a tendency for all of us to forget who it is that is suffering as the rest of us toss our brickbats; for it is our people, black people, those on whose behalf all of us claim to be laboring, who are withering in the violent prisons that many of our inner cities have become.

It is worst of all for our children, our future, the leaders of the generations of black people to come, more than half of whom are now born into poverty and few of whom have much hope for anything resembling the American Dream that so many of the rest of us have lived. If we cannot stop our bitter internecine warfare for ourselves, then perhaps we can stop it for the children, for in the time that it takes the rest of us to figure out who called whom the nastiest name first, countless more of them will likely fall.

IV

Very well: it is off my chest. A book within a book, a dissenting view about dissenting views. I have written this book as I do all of my scholarship: to spark a dialogue. To be sure, I believe that what I say is right. But I willingly accept correction, too, and I have erred often and will err again. So, like Montaigne, I offer my opinions as what I believe, not as what is to be believed.

Writing at the turn of the century, W. E. B. DuBois opened *The Souls of Black Folk* with a question: How does it feel to be a problem? He answered it too: "[B]eing a problem is a strange experience."[7] DuBois's question, and his answer, ought to be much on the minds of black intellectuals, for as the twentieth century lurches violently toward its close, we are each of us a problem. We are a problem because our training, if we have been trained well, is in thinking independently. Nothing is harder (or more awkward) for an intellectual than to be part of a political movement. In the nineteenth century, Karl Marx thought that he had surely sundered for all time the wall that traditionally kept those who lived the life of the mind separate from the world in which they lived it; he thought that a philosopher not willing to make theory into practice was not worthy of the name. And Marxism is the embarrassing result of entire generations of intellectuals deciding not to think for themselves but to bend their minds instead to the construction of the better world that Marx promised.

I am an intellectual, not a leader. I observe what others are doing and try to stand apart from it as I analyze it. And I assume that others will analyze what I have written and point out my errors as well. That's fine: as I have said, I write less to persuade than to participate in a dialogue. My criticism is meant to be constructive, and I hope that it is taken, and also answered, in that spirit. My fear, however, is that as a result of this book, only one thing will change: far from releasing me from my intellectual box, the labelers from both camps will simply change the legend on the outside. The new label will read "BLACK NEOCONSERVATIVE." And that new label will be just as inaccurate, just as stifling, just as painful, and just as much a denial of my right to think.

DuBois, as so often, was right about this, too: it does feel strange to be a problem. Strange, but also oddly exhilarating. Necessary. Right. To our discredit, we Americans have never fully appreciated what the rest of the democratic world knows so well: reflective and open dissent is an act of loyalty. To take the needed pains to try to point out to the body politic what might be error is itself a pledge of allegiance, one with far more meaning than the often empty words of enthusiastic agreement that every community likes to hear. And for the dissenter who happens to be black, the act of dissent can be even more. An avowal of race. An acknowledgment of solidarity. An act of hope.

An act of love.

Notes

INTRODUCTION

1. William Julius Wilson, *The Declining Significance of Race,* 2nd ed. (Chicago: University of Chicago Press, 1980), pp. 110–11.
2. *Regents of the University of California v. Bakke,* 438 U.S. 265 (1978).
3. Robert L. Allen, "The Bakke Case and Affirmative Action," *Black Scholar* (September 1977): 9.

CHAPTER 1

1. Derek Bok, "Admitting Success," *New Republic,* 4 February 1985, p. 14. For the past several years, Scholastic Aptitude Test scores and scores on other standardized tests taken by black candidates have been improving both in absolute terms and relative to scores of white candidates. (National Research Council, *A Common Destiny: Blacks and American Society* [Washington, D.C.: National Academy Press, 1989], pp. 348–52.)
2. Quoted in Colin Leinster, "Black Executives: How They're Doing," *Fortune,* 18 January 1988, p. 109.
3. Anthony Borden, "Baker & McKenzie Gives a Lesson in Damage Control," *American Lawyer* (April 1989): 30.
4. For discussions of the aftermath, see, for example, Lisa Green Markoff, "Employers Learn the Hard Way About What Campuses Will Allow," *National Law Journal,* 13 March 1989, p. 4;

Lisa Green Markoff, "Stanford Bars Firm," *National Law Journal,* 24 April 1989, p. 4.

5. The legal scholar Charles Black suggested long ago that the personal sacrifice entailed by preferential policies is an obligation of citizenship, just as taxes are: everyone has a role to play in reducing the debts that the society has undertaken, and the debts may be moral as well as financial. See Charles Black, "Civil Rights in Times of Economic Stress—Jurisprudential and Philosophic Aspects," *University of Illinois Law Forum* (1976): 559. According to Black, this line of argument also answers the claim that white immigrants and their children should not be made to suffer a detriment for wrongs done before their arrival in America. One who takes up the benefits of citizenship, says Black, takes up the burdens as well.

   To be sure, Black's thesis is not a perfect one. The costs of preferential admissions, for example, may fall with special force on relatively disadvantaged whites, which would make the programs in some sense regressive. Moreover, in economic terms, if the resources transferred through preferential programs are less valuable (that is, less productive) in the hands of the favored than the disfavored group, there will be a net societal loss from the transfer. (I take no position here on who will put the resources to a more productive use.) Those distinctions, however, at best make affirmative action an extreme case of a form of social transfer that takes place all the time; so even if it appears that the singling out of white males (or subgroups of white males) for special disfavoring is in a sense less fair than some other societal transfers, the similarities may outweigh the differences.

6. Seymour Martin Lipset, *Political Man: The Bases of Politics,* rev. ed. (Baltimore: Johns Hopkins University Press, 1981). For my own views on this proposition, see Carter, "The Constitution, the Uniqueness Puzzle, and the Economic Conditions of Democracy," *George Washington Law Review* 56 (1987): 136.

7. Maria Markham Thompson, letter to the editor, *Bond Buyer,* 18 June 1990, p. 22.

8. Randall Kennedy, quoted in Ethan Bronner, "High Court's Split on Affirmative Action Echoes Nation's Division," *Boston Globe,* 29 June 1990, p. 1.

9. R. Richard Banks, "Affirmative Action—The Blacks 'Burden,'" *San Francisco Chronicle,* 26 July 1990, p. A19. For further examples of this line of argument, see, for example, Richard Wasserstrom, "One Way to Understand and Defend Programs of Preferential Treatment," in *The Moral Foundations*

of Civil Rights, ed. Robert K. Fullinwider and Claudia Mills (Totowa, N. J.: Rowman & Littlefield, 1986), p. 46; Ian Waldon, letter to the editor, *Newsday,* 19 August 1988, p. 82; Rosenfeld, "Decoding *Richmond:* Affirmative Action and the Elusive Meaning of Constitutional Equality," *Michigan Law Review* 87 (1989): 1729.

10. See, for example, Thomas Sowell, *Preferential Policies: An International Perspective* (New York: William Morrow, 1990).
11. Ibid., page 160.
12. Robert L. Allen, *Black Awakening in Capitalist America* (New York: Anchor, 1970), p. 262.
13. Anne Kelley, "Book Review," *Black Scholar* (October 1971): 50, 52.
14. As of 1980, some 56 percent of white students who began four-year college programs directly out of high school, as against 31 percent of black students, completed their degrees in less than six years. (Chester E. Finn, Jr., "The Campus: 'An Island of Repression in a Sea of Freedom,'" *Commentary* [September 1989]: 17, 22, analyzing figures from the United States Department of Education.) The other way of putting the point is that 44 percent of white students and 69 percent of black students failed to finish within six years. Another sensitive measure of college completion is the "persistence rate," the percentage of students enrolled in college in one October who enroll again the following October. As of 1986, the persistence rate of white students was 81.9 percent, and the persistence rate of black students was 72.7 percent. (National Center for Education Statistics, *The Condition of Education 1990,* vol. 2 [Postsecondary Education]: 28.) This difference becomes much greater when the rates are cumulated over four years; by my own calculations, only 55 percent of white students and 38 percent of black students would return for a fourth year, and, at the end, only 45 percent of white students and 27 percent of black students would be left. It is widely assumed that the persistence rate for black students is particularly low at the elite schools where affirmative action is most in issue. For example, much has been made of figures collected by the *San Francisco Examiner* in a study of the University of California at Berkeley purporting to show that 70 percent of black students fail to graduate at all. See, for example, Sowell, *Preferential Policies,* p. 109; John H. Bunzel, "Affirmative-Action Admission: How It 'Works' at U.C. Berkeley," *Public Interest* (Fall 1988): 111. The *Examiner* study, however, covered only graduation within five years of entrance, and found that 27 percent of black students graduate

Berkeley within that period. This graduation figure is the same as the aggregate five-year persistence rate figure I calculated above, and therefore cannot without more serve as evidence that there are particular problems for black students on the campuses of predominantly white elite schools. It remains true, nevertheless, that the substantial spread between black and white five-year persistence rates should be troublesome to those who support affirmative action in higher education.

I am aware of no comparable figures for elite law schools like Yale, but my anecdotal observations reassure me that the results would be very different. Yale's students of color, like its white students, are carefully chosen and highly motivated—and they rarely drop out. So the difficulties might be exaggerated, or the problems, whatever they are, might have less application to professional schools than to undergraduate colleges, perhaps because students who attend professional school have already displayed an unusual degree of motivation: after all, they have completed their undergraduate degrees.

15. 438 U.S. 265 (1978).
16. Alex M. Johnson, Jr., "The New Voice of Color," *Yale Law Journal* 100 (1991). For my response to Professor Johnson, see Carter, "Academic Tenure and 'White Male' Standards: Some Lessons from the Patent Law," *Yale Law Journal* 100 (1991).
17. Richard H. Chused, "The Hiring and Retention of Minorities and Women on American Law School Faculties," *University of Pennsylvania Law Review* 137 (December 1988): 537.
18. Association of American Medical Colleges, *Women and Minorities on U.S. Medical School Faculties* (1989), pp. 6–12.
19. Statistics from United States Department of Commerce, *Statistical Abstract of the United States* (Washington, D.C.: U.S. Government Printing Office, 1990), p. 389.

CHAPTER 2

1. "For Congress in Connecticut," *New York Times,* 25 October 1990.
2. Lester Ross, "How to Characterize Black Conservatives," letter to the editor, *New York Times,* 15 November 1990.
3. "Lawmaker Assails Health Chief," *New York Times,* 3 August 1990, p. A16.
4. Alison Leigh Cowan, "The New Wave Directors," *New York Times,* 1 April 1990, sec. 6, pt. 2, p. 28; Caroline Price, "Minorities Still a Small Percentage of Board Membership," *Michigan Business,* July 1990, p. 24. The recruitment of people of color as

executives and board members in order to gain access to a particular perspective should not be confused with the sensible encouragement of managers to understand the diversity of perspectives in the professional work force—provided always that managers are not taught to *assume* that race is a proxy for perspective. For sympathetic discussions of the "managing diversity" phenomenon, see, for example, Don J. DeBenedictis, "Changing Faces: Coming to Terms with Growing Minority Populations," *ABA Journal* (April 1991): 54; Sheryl Hilliard Tucker and Kevin D. Thompson, "Will Diversity=Opportunity+Advancement for Blacks?" *Black Enterprise* (November 1990), p. 50.

5. For news reports of the FAIR studies, see, for example, Judith Michaelson, "Media Group Assails 'Nightline' for Being Too Narrow," *Los Angeles Times,* 6 February 1989, pt. 6, p. 1; James Warren, "Narrow Spectrum: Study Finds 'MacNeil/Lehrer' as Bad as Networks at Reflecting Diversity," *Chicago Tribune,* 21 May 1990, Tempo sec., p. 7.

6. For example, according to the Gallup poll, only 16 percent of black respondents, as against 24 percent of white respondents, say that their sympathies in the Middle East lie more with the Palestinian Arabs than with the Israelis. Black people are slightly less likely than white people (70 percent to 73 percent) to approve negotiations with the Palestine Liberation Organization. (*The Gallup Poll 1989,* pp. 13–16.) On what is probably the most divisive current social issue, abortion, different surveys have reached different results, some showing that black people are more pro-life than white people, some showing that the views are about the same, but none showing black people as significantly more pro-choice than white people. For data suggesting that black respondents are much less likely than white respondents to approve abortion on demand, see National Research Council, *A Common Destiny: Blacks and American Society* (Washington, D.C.: National Academy Press, 1989), p. 215. For data suggesting that black people and white people are about equally opposed to overturning *Roe v. Wade,* the Supreme Court's principal abortion decision, see *The Gallup Poll 1989,* pp. 20–21. And, to take an equally current but perhaps less controversial domestic issue as an example, black people are almost twice as likely as white people to describe themselves as not being strong environmentalists. (*The Gallup Poll 1989,* p. 121.)

7. "Statement of Derrick Bell," reprinted in *Association of American Law Schools Section on Minority Groups Newsletter,* May 1990, pp. 4, 5.

8. Ibid., p. 4.
9. Quoted in Glenn Loury, "Who Speaks for American Blacks?" *Commentary* (January 1987): 34, 36.
10. Huey P. Newton, *Revolutionary Suicide,* paperback ed. (New York: Ballantine Books, 1974), p. 175.
11. *Metro Broadcasting, Inc. v. Federal Communications Commission,* 110 S. Ct. 2997, p. 3010 (1990).
12. Ibid., p. 3011.
13. Ibid., p. 3029 (O'Connor, J., dissenting).
14. For my views on the constitutionality of affirmative action generally, see Carter, "When Victims Happen to Be Black," *Yale Law Journal* 97 (February 1988): 420, 431-39.
15. *Metro Broadcasting,* p. 3016.
16. For a forceful statement of this possibility, see Patricia J. Williams, *"Metro Broadcasting, Inc. v. FCC:* Regrouping in Singular Times," *Harvard Law Review* 104 (1990): 525.
17. Anthony Appiah, "The Uncompleted Argument: DuBois and the Illusion of Race," in *"Race," Writing, and Difference,* ed. Henry Louis Gates, Jr. (Chicago: University of Chicago Press, 1986), pp. 21, 36.
18. "Minority Students at Harvard Protest Boycott," *New York Times,* 9 August 1982, p. A9.
19. "Blacks to Press Boycott of Law Course at Harvard," *New York Times,* 15 September 1982, p. A15.
20. Quoted in John Gregory Dunne, "An American Education," in *Crooning* (New York: Simon & Schuster, 1990), p. 21.
21. For a debate on a related issue, the role of white reporters in covering black communities, see Cathy Corman, "The Reporter as 'Lightning Rod,'" *Christian Science Monitor,* 31 January 1991, p. 12.
22. Townsend Davis, letter to the editor, *New York Times,* 19 May 1989, p. A34.
23. Richard Rodriguez, *Hunger of Memory* (Boston: David R. Godine, 1981), pp. 167-172.

CHAPTER 3

1. See, for example, the account of the debate in Maryland in *Bond Buyer,* 31 July 1990, p. 32.
2. Ira Glasser, "Affirmative Action and the Legacy of Racial Injustice," in *Eliminating Racism: Profiles in Controversy,* ed. Phyllis A. Katz and Dalmas A. Taylor (New York: Plenum Press, 1988), pp. 341, 350.
3. Stanley Crouch, *Notes of a Hanging Judge* (New York: Oxford University Press, 1990).

4. The most recent General Social Survey, a regular report of the widely respected National Opinion Research Center, found that 53 percent of white respondents consider black people generally less intelligent than white people. ("Whites Retain Negative View of Minorities, a Survey Finds," *New York Times,* 10 January 1991, p. B10.) Prior surveys through the late 1960s had shown a decline in the percentage of white respondents who consider black people less intelligent. Historical polling results on the attitudes of white Americans about black Americans are collected in National Research Council, *A Common Destiny: Blacks and American Society* (Washington, D.C.: National Academy Press, 1989), pp. 120–23. For a more detailed discussion of data collected during the 1980s, see Lee Sigelman and Susan Welch, *Black Americans' Views of Racial Inequality* (Cambridge: Cambridge University Press, 1991), esp. pp. 85–100.

5. Quoted in Colin Leinster, "Black Executives: How They're Doing," *Fortune,* 18 January 1988, p. 109.

6. John Hope Franklin, "The Dilemma of the American Negro Scholar," in *Race and History: Selected Essays 1938–1988* (Baton Rouge: Louisiana State University Press, 1989), p. 295. The essay was originally published in 1963.

7. My description of the star system might usefully be compared to the French sociologist Pierre Bourdieu's analysis of the role of "cultural capital" and "social capital" in the maintenance of the class structure: Pierre Bourdieu, "Cultural Reproduction and Social Reproduction," in *Power and Ideology in Education,* ed. J. Karabel and A. H. Halsey (New York: Oxford University Press, 1977), p. 487. I am less sure than Bourdieu is that the system works principally to the benefit of the children of those already part of it; my concern with the star system is that it is exclusionary and at the same time a distortion of the meritocratic ideal.

8. Mari Matsuda, "Affirmative Action and Legal Knowledge: Planting Seeds in Plowed-up Ground," *Harvard Women's Law Journal* 11 (Spring 1988): 5–6.

9. Although it is sometimes said that racial discrimination serves the interests of capitalism, the inefficiency of prejudice in the market is well understood in economics. The classic analysis of the market costs of discrimination on the basis of race is Gary S. Becker, *The Economics of Discrimination* (Chicago: University of Chicago Press, 1957). Much of the analysis in Becker's book is mathematical and may be inaccessible to the lay reader. A recent and more accessible treatment of the same issue is Thomas Sowell, *Preferential Policies: An International Perspective* (New

York: William Morrow, 1990), esp. pp. 20–40. For a discussion of the way that racial discrimination following the Civil War retarded the growth of the Southern economy, see Roger L. Ransom and Richard Sutch, *One Kind of Freedom: The Economic Consequences of Emancipation* (Cambridge: Cambridge University Press, 1977).

10. Quoted in Adam Begley, "Black Studies' New Era: Henry Louis Gates Jr.," *New York Times Magazine,* 1 April 1990, p. 24.
11. Franklin, "The Dilemma of the American Negro Scholar," p. 305.

CHAPTER 4

1. For general discussions of this phenomenon, see National Research Council, *A Common Destiny: Blacks and American Society* (Washington, D.C.: National Academy Press, 1989), pp. 274–94; Kevin Phillips, *The Politics of Rich and Poor* (New York: Random House, 1990), pp. 207–8. From 1959 through 1982, the income gap grew in absolute but not relative terms; that is, the dollar size of the income spread between the poorest and richest families grew, whereas their relative shares of total income stayed about the same. (Reynolds Farley, *Blacks and Whites: Narrowing the Gap?* [Cambridge: Harvard University Press, 1984], pp. 181–83.) During the 1980s, the size of the gap grew larger still. In a somewhat more revealing statistic on income stratification, the income of black married couples in 1986 was nearly three times the income of black female-headed households with no spouse, the majority of which are below the poverty line. (In white households, the ratio was slightly more than two to one.) (National Research Council, *A Common Destiny,* p. 282.)
2. Reynolds Farley and Walter Allen, *The Color Line and the Quality of Life in America* (New York: Russell Sage, 1987).
3. Robert Klitgaard, *Choosing Elites* (New York: Basic Books, 1985).
4. William Julius Wilson has been especially forceful and persistent in making this point. See, for example, *The Truly Disadvantaged* (Chicago: University of Chicago Press, 1978), and *The Declining Significance of Race* (Chicago: University of Chicago Press, 1978).
5. Roger Wilkins, "Uncommon Ground," *Mother Jones,* July/August 1990, p. 10.
6. National Research Council, *A Common Destiny,* pp. 280, 281.
7. Joel Dreyfuss and Charles Lawrence III, *The Bakke Case: The Politics of Inequality* (New York: Harcourt Brace Jovanovich, 1979), p. 228.

8. Stokely Carmichael and Charles V. Hamilton, *Black Power: The Politics of Liberation in America* (New York: Vintage, 1967), p. 4.

9. Ibid., p. 22.

10. See, for example, George Gilder, *Wealth and Poverty* (New York: Basic Books, 1981), esp. pp. 169–82; and Charles Murray, *Losing Ground: American Social Policy 1950–1980* (New York: Basic Books, 1984), esp. pp. 96–112, 172–75.

11. See, for example, Richard Herrnstein, "Still an American Dilemma," *Public Interest* (Winter 1990): 3.

12. National Research Council, *A Common Destiny,* pp. 333, 346–47. See also Nathan Glazer, "Education and Training Programs and Poverty," in *Fighting Poverty,* ed. Sheldon H. Danziger and Daniel H. Weinberg (Cambridge: Harvard University Press, 1986), p. 152. Richard Herrnstein has challenged the normative value of these studies. Assuming that all students benefit equally from early schooling, and if (as he seems to think is likely) racial differences in measured intelligence are innate, Herrnstein makes the remarkable suggestion that we might be better off spending the money on the students with the higher rather than the lower measured aptitude. (Herrnstein, "Still an American Dilemma.")

13. National Research Council, *A Common Destiny,* p. 360.

14. This research is summarized in ibid., pp. 369–70. See also Reginald M. Clark, *Family Life and School Achievement: Why Poor Black Children Succeed or Fail* (Chicago: University of Chicago Press, 1983). For a moving account of the successes (and complexities) of the "A Better Chance" (ABC) program, aimed at overcoming some of these difficulties, see Richard L. Zweigenhaft and G. William Domhoff, *Blacks in the White Establishment?* (New Haven: Yale University Press, 1991).

15. National Research Council, *A Common Destiny,* pp. 338–54.

16. The figures for high school graduation and college enrollment rates are Commerce Department figures discussed in Reginald Wilson, "Black Higher Education: Crisis and Promise," in *The State of Black America 1989* (New York: National Urban League, 1989). The figures on percentage of high school graduates attending some college are my own, calculated from Wilson's data.

17. J. R. Pole, *The Pursuit of Equality in American History* (Berkeley: University of California Press, 1978).

18. See, for example, Stephen J. Gould, *The Mismeasure of Man* (New York: W. W. Norton, 1981).

19. Derrick Bell, "Whites Make Big Gains Under Broadened Selection Criteria," *Los Angeles Daily Journal,* 1 September 1987, p. 4.

20. National Research Council, *Fairness in Employment Testing* (Washington, D.C.: National Academy Press, 1989), p. 185.

21. Ibid., p. 6. Another important report that tries to deal in similar ways with similar statistical difficulties is National Commission on Testing and Public Policy, *From Gatekeeper to Gateway: Transforming Testing in America* (Chestnut Hill, Mass.: National Commission on Testing and Public Policy, 1990). Although the National Commission on Testing report discusses racial differential in scoring in terms of cultural bias, it does not seriously defend an underprediction claim, choosing instead—correctly, in my judgment—to warn against an overreliance on scores alone in evaluating *all* candidates, not just those whose presence is said to lend diversity.

22. National Research Council, *Fairness in Employment Testing,* p. 186. This is not to suggest that race and other irrelevant characteristics play no role in any evaluations. On the contrary, the social psychology literature suggests that they frequently do, although predicting whether the role will be positive or negative is not easy. See, for example, John B. McConahay, "Modern Racism and Modern Discrimination: The Effects of Race, Racial Attitudes, and Context on Simulated Hiring Decisions," *Personality and Social Psychology Bulletin* 9 (1983): 551; Eve Spangler, Marsha A. Gordon, and Ronald M. Pipkin, "Token Women: An Empirical Test of Kanter's Hypothesis," *American Journal of Sociology* 84 (1978): 160.

23. For a thoughtful discussion of these "later-life" predictions, see Robert Klitgaard, *Choosing Elites* (New York: Basic Books, 1985), pp. 116–53.

24. Nathan Glazer, "The Future of Preferential Affirmative Action," in *Eliminating Racism: Profiles in Controversy,* ed. Phyllis A. Katz and Dalmas A. Taylor (New York: Plenum Press, 1988), pp. 329, 339.

CHAPTER 5

1. Judges 12:16. I recognize that the King James Version of the Bible is not accepted by serious biblical scholars as a very accurate translation. But I have selected this language not because it accurately represents the original text, but because it is from this popular version that the word *shibboleth* came into the language.

2. Quoted in William Raspberry, "Much Worse Than Meese," *Washington Post,* 16 December 1983, p. A23.

3. Glenn Loury, "Hunger and Politics," *Business and Society Review* (Spring 1984): 60, 61.

4. William Julius Wilson, *The Declining Significance of Race* (Chicago: University of Chicago Press, 1978), p. 144.

5. William Julius Wilson, *The Truly Disadvantaged* (Chicago: University of Chicago Press, 1978), p. viii.

6. For a detailed discussion of my reasons for thinking Steele too optimistic, see my book review in *Transition* 1 (1991).

7. Quoted in Gene Seymour, "The Great Debate," *Newsday,* 10 October 1990, part 2, p. 8.

8. Quoted in Peter Applebome, "Stirring a Debate on Breaking Racism's Shackles," *New York Times,* 30 May 1990, p. A18.

9. Thomas Sowell, *Preferential Policies: An International Perspective* (New York: William Morrow, 1990), p. 150.

10. Carl T. Rowan, "———or Quisling?" *Washington Post,* 29 September 1981. In the same column, Rowan compared Sowell to Aunt Jemima and Stepin Fetchit.

11. Quoted in Jacob V. Lamar, Jr., "Redefining the American Dilemma: Some Black Scholars Are Challenging Hallowed Assumptions," *Time,* 11 November 1985, p. 33.

12. Martin Kilson, letter to the editor, *New Republic,* 11 November 1985, p. 6.

13. Randall Kennedy, "Racial Critiques of Legal Academia," *Harvard Law Review* 102 (June 1989): 1745.

14. Julius Lester, *Lovesong: Becoming a Jew* (New York: Henry Holt, 1988), p. 210.

15. Quoted in Elizabeth Mehren, "The Baldwin Blowup," *Los Angeles Times,* 10 July 1988, pt. 6, p. 1.

16. For an extended discussion of this episode, and sources for these and other quotations, see Stephen L. Carter, "Loving the Messenger," *Yale Journal of Law and the Humanities* (May 1989): 317, 344.

17. Stanley Crouch, *Notes of a Hanging Judge* (New York: Oxford University Press, 1990), p. 239.

18. Judith N. Shklar, *Ordinary Vices* (Cambridge: Harvard/Belknap, 1984) p. 131.

19. Glenn Loury, "Who Speaks for American Blacks?" *Commentary* (January 1987): 34, 38.

20. Quoted in Henry Allen, "Hot Disputes and Cool Sowell," *Washington Post,* 1 October 1981, p. C1.

21. Shelby Steele, *The Content of Our Character* (New York: St. Martin's Press, 1990), p. 72.

22. Quoted in Eric Harrison, "Economics Is Key Element as Black Leaders Set Goals," *Los Angeles Times,* 24 April 1989, p. 1.

23. Quoted in E. J. Dionne, "Red Hot Ideas on Black and White," *Washington Post,* 10 October 1990, p. D1.

24. Stephen L. Carter, "Racial Preferences? So What?" *Wall Street Journal,* 13 September 1989, p. A20.

25. Affirmative action, like abortion, is an issue on which poll results depend a great deal on precisely how the question is worded. For example, when asked whether an employer faced with two equally qualified applicants, one white and one black, should choose the black applicant because of historical racism, 80 percent of white respondents and 50 percent of black respondents said no. (*Newsweek,* 7 March 1988, p. 23.) Lee Sigelman and Susan Welch, who have collected survey results concerning preferential policies, have made some interesting findings. In 1984, only 23 percent of black respondents and 10 percent of white respondents supported the idea that black people and women should receive "preferential treatment in getting jobs and places in college as opposed to mainly considering ability as determined by test scores." In 1988, however, asked whether they favored "affirmative action programs in employment for blacks, provided there are no rigid quotas," 78 percent of black respondents and 73 percent of white respondents said yes. Other answers cover a similar range, but it is clear that the more one describes affirmative action as a way to get hired, the lower the support from black and white respondents alike; the more one describes it as a way to get trained, the greater the support from black and white respondents alike. Lee Sigelman and Susan Welch, *Black Americans' Views of Racial Inequality: The Dream Deferred* (Cambridge: Cambridge University Press, 1991), p. 129.

26. Quoted in Robert Marquand, "New Education Appointee," *Christian Science Monitor,* 27 March 1987, p. 21.

27. For an evocative account of the battle between Booker T. Washington and the radical intellectuals, see Stephen Fox, *The Guardian of Boston: William Monroe Trotter* (New York: Atheneum, 1970).

28. Quoted in Samuel P. Spencer, *Booker T. Washington and the Negro's Place in American Life* (Boston: Little, Brown, 1955).

29. All quotations from correspondence to or from George A. Towns are taken from letters found in the George A. Towns Papers, Atlanta University Archives, Atlanta, Georgia.

30. W. E. B. DuBois, *The Autobiography of W. E. B. DuBois* (New York: International Publishers, 1968), p. 241 (emphasis in original).

31. Quoted in E. David Cronon, *Black Moses* (Madison: University of Wisconsin Press, 1955), p. 131.

32. Ibid., p. 192.

CHAPTER 6

1. Langston Hughes, "Professor," in *Laughing to Keep from Crying* (New York: Henry Holt, 1952), p. 105.
2. Derrick Bell, letter to the editor, *New York Times,* 26 January 1990, p. A30.
3. Harold Isaacs, "Group Identity and Political Change: The Role of Color and Physical Characteristics," *Daedalus* 353 (Spring 1967).
4. This research is summarized in National Research Council, *A Common Destiny: Blacks and American Society* (Washington, D.C.: National Academy Press, 1989), pp. 371-73.
5. Derrick Bell, *And We Are Not Saved: The Elusive Quest for Racial Justice* (New York: Basic Books, 1987), p. 14.
6. Girardeau Spann, letter to the editor, *Reconstruction* 1, no. 2 (1990): 3.
7. For a sensitive discussion of the rejection of the terms *negritude* and *African personality* by an earlier generation of black intellectuals, see St. Clair Drake, " 'Hide My Face?' On Pan-Africanism and Negritude," in *The Making of Black America,* vol. 1, ed. August Meier and Elliott Rudwick (New York: Atheneum, 1971), p. 66.
8. Quoted in Paul Weyrich, "Clarence Thomas: Here Comes the Judge," *Washington Times,* 1 March 1990, p. E1.
9. Christopher Hitchens, "How Neoconservatives Perish," *Harper's,* July 1990, p. 65.
10. These figures are drawn from United States Department of Commerce, *Statistical Abstract of the United States 1990,* pp. 66, 459-60.
11. Quoted in Paul Weyrich, "Clarence Thomas: Here Comes the Judge," *Washington Times,* 1 March 1990, p. E1.
12. Quoted in Gene Seymour, "The Great Debate," *Newsday,* 10 October 1990.
13. Quoted in Peter Applebome, "Stirring a Debate on Breaking Racism's Shackles," *New York Times,* 30 May 1990, p. A18.
14. Quoted in Clarence Page, "A Summit Should Harness Diversity, Not Harden Discord," *Chicago Tribune,* 26 April 1989, p. 19.
15. "Clarence Thomas, in His Own Words," *Legal Times,* 16 October 1989, p. 11.
16. Thucydides, *History of the Peloponnesian War,* Book 8, tr. Rex Warner (New York: Penguin Books, 1954), p. 588.
17. Roy Wilkins, *Standing Fast,* p. 51.

CHAPTER 7

1. Quoted in Paul Weyrich, "Getting Serious About Blacks," *Conservative Digest* (July/August 1989): 11, 13.

2. John Dillin, "Pro-Choice Stance Helps Wilder," *Christian Science Monitor,* 27 September 1989, p. 8. See also James N. Baker, "Blacks Agonize over Abortion," *Newsweek,* 4 December 1989, p. 63.

3. This research is summarized in National Research Council, *A Common Destiny: Blacks and American Society* (Washington, D.C.: National Academy Press, 1989), p. 215.

4. Ibid.

5. Ibid.

6. Quoted in E. J. Dionne, Jr., "Red-Hot Ideas on Black and White," *Washington Post,* 10 October 1990, p. D1.

7. Stephen Carter, "The Confirmation Mess," *Harvard Law Review* (April 1988): 1185, and Stephen Carter, "The Constitution, the Uniqueness Puzzle, and the Economic Conditions of Democracy," *George Washington Law Review* 56 (November 1987): 136.

8. Glenn Loury, "The Saliency of Race," *Second Thoughts* 1, no. 3 (Summer 1990): 1, 6.

9. Quoted in William Raspberry, "Reaching Out to Blacks," *Washington Post,* 14 July 1989, p. A21.

10. Clarence Thomas, "Why Black Americans Should Look to Conservative Policies," *Heritage Lectures,* no. 119 (Washington, D.C.: Heritage Foundation, 18 June 1987), p. 5.

11. Quoted in Robert Shogan, "Blacks Threaten Suit," *Los Angeles Times,* 11 August 1988, p. 24.

12. Thomas, "Why Black Americans Should Look to Conservative Policies," p. 5.

13. William O. Douglas, *The Court Years 1939–1975* (New York: Random House, 1980), p. 241.

14. Quoted in Henry Allen, "Hot Disputes and Cool Sowell" *Washington Post,* 1 October 1981, p. C1.

15. Adam Clymer, "Problem for the G.O.P.: Views and Woes of Blacks," *New York Times,* 5 October 1981, p. B16.

16. Fred Barnes, "George Bush 'Schmoozes' Afro-Americans Effectively," *New Republic,* 28 May 1990, p. 11.

17. Richard Lacayo, "Back to the Party of Lincoln?" *Time,* 2 January 1989, p. 79.

18. Thomas, "Why Black Americans Should Look to Conservative Policies," p. 4.

19. Quoted in Fred Barnes, "Party of Lincoln," *New Republic,* 20 March 1989, p. 10.

20. This argument was put forward by Edward Rollins, who was at the time executive director of the House Republican campaign committee. Quoted in Fred Barnes, "Party of Lincoln," *New Republic,* 20 March 1989. p. 10, 12.

21. "Blacks and the GOP," *National Review,* 30 September 1988, pp. 15, 16.

22. See "Eyeing the Prize: GOP Sets Sights on Blacks," *Black Enterprise,* May 1989, p. 35; "From Two New Party Chairmen: Plans to Woo and Keep the Black Vote," *American Visions,* June 1989, p. 16.

23. See George E. Curry, "Black Republicans: Who They Are, What They Want," *Emerge* (March 1990): 20. See also "Dems Win Congress But Will They Lose Blacks?" *Black Enterprise,* January 1989, p. 13. In the 1990 mid-term elections for the House of Representatives, Republican candidates received 22 percent of the black vote, compared with 14 percent (1986) and 11 percent (1982) in the two mid-term elections during Ronald Reagan's term as president. "Portrait of the Electorate: U.S. House Vote," *New York Times,* 8 November 1990, p. B7.

24. Between 1960 and 1984, in fact, the percentage of black people identifying themselves as Republicans plummeted from 22 to 5—a statistic that speaks volumes about perceptions during some of the most trying years of the civil rights movement. Curry, "Black Republicans: Who They Are, What They Want," p. 21.

25. Weyrich, "Getting Serious," pp. 12–14.

26. Thomas, "Why Black Americans Should Look to Conservative Policies," p. 8.

27. Quoted in Jack Bass, "End of the Southern Strategy," *New York Times,* 12 January 1991, Sec. 1, p. 25.

28. Thomas, "Why Black Americans Should Look to Conservative Policies," p. 2.

29. Quoted in Weyrich, "Getting Serious," p. 13.

30. Thomas, "Why Black Americans Should Look to Conservative Policies," p. 2.

31. William P. Barr, letter to the editor, *New York Times,* 5 October 1990, p. A36.

32. The most extensive study of the relevance of race in the administration of capital punishment is David C. Baldus, George Woodworth, and Charles A. Pulaski, Jr., *Equal Justice and the Death Penalty: A Legal and Empirical Analysis* (Boston: Northeastern University Press, 1990). The Supreme Court rejected a constitutional claim based on these and similar disparities in *McCleskey v. Kemp,* 481 U.S. 279 (1987), which is discussed in Stephen L. Carter, "When Victims Happen to Be Black," *Yale Law Journal* 97 (February 1988): 420, and Randall Kennedy, *"McCleskey v. Kemp:* Race, Capital Punishment, and the Supreme Court," *Harvard Law Review* 101 (1988): 1388.

33. John B. Judis, "Black Donkey, White Elephant," *New Republic,* 18 April 1988, p. 25.

34. Henry Klingeman, "The GOP's Black Eye," *National Review,* 30 January 1987, p. 31.

35. Cato, "Letter from Washington," *National Review,* 9 December 1988, p. 11. The editorial was couched in language illustrating how awkward a point this is for the Republican party: "The Republicans' challenge is to eradicate that dimwitted notion, without alienating southern whites"—the group that, in the previous sentence, the writer had said was attracted to the GOP by the "incorrect view . . . that Republicans are hostile to the rights of minorities."

36. See, for example, Bruce Fein, "Choosing by Race Is Doing the Wrong Thing," *U.S.A. Today,* 29 June 1990, p. 10A, and Clint Bolick, "Fulfilling America's Promise, A Civil Rights Strategy for the 1990s," *Heritage Foundation Reports* 773 (Heritage Foundation, 1990). I am concerned only with the polemical use of the comparison. I have no quarrel with the scholarly and, in its way, reasonable comparison (which also cites the difference between the two) made by Thomas Sowell in his book *Preferential Policies: An International Perspective* (New York: William Morrow, 1990).

CHAPTER 8

1. See *Dictionary of Cautionary Words and Phrases* (Columbia: University of Missouri School of Journalism, 1989).

2. Richard Herrnstein, "Still an American Dilemma," *Public Interest* (Winter 1990): 3.

3. For discussions of this effort, see Richard Bernstein, "The Rising Hegemony of the Politically Correct," *New York Times,* 28 October 1990, sec. 4, p. 1, and Chester E. Finn, Jr., "The Campus: 'An Island of Repression in a Sea of Freedom," *Commentary,* September 1989, p.17.

4. For catalogues of several of the worst incidents, see, for example, Steve France, "Hate Goes to College," *ABA Journal* (July 1990): 44; Mari Matsuda, "Public Response to Racist Speech: Considering the Victim's Story," *Michigan Law Review* 87 (August 1989): 2320; Jon Wiener, "Reagan's Children: Racial Hatred on Campus," *The Nation,* 27 February 1989, p. 260.

5. Quoted in Felicity Barringer, "Campus Battle Pits Freedom of Speech Against Racial Slurs," *New York Times,* 25 April 1989, p. A1.

6. Quoted in Nadine Strossen, "Regulating Racist Speech on Campus: A Modest Proposal?" *Duke Law Journal* (1990): 484.

7. Quoted in Jon Wiener, "Free Speech for Campus Bigots?" *The Nation,* 26 February 1990, p. 272.
8. For a discussion of the Goetz case in this context, see Stephen L. Carter, "When Victims Happen to Be Black," *Yale Law Journal* 97 (February 1988): 420.
9. Patricia Williams, "On Being the Object of Property," *Signs* 14 (1988): 5, 17.
10. *Doe v. University of Michigan,* 721 F. Supp. 852 (E. D. Mich. 1989).
11. See, for example, Matsuda, "Public Response to Racist Speech," and Charles R. Lawrence III, "If He Hollers Let Him Go: Regulating Racist Speech on Campus," *Duke Law Journal* (1990): 431.
12. Quoted in Wiener, "Free Speech for Campus Bigots?" p. 274.
13. Sarah Lawrence Lightfoot, *Balm in Gilead: Journey of a Healer* (Reading, MA: Addison Wesley/Merloyd Lawrence, 1988), p. 105.
14. William Shockley, "Dysgenics, Geneticity, Raceology: A Challenge to the Intellectual Responsibility of Educators," *Phi Delta Kappan,* January 1972, p. 297.
15. Ibid., pp. 303–4.
16. Matsuda, "Public Response to Racist Speech," pp. 2364–65.
17. For a forceful rejection of Shockley's thesis, see, for example, Stephen Jay Gould, *The Mismeasure of Man* (New York: W. W. Norton, 1981). A useful collection of essays on the same subject is Ashley Montagu, ed., *Race and IQ* (London: Oxford University Press, 1975).
18. Loren Graham, "Political Ideology and Genetic Theory: Russia and Germany in the 1920's," *Hastings Center Report* (October 1977): 30.
19. Shelby Steele, *The Content of Our Character* (New York: St. Martins Press, 1990).

CHAPTER 9

1. Alice Walker, "The Civil Rights Movement: What Good Was It?" in *In Search of Our Mothers' Gardens* (New York: Harcourt Brace Jovanovich, 1983), pp. 119, 127–28.
2. Quoted in Ethan Bronner, *Battle for Justice: How the Bork Nomination Shook America* (New York: W. W. Norton, 1989), p. 279.
3. I have written about the Bork hearings elsewhere in considerable detail. See, for example, Carter, "The Confirmation Mess," *Harvard Law Review* 101 (1988): 1185; Carter, "Bork Redux," *Texas Law Review* 69 (February 1991): 751.
4. Carol Gilligan, *In a Different Voice* (Cambridge: Harvard Uni-

versity Press, 1982). For a similar argument, see Gibbs, Arnold, and Burkhart, "Sex Differences in the Expression of Moral Judgment," *Child Development* 55 (1984): 1040.

5. See Lawrence Walker, Brian de Vries and Shelley Trevethan, "Moral Stages and Moral Orientations in Real-Life and Hypothetical Dilemmas," *Child Development* 58 (1987): 842; idem, "Sex Differences in the Development of Moral Reasoning: A Critical Review," *Child Development* 55 (1984): 677 (asserting that substantial evidence of lack of sex differences in moral development is disregarded); Catherine Greeno and Eleanor Maccoby, "How Different Is the "Different Voice"?," *Signs* 11 (1986): 310 (questioning Gilligan's methodology and citing contrary evidence); Zetta Luria, "A Methodological Critique," *Signs* 11 (1986): 316 (rejecting Gilligan's methodology). For Gilligan's response to her critics, see, for example, "Reply by Carol Gilligan," *Signs* 11 (1986): 324.

6. See, for example, Catherine MacKinnon, *Feminism Unmodified* (Cambridge: Harvard University Press, 1982), pp. 38–39 (arguing that Gilligan's work affirms difference "when difference means dominance" and therefore affirms "the qualities and characteristics of powerlessness"); and Linda Kerber, "Some Cautionary Words for Historians," *Signs* 11 (1986): 304 (assessing dangers in suggesting biological source of differences). Some feminists who have embraced her conclusions have been critical of her methodology or style. See, for example, Judy Auerbach, Linda Blum, Vicki Smith, and Christine Williams, "Commentary: On Gilligan's *A Different Voice,*" *Feminist Studies* (Spring 1985): 149, 160 ("The problem with her book is not that its politics are bad, but that it lacks a politics altogether"). Others have accepted the work, and considered principally its implications. See, for example, Jessica Benjamin, "Book Review," *Signs* 8 (Winter 1983): 297, 298 ("Gilligan's work . . . points to the radical potential of women's search for universal norms through a psychological rather than a formal logical mode of thought"); Suzzana Sherry, "Civic Virtue and the Feminine Voice in Constitutional Adjudication," *Virginia Law Review* 72 (1986): 543, 591 (Gilligan's work implies "a feminine vision" of "a mature virtue-based ideology" that "has been conspicuously absent from the shaping of [American] moral or political traditions"). Cf. Lindsy Van Gelder, "Carol Gilligan: Leader for a Different Kind of Future," *Ms.* (January 1984): 37 (uncritical acceptance of the work).

7. Stokely Carmichael and Charles V. Hamilton, *Black Power: The Politics of Liberation in America* (New York: Random House, 1967), pp. 61–62.

8. See, for example, Stanley Crouch, *Notes of a Hanging Judge* (New York: Oxford University Press, 1990); Randall Kennedy, "Racial Critiques of Legal Academia," *Harvard Law Review* 102 (1989): 1745.

9. Harold Cruse, *The Crisis of the Negro Intellectual* (New York: William Morrow, 1967), p. 475.

10. Edward Shils, "Color and the Afro-Asian Intellectual," *Daedalus,* (Spring 1967): 279, 288.

11. Ibid., p. 293.

12. This story is recounted by Peter Brimelow in "A Man Alone," *Forbes,* 24 August 1987, p. 40. According to Brimelow, Sowell refused to confirm or deny it.

13. Julius Lester, *Lovesong: Becoming a Jew* (New York: H. Holt, 1988), p. 172.

14. Quoted in Edwin McDowell, "A Noted 'Hispanic' Novelist Proves to be Someone Else," *New York Times,* 22 July, 1984. p. 1.

15. David Tracy, *Plurality and Ambiguity: Hermeneutics, Religion, Hope* (San Francisco: Harper & Row, 1987), pp. 20-21.

16. Alexander M. Bickel, *The Morality of Consent* (New Haven: Yale University Press, 1975), p. 111.

17. See, for example, Thomas Sowell, *Ethnic America* (New York: Basic Books, 1981).

18. See, for example, Richard Wasserstrom, "One Way to Understand and Defend Programs of Preferential Treatment," in Robert K. Fullinwider and Claudia Mills, eds., *The Moral Foundations of Civil Rights* (Totowa, N. J.: Rowman & Littlefield, 1986); Carter A. Wilson, "Affirmative Action: Exploding the Myths of a Slandered Policy," *Black Scholar* (May/June 1986): 19.

19. I discuss the problem of black anti-Semitism in Stephen L. Carter, "Loving the Messenger," *Yale Journal of Law and the Humanities* (May 1989): 317.

20. Lester, *Lovesong,* p. 65.

21. Quoted in William L. Shirer, *The Rise and Fall of the Third Reich: A History of Nazi Germany* (New York: Simon and Schuster, 1960), p. 895*n.*

22. Judith N. Shklar, *Ordinary Vices* (Cambridge: Harvard/Belknap, 1984), p. 17.

23. J. R. Green, letter to the editor, *New York Times,* 22 March 1990, p. A26.

24. Gordon Allport, *The Nature of Prejudice* (Garden City, NY: Doubleday, 1955), p. 9.

25. A detailed reminder of this stark fact is Thomas Sowell's *Preferential Policies: An International Perspective* (New York: William Morrow, 1990).

CHAPTER 10

1. Jason DeParle, "Talk of Government Being Out to Get Blacks Falls on More Attentive Ears," *New York Times,* 29 October 1990, p. B7. Recounting results of *New York Times*/CBS poll.

2. This argument is developed in some detail, with the citation of evidence, in Thomas Sowell, *Preferential Policies: An International Perspective* (New York: William Morrow, 1990).

3. Letter of Adelaide Casely–Hayford to Anna Melissa Graves, 7 November 1942, quoted in Anna Melissa Graves, *Benvenuto Cellini Had No Prejudice Against Bronze* (Baltimore: Waverly Press, 1943), p. 87. Graves, who edited this fascinating book of letters from correspondence in West Africa, spent the first half of the twentieth century traveling the world to get to know as many different cultures as possible, the better, she explained, to demonstrate the brotherhood of man.

4. See Stephen L. Carter, "When Victims Happen to Be Black," *Yale Law Journal* 97 (1988): 420.

5. James Blanton, "A Limit to Affirmative Action?" *Commentary* (June 1989): 28. For a similar discussion of faculty hiring and the shrinking pool of nonwhite candidates with Ph.D.'s, see John H. Bunzel, "Minority Faculty Hiring: Problems and Prospects," *American Scholar* (Winter 1990): 39.

6. Bella Stumbo, "Where There's Smoke: On the Front Line with the Tobacco Lobby," *Los Angeles Times,* 24 August 1986.

7. Mary A. Dempsey, "Smoking Growing Among Blacks, Expert Says," United Press International, 19 June 1987, BC cycle.

8. Robb London, "Judge's Overruling of Crack Law Brings Turmoil," *New York Times,* 11 January 1991, p. B5.

9. Quoted in Susan Milligan, "Eyes on the Lies: How Black Leaders and Cigarette Companies Have Turned Indoor Smoking into a Civil Rights Issue," *Washington Monthly* (June 1987): 39.

10. For a perhaps overly sarcastic account, see Richard Blow, "Blackstabbers," *New Republic,* 29 May 1989, p. 16.

11. William H. Hastie, "Observations on the Judicial Process," in *From the Black Bar: Voices for Equal Justice,* ed. Gilbert Ware (New York: Putnam, 1976), p. 177.

12. DeParle, "Talk of Government," p. B7.

13. Carter A. Wilson, "Affirmative Action: Exploding the Myths of a Slandered Policy," *Black Scholar* (May/June 1986): 19, 20.

14. Thomas Sowell, "Affirmative Action in Faculty Hiring," in *Education: Assumptions vs. History* (Stanford, CA: Hoover Institution Press, 1986), p. 76.

15. Martha Minow, *Making All the Difference: Inclusion, Exclusion,*

and American Law (Ithaca: Cornell University Press, 1990), p. 387.

16. Quoted in Ellen Hopkins, "Blacks at the Top: Torn Between Two Worlds," *New York,* 19 January 1987, pp. 21, 28.

17. Ibid.

18. Kenneth B. Clark, "The Duty of the Intellectual," in *Pathos of Power* (New York: Harper & Row, 1974), p. 20.

19. See Robert Klitgaard, *Choosing Elites* (New York: Basic Books, 1985).

20. Vincent Harding, *There Is a River: The Black Struggle for Freedom in America* (New York: Harcourt Brace Jovanovich, 1981), pp. 260–61.

21. Quoted in Colin Leinster, "Black Executives: How They're Doing," *Fortune,* 18 January 1988, p. 109.

CHAPTER 11

1. Alice Walker, "The Civil Rights Movement: What Good Was It?" in *In Search of Our Mothers' Gardens* (New York: Harcourt Brace Jovanovich, 1983).

2. Shelby Steele, *The Content of Our Character* (New York: St. Martin's Press, 1990), pp. 106, 171, 172.

3. Price M. Cobbs, "Valuing Diversity: The Myth and the Challenge," in *The State of Black America 1989* (National Urban League, 1989), pp. 151, 153.

4. Anthony Appiah, "The Uncompleted Argument: DuBois and the Illusion of Race," in Henry Louis Gates, Jr., ed., *"Race," Writing, and Difference* (Chicago: University of Chicago Press, 1986), p. 21.

5. Appiah, "The Uncompleted Argument," p. 27.

6. Quoted in George E. Curry, "GOP Reaching Out to Blacks," *Chicago Tribune,* 14 August, 1989.

7. W. E. B. DuBois, "Of Our Spiritual Strivings," in *The Souls of Black Folk* (New York: New American Library, 1969) pp. 43, 44. The book was first published in 1903.

Index

"A Better Chance" (ABC) program, 263*n*14
Abortion, 133, 145, 259*n*6, 266*n*25
Academic tenure, 90
Affirmative action, 1–8, 146, 229, 230, 246; ambivalence of role of beneficiary of, 3, 11–27, 47–49, 52; backlash against, 25–26, 166, 211; and "best black" syndrome, 47–69; and black middle class, 18, 71, 232, 233, 249; conservative critics of, 160–61, 167, 168; costs of, 17–21, 72, 256*n*5; defended as compensation, 72, 74, 79, 84, 86–87, 198; demise of, 7, 26, 94, 232–35; and difference theory, 207, 210–11; diversity approach to, 34–36, 44–45, 128, 198–99; 207, 210–11, 233; future of, 3, 5–7, 94–95, 227, 232–35; and "hate speech" rules, 171; inequalities not addressed by, 71–84, 133, 233, 252; and market behavior, 224–27; once opposed by black left, 20, 134–35; performance of beneficiaries of, 17*n*, 21, 67, 257*n*–58*n*14; polling data on attitudes of black and white Americans toward, 118, 266*n*25; and qualification question, 12–17, 17*n*, 22–24, 44, 45, 95, 170, 171; as redistributive, 18, 39; silencing of critics of, 101–19, 125–36; and social construction of race, 247; and standards for achievement, 84–95; and stereotype of the minority viewpoint, 5–6, 29–45
Affirmative action babies, as term, 4–5
Affirmative action pyramid, 89–90
African-American, as term, 128, 246
African-American summit (1989), 112, 139
African National Congress (ANC), 143, 144
Afro-American Studies departments, 57–58
AIDS virus, 215
Ailes, Roger, 156
Alcibiades, 140, 141
Alien and Sedition Acts, 176–77